Bird of Paradise
Drums Beating

Copyright © 2012 Penny Ross

All rights reserved. No part of this publication may be reproduced or transmitted in any form or by any means, graphic, electronic or mechanical, including photocopying, recording or by any information storage and retrieval system now known or to be invented, without permission in writing from the publisher, except in the case of brief quotations embodied in reviews.

This novel is a work of fiction. Names, characters, places and incidents either are the product of the author's imagination or are used fictitiously. Any resemblance to actual persons, living or dead, is coincidental.

Cover design by Cathy Wickett
Printed and bound in the United States

Published by Butterfly Dreams Publishing

[Summary: Brittany and Amy sift through the secret lives of Kara who claims she was Cleopatra, Nellie McClung, Marie-Anne Lagimodière and other legendary women.]

Library and Archives Canada Cataloguing in Publication

Ross, Penny, 1962-
Bird of paradise drums beating / Penny Ross.

Issued also in electronic format.
ISBN 978-0-9869033-3-5

I. Title.

PS8635.O696B57 2012   C813'.6   C2012-905248-5

ISBN: 0-9869-0333-7
ISBN-13: 9780986903335

Bird of Paradise Drums Beating

Penny Ross

Dedication

To my merry band of women Tanya, Ann & Frances

1

Brittany was in a hurry. She had to fit this power walk in before her class tonight. She hadn't gotten any exercise in yesterday and felt sluggish. Now, partway through her walk, Brittany was invigorated. Arms pumping, head bobbing to her music, legs stretched, she moved with purpose.

As she passed a bend in the path something colourful caught her eye. Brittany turned her head but didn't slow her pace. In the distance she saw what could have been a bird. It was vibrant though, not drab like the other birds that hung around Kildonan Park.

Brittany smiled. She had a sudden memory of a trip to Mexico with her parents and grandparents. They'd gone to one of those bird places. It might have been an aviary. Brittany had loved the colours of the parrots and a pretty yellow bird she'd called Kissakee. That wasn't the real name of the bird though. What had it been called? Her mother would know. She'd have to ask later.

Brittany rounded the corner. Her eyes widened as she saw what appeared to be a Mexican parrot sitting directly in front of her on the path. "Wow," she murmured as she pulled her earbuds out then slowed her pace. The bird bobbed its head then did this strange little jumping motion.

Brittany laughed. What a riot! This was priceless. She was about to grab her iPod to videotape the show then decided against it. She didn't want to spook the bird.

The bird appeared to be dancing to Brittany's music. The beat was definitely the same. As Brittany stopped to watch this spontaneous performance the song ended. The bird did a little curtsey. It was so cute. Brittany clapped her hands then gasped as the bird nodded in her direction.

Penny Ross

What kind of bird was this? Someone must have trained it to perform.

The bird turned away, ran forward a few steps then took to the air. It circled over Brittany's head once then disappeared into the trees. As the bird rose into the air Brittany heard the words, *'What about the pain?'*

"That's a weird sendoff," Brittany said aloud. "What's pain got to do with it?" She chuckled as the words reminded her of the song, *'What's love got to do with it?'*

Brittany replaced her ear buds then picked up her pace again. She glanced at her watch, noted she still had time to finish her usual circuit then smiled as she mentally picked out an outfit for tonight. There was this really cute guy in her Biology class that had caught her eye the other day. Maybe they'd talk tonight at their lab … .

༄

"Have you got time for supper?" her mom called out as Brittany closed the door.

Brittany glanced at her watch. "Can I take your car to class?"

"Sure, I don't need it."

"Yeah, then I've got time. Thanks mom." Brittany gave her mom a quick kiss on the cheek then scurried off. "Gotta jump in the shower, change and get ready. I can eat before I leave. Later … "

Amy laughed then shook her head fondly. That one was always off to do something. Classes, power walks, studying, she had taken to university well. Even though it was early in the school year Brittany was sure to meet tons of people and then juggle her friends into the mix.

Andy walked in the door moments before Amy heard Brittany on the stairs.

"Perfect timing." Amy beamed at Andy and Brittany. "Supper's on."

They chatted about what they'd done throughout the day over their meal.

Bird of Paradise Drums Beating

"You're especially pretty tonight Brittany, I like your outfit," Amy commented as she watched Brittany shoveling food into her mouth. What Amy wanted to say was *'slow down, eat slower,'* but she refrained since she knew that wouldn't be a welcome comment.

"I'm glad your hair has grown out, I like it long like that," Andy added. Brittany's chestnut hair was currently shoulder length. Cropped short the year before the family had expressed mixed feelings about her hair length.

"Thanks mom, thanks dad." Brittany grinned. "Hey, remember those birds we saw in Mexico when I was really little? Eric and Sam weren't born yet. We went there with grandma and grandpa. There were parrots and cute tiny yellow ones I named Kissakee. That wasn't their real name though. Do you remember what they were called?"

Andy laughed. "The ones that resemble Orioles, you followed them around whenever we spied one."

They gazed at Amy, expectant.

Amy was the keeper of facts in the family. She stored away information to be brought out later when someone in the family asked about a specific event, person, animal or whatever.

"Yes, their name is Kiskadee."

"I knew you'd know that." Brittany beamed at her mother. "I saw this bird today in Kildonan Park that reminded me of Kissakee. It wasn't the same colour though, it was ... " Brittany glanced at the clock on the wall then jumped up. "Oops, gotta run, see you guys later."

She grabbed her purse, jacket and car keys then ran to the hall to get her shoes. Moments later they heard the door slam.

"She must have seen another Oriole." Andy grinned. "Even though their yellow isn't nearly as brilliant as they are in Mexico Brittany has always thought they were the same bird."

They smiled as they shared the memory and gathered up the dishes.

Penny Ross

Brittany walked into her lab class then glanced around before she headed toward a chair. Great, the cute guy was already seated. She headed in his direction, careful to appear nonchalant, not like a stalker.

"Is this seat taken?" She pointed at one of the seats beside him.
"No, go for it."

Brittany smiled at him then got settled. It was great this bio class had a lab component. Maybe she'd get to be partners with the cute guy. The thought brought another smile to Brittany's face as she reached down to grab her backpack. She laid out her notebook and a pen then threw the pack back on the floor. The prof walked in moments later followed by some last minute students. The remaining chairs filled up quickly.

It was about an hour into the class. Brittany was daydreaming about the cute guy when something the prof said caught her attention.

"So take a quick break. Starting at the far wall the three people from the end will be lab partners tonight, then the next three and so on. This will be the same seating arrangement for all your labs. Take a moment to meet your new lab partners then grab a sheet for tonight's assignment. You'll measure sucrose solutions with the scale. You can take your break now. Be back in fifteen minutes." The prof nodded then left the room.

Brittany turned toward the far wall then began to count three's off in her head. Yes, cute guy was one of her partners. How cool was that?

"Guess we're lab partners," the man of her dreams said, "I'm Brad."

"Brittany," she replied.

"I'm Caitlin," the girl on Brittany's other side piped in. "Gotta go phone my boyfriend. See ya in fifteen."

The rest of the class was like a scene out of a movie. At least it felt that way to Brittany. She was hyperaware of Brad as they measured and recorded each solution. Caitlin chattered away which helped ease any awkwardness that might have come up. Brittany learned way more about Caitlin than she needed to know but had to admit Caitlin did seem friendly, outgoing and pleasant. She also had a wicked sense of humour which resulted in the three of them bursting into laughter at the most inappropriate times. It turned out to be a fun lab and they even managed to finish their assignment on time.

Brittany replayed the conversation in her mind as she drove home to her grandparents' house. She was glad she lived in Winnipeg with her grandparents while she went to university. If she had commuted from Gimli she likely wouldn't run into Brad as much. She made a mental note to hang around campus more as she daydreamed about Brad.

Brad had gorgeous dark hair, it curled every which way and she'd had to control herself not to run her fingers through it as they'd bent over their work. His voice was deep and husky. Shivers ran up and down her spine as she listened to him. She was glad Caitlin cracked so many jokes and kept up a running commentary so Brittany could covertly watch Brad. Every time he laughed she'd joined in, pleased he had a similar sense of humour.

She could hardly wait until their next biology lecture. Should she sit next to him or just nearby?

"I'm going for a walk. Do you want to join me?" Amy called to Andy as she prepared to go out.

"No, you go ahead."

Amy shook her head. She knew Andy would say that. What a creature of habit. She headed out the door, strode down the sidewalk then cut over toward the park.

The sudden effect of pain ripped through Amy's head then stopped her forward motion. Brilliant white lights flashed beyond her vision. Amy stumbled, blinded. She gasped as her head throbbed. Pain seared her left temple as it spread across the top of her skull. Thump, thump, thump. Amy brought her hand up in a reflex motion, groaned then closed her eyes.

Penny Ross

Amy frowned when she heard a distant voice call, '*What about the pain?*' She tried to focus in spite of her sudden headache. Startled, Amy's eyes flew open again. The overwhelming sense of pain passed, as if it had never been.

Amy was confused by the sudden absence of pain. It had been complete. It had overwhelmed her. Now .... there was nothing.

"Ow. What happened?" Amy uttered aloud. "The pain came from nowhere. Ow, that hurt. Is this something I need to worry about? How odd." Amy massaged her temple. She was careful at first then used more pressure when she realized the pain hadn't returned.

"Did you say something? I heard you talking. Hey, are you all right?" a woman called. The level of her voice rose with the last question.

Dazed, Amy slowly lifted her head. She turned toward the woman who stood a few feet away on the pathway.

"Have we met before?"

"No, I don't think so," the woman replied. "Are you OK?" she persisted. "You don't appear to be well. Maybe you should sit down."

The woman pointed to a nearby bench.

Grateful, Amy moved forward to take a seat. Her knees were shaky and her head tender. She touched the pain spot. It was gone but would it return? She made a mental note to book a doctor's appointment when she got home.

Amy stared at the woman before good manners intruded.

"I'm Amy. Thanks for helping me out there," she said by way of introduction.

"No problem. I'm Kara."

She joined Amy on the bench.

"You said something a moment ago?"

"No, it was nothing."

"Are you sure?"

Amy was surprised at the tone. Kara sounded skeptical.

"Well, no, it was just," Amy's words trailed off as she stared at Kara. Amy remembered the words '*what about the pain?*' then the

Bird of Paradise Drums Beating

searing sensation. Had Kara been nearby when Amy felt the pain and heard the words? Yes, Amy thought she had.

Did it mean something?

Kara interrupted Amy's thoughts. "I thought I heard you mumble something about pain. Was that it?"

Shocked by Kara's ability to read her mind, Amy hesitated. She sat upright then mumbled, "Yeah, well, I mean, no, well, yeah."

Kara crossed her arms, her expression puzzled.

"Which one is it?"

"I'm not sure," Amy hedged. "What I mean is, well, it's like this." Amy spread her hands out. "I heard something, a distant voice. I don't know what, exactly. It was about pain and it floated by on the breeze. It happened just before you called to me on the pathway."

It was Amy's turn to stare. Amy didn't want to mention what she'd heard and felt aloud. To talk about it would make it more real. She bit her lip to stop the further flow of words.

Kara was startled. With wide eyes she covered her hand with her mouth. A troubled "Oh," escaped from Kara's mouth in spite of the hand that covered it.

Amy waited but Kara didn't elaborate.

As she observed Kara, Amy pegged her somewhere in her late thirties. She had clear skin, no wrinkles and striking blue eyes. Kara's dark hair was long, past her shoulders. Her outfit was questionable from a fashion standpoint. A black cardigan covered her shoulders like a shawl. It complimented her red, violet and blue tee-shirt dress. A wide green belt cinched at her waist and yellow high top sneakers completed the ensemble. Amy thought the clothes were eccentric. Kara did have flair though. Amy never would have worn the outfit yet Kara managed to carry it off.

How did clothes suit one woman while they were ridiculous on others? Stature seemed to have something to do with it. Kara was taller than the average woman and held herself very erect.

Amy shook her head. Who cared about clothes? Why was she unfocused? Had the pain made her woozy? What had they been discussing?

Ah, the pain, that was it. Amy's pain remark had bothered Kara. Amy shrugged. So what? She may as well leave. Kara meant nothing to her. They'd only just met.

Amy stood. "It was good to meet you. I have to go." She strode off, quick, feeling a bit rude, not enough to turn back though.

Amy rolled her head in one direction then the other while she walked. Pleased to note she felt no ill effects from her earlier discomfort Amy continued her fitness walk. Her pace was more relaxed than before.

Amy heard footsteps pound behind her. Rather than move to one side, she quickened her pace. She put her head down then forged ahead. She'd rise to the challenge and walk faster than the person behind her.

The person behind increased their pace. She heard the stranger gain on the short distance between them. Amy slowed then moved to one side to allow the person behind her to pass.

Amy was taken aback when Kara drew up alongside her.

"Oh, it's you. What a surprise."

Kara stopped dead in her tracks then glared at Amy.

"I'm sorry," Amy apologized. "Did you want to talk to me? I know I left but I had to get away."

Kara frowned.

Amy's mother claimed frowning increased wrinkles. From what she'd witnessed so far, Kara should be covered in creases. Instead, Kara had skin smooth as satin. Had Kara taken advantage of cosmetic surgery? Who cared? When had she become so unfocused? It was annoying.

"Why did you leave?" Kara blurted.

"I don't know. I told you. I just needed to get away. I mean, well…" Amy stopped. Why did she feel it necessary to explain her actions to a stranger?

Bird of Paradise Drums Beating

Kara stared at Amy. Her gaze penetrated Amy's foggy thoughts.

Against her better judgment Amy rushed to talk. Words tumbled out of her mouth as if separate from her thoughts, torn from her without prior knowledge. "I had to get away. It's strange. I mean, I don't even know you but I had to escape. I'm sorry."

"Tell me more."

Amy blurted out, "All right, it's like this." She stopped, shuffled from one foot to the other, hesitated. Amy knew procrastination put off the inevitable. "I don't know how to say this so I just will." Amy felt like a wild woman and knew her eyes bulged out in an unbecoming manner. Her voice rose. It was unsteady.

"When I passed you on the path I heard, *'what about the pain?'* float by on the breeze. Then I experienced a searing pain from my temple to the top of my skull." Amy touched the spot with her hand. When she removed her hand Amy stared at it, as if unaware her hand was an extension of her body.

Kara narrowed her eyes, stared at Amy for a moment then turned and headed over to a nearby bench.

With reluctance Amy joined Kara.

Amy watched people walk by. They laughed and carried on conversations. The normal actions reassured her.

In contrast, Kara and Amy sat in silence for a while. The quiet settled over them. Amy began to feel at peace, companionable almost with this stranger. How odd.

When Kara spoke, Amy was sure something cold and unwanted joined them.

"You could have the gift," Kara announced.

"What?" Amy croaked. She crossed her arms for warmth as a sudden chill penetrated her skin. Goosebumps rose on her arms as if a great gust of wind passed by. Yet when Amy glanced up, the trees had an unnatural stillness. The sensation was eerie. She shuddered.

"You felt the pain and heard those words on the wind, didn't you?"

Penny Ross

Reluctant to admit it Amy bent her head down then murmured, "Yes."

"That's it then."

"What do you mean, that's it? What's it?"

Amy locked eyes with Kara. She felt as if her soul was exposed to this stranger. Each layer was peeled away in a gentle yet insistent strip until only her essential core remained. The exploration didn't feel like a violation, more like a sociable investigation. Amy was amazed she'd allowed a stranger this depth of scrutiny. It was alien to her nature. Amy felt as if she'd just been probed.

Kara broke contact first. She stood up then announced, "I have to go. We'll talk again another day."

Startled, Amy jumped up.

Kara turned to walk up the path.

"But," Amy stammered.

Torn between following Kara and heading back to Andy, Amy felt deflated, like something momentous had been about to happen then got ripped away. The suddenness made Amy tired. Disheartened, Amy headed back to her parents' house. Not wanting to appear rude again, she turned to bid Kara good-bye.

Kara had disappeared.

Instead, a bird stood on the path. It held Amy's gaze.

Amy stared at the bird, intrigued by its brilliant colours. Red, blue, violet, green and yellow melded with black like a kaleidoscope. It couldn't live here in the park. It appeared to be a tropical bird. While she stared, Amy heard something beat in the background. Intent now, she raised her head to listen.

Amy heard the beat of a drum far off in the distance.

There was something about the colour combination of the bird. Whatever it was eluded Amy. It nagged at her. There was some link, an item it reminded her of. The thought fluttered, vague like a cobweb trembling in the shadows.

The bird had a lot of colours. What country had that flag? Amy conjured up countries and their appropriate flag colours. She shook

Bird of Paradise Drums Beating

her head then murmured, "No, that's not it. It's something more immediate."

She glanced across to houses in the distance. Flowers, hedges, a fence, bordered the walkway. If she focused, perhaps the image would become clearer.

"Red, blue, violet, green, black and yellow," Amy whispered hoping for a clue. Nothing nearby had that colour combination. It was something else then. She must have seen it earlier. Not too long ago though.

"Ah hah." Amy felt triumphant as she raised her arm to congratulate herself. "Nah can't be." Amy lowered her arm again. What an outrageous idea!

As Amy dismissed the thought, she heard the drumbeat fade away.

Amy turned then headed off, tired and ready for bed. Her feet dragged and shoulders ached as if a great burden had been laid upon them. Her earlier feeling of elation had been replaced by disappointment.

If Amy and her daughter Brittany had shared notes about the bird that night it would have avoided a lot of confusion over the next few days.

2

The following evening, Amy was drawn to the pathway at Kildonan Park again. Amy loved how Winnipeg had so many walking trails. She'd walked a short distance when a musical sound caught her attention.

It was a bird, singing a song of sweetness, love and harmony. The pureness of the melody made her heart ache. Closing her eyes, Amy focused on the song, her mind a blank canvas open to the harmonious tune.

Amy had never heard such emotion from a bird. Lifted to an ultimate height she crashed down when the birdsong turned sad and painful. Tender notes seemed to reach within the depth of Amy's core. On the verge of fulfillment she craved more. When the sound broke off without warning, Amy cried out. Her heart ached as if a great love had turned from her affection without explanation. How could something so simple make you hurt when it ceased to exist?

Amy's eyes flew open. A bird sat on the path in front of her. She assumed it was the same bird that had sung the melodious notes. Curious now, Amy watched it. It could be the vibrant bird she'd seen the day before.

Intrigued by the bird, Amy stared. Where had it come from? As she contemplated it Amy was distracted by a distant sound. It was a drum, the same as yesterday. Was the drum real or the pounding of blood in her ears? Why had this bird popped up two days in a row in the same spot? Were the two events related?

Amy meant to go but her hand reached out of its own accord toward the bird. The drumming increased in tempo. With a start, Amy realized her posture implored the bird to come closer. Why was she drawn to it?

Bird of Paradise Drums Beating

She trembled then drew her hand back. "No," she said aloud then turned to go. Amy wavered as she realized the bird frightened her. Desperate, she opened her mouth to talk to it. Part of her longed to approach the bird yet her logical part wanted to flee and never see it again. In turmoil, Amy walked forward then stepped back.

Frightened by the intensity of her feelings, unsure what to do next, Amy stumbled about like a sleepwalker. She turned from the bird convinced she should leave. Again she wandered back, pulled by an invisible string like a reluctant puppet guided by its master.

Throwing her hands up, Amy covered her face, almost weeping with frustration. Why did she feel this way? It was as if the bird controlled her or had set up a force field Amy had walked into. Powerless, she was torn by conflicting emotions.

"Do you like it?" someone asked behind her.

The drums faded…...

─────

Amy tore her hands from her face then whirled to confront the speaker. Speechless, Amy stared at the woman before her.

"It's a paradise tanager. There's no difference between the male and female birds. I like that. Most female birds are dull compared to the brilliant colours of the males. She sings, chirps and flocks together with the male species. That's rare."

"Huh? What?"

Shaking herself like a wet dog just out of water, Amy tried to focus on Kara. Where had she come from?

With a quick glance over her shoulder Amy's eyes scanned the area behind her. She needed to see the bird, now.

A blank path greeted Amy like a slate wiped clean of memories. The air was silent, the birdsong and drums had both faded away. Had she dreamt them?

Disappointment washed over Amy. She felt like a child eagerly waiting for a present that finds out today is not the day for gifts. She had to sit down.

Amy spied a nearby bench then headed toward it. Her knees shook and her body felt quivery. Amy wished she were alone. She needed time to recover, to ponder why she'd felt so overpowered by the bird. Instead, she'd have to talk to this stranger again. With reluctance, Amy lifted her head then gazed at Kara.

Piercing blue eyes met Amy's.

Amy sighed. With little enthusiasm she uttered, "Hello Kara."

Why had this woman popped up again and where had the bird gone? Twice they'd met at the same spot. Although she didn't believe in coincidence, Kara stood before Amy, a living, breathing, twist of fate.

Amy stared at Kara. Something about her was intriguing. Yet Amy felt repelled at the same time. Puzzled, Amy continued to scrutinize Kara.

Kara stood there. She held her head to one side as if curious about something. The movement reminded Amy of the bird.

The bird confused Amy. Did a connection exist between Kara and the bird? What was up with the same colour combination? Yesterday Kara had worn red, blue, violet, green, black and yellow. Amy noted Kara wore the identical shades today. They were the same colours as the bird.

Kara was quiet while Amy stared at her. Kara reminded her of a butterfly, poised to flutter by flowers just before it settled on the petal of its choice. Why had Kara mentioned a gift yesterday? Amy had never had special powers.

Amy frowned. Why was she so unfocused, doubting everything? As questions piled up, they cluttered her mind like newspapers in need of the recycle bin.

Kara broke into her thoughts. "I should go. Perhaps we'll meet again tomorrow night? Bye."

Kara walked away without another word.

Amy turned to say good-bye but Kara had disappeared again.

Bird of Paradise Drums Beating

With weary limbs, Amy stood to retrace her steps back to her parent's house. Desperate and tired, she longed to talk to her husband Andy.

As she walked home in the evening twilight Amy watched lights of the city blink around her. They reminded her of twinkling stars dancing in the sky. It was hard to see stars in the city. There were too many lights.

At home, in Gimli, the stars were plentiful on any given night. Even though it was nice of Amy's parents to let her and her husband Andy stay in their house in Winnipeg, Amy preferred her home in Gimli. Of course staying at her parent's house instead of a hotel was a better option. She couldn't complain. So what if the stars were less ample in Winnipeg?

Relieved to be away from Kara, Amy increased her pace, eager to join Andy and share her strange meeting. She wanted to hear what Andy thought of Kara and the bird.

Andy listened to Amy's version of her chance meetings with Kara. A curious man, he held his head to one side. It reminded Amy of Kara and the bird. Andy focused his clear blue eyes on her. It was one of the things Amy loved about Andy. He paid rapt attention when she spoke.

"The bird seems to be the key to your puzzle. Perhaps the complexity of the bird expresses the interrelated parts of the woman Kara."

"Huh? What?"

At times Andy talked like a psychology professor. He had an amazing ability to reason things out but didn't always explain himself in simple, direct terms.

"Maybe Kara relates to the bird somehow. The bird could be significant to her. You've seen Kara and the bird twice on the same path. When Kara mentioned your hidden gift she could have been inviting you to ask questions or help solve her puzzle.

I think you're right Amy. There's more to Kara than you've seen so far. I wonder if Kara wears the same colours every day or it's a coincidence she's worn them yesterday and today. If you see her again you'll have to note how she's dressed."

"What about the drum I hear when I see the bird?"

"Ah, well that's another part of the mystery, isn't it?"

Unsure if the conversation with Andy cleared matters up or raised more questions Amy was torn. Should she walk by the river again tomorrow night? Did she want to cultivate a relationship with Kara or avoid her? Amy went to bed unsure what to think.

Amy awoke from a nightmare near dawn. Bathed in sweat, words echoed in Amy's mind. They reminded her of Kara. *'The pain, the pain is unbearable.'*

"What pain?" Amy uttered.

While she lay in bed images from her nightmare filtered through Amy's mind. They reached out, tantalizing, yet ambiguous. Amy recalled hazy clouds. Surrounded by women, they'd tried to grasp at her. With arms outstretched, muscles taut and mouths wide open the women implored Amy to come closer. United as one, they uttered a soulful litany, an aching epitaph. *'The pain, help us with the pain. It's unbearable … … '*

Ripples coursed through Amy's body, an electric current generated by the agony of generations. The sensation ceased, as suddenly as it had begun. Her mind cleared.

The anguish evaporated into thin air, back to where it had come, like a wisp in the dawn. Amy realized the nightmare and her encounters with Kara had to be related. A visit to Kara seemed in order. Amy had to know more about *'the pain.'* It didn't matter if she was ambivalent about Kara. Amy's curiosity had been aroused … ..

3

That evening Amy went for another walk. She liked to exercise after dinner while Andy preferred to watch TV. Andy encouraged her to walk in Kildonan Park to see if she met Kara again. Amy ventured out. Part of her hoped she wouldn't bump into Kara while she had to admit part of her was eager.

Amy hadn't gone far when Kara appeared out of nowhere.

"Mind if I walk with you?"

"No, I guess not."

Turning, they continued along the pathway. They didn't speak until they reached a second path that intersected theirs and led toward Rainbow Stage. Amy turned to Kara who was focused on the platform in front of them.

"Do you live around here?" Amy hadn't meant to be harsh yet the words flew from her lips, sounding abrupt even to Amy's ears.

Kara's gaze was sharp as she answered, "Back there." She pointed across the park in the direction they'd come from.

Amy knew there were blocks of houses within walking distance. Her parents' house was nearby and she stayed there a lot. Amy had walked in the area for years now.

"Have you ever seen entertainers here on the weekend?" Kara asked. "I've noticed magicians and sometimes there are puppet shows for children in the afternoon."

"Yes, we've taken our kids to those before. Of course that was when they were younger. My mom and I went to the Wizard of Oz and I took my daughter Brittany to Cats so we've been to a few performances at Rainbow Stage. How about you?"

"My husband insisted we attend Joseph and the Amazing Technicolour Dreamcoat. I'm not much for crowds these days so I didn't know what to expect. It was enjoyable in the end though. Footloose and Annie were showcased this year. We didn't go though."

"Yes, my daughter Brittany and I went to Footloose. Boy those actors had energy! They had quite the dance moves," Amy added.

Kara moved toward a bench then sat down. Amy joined her.

"So you must live nearby," Kara noted as she turned toward Amy.

"No, we're just visiting. We live an hour away from here, in Gimli. My husband and I are here for a business conference. I like to walk and it's a beautiful evening. We stay at my parents' house nearby."

"What sort of business are you in?"

"My husband Andy and I are technical computer consultants. We set up computer programming for mid-sized companies then train their staff to use the equipment. This conference happens to be sponsored by IBM. They encourage people like us to attend since they manufacture computers and provide computer products. Most people think we're in competition. We're not though, since they're dominant in the global market and people like us enhance their company not detract from it."

"Sounds fascinating, what's it like working with your spouse?"

"Different from how I thought it would be. He specializes in the computer area and bookwork while I deal more with the clients. My work involves administration and PR so we compliment one another. We haven't had many of the typical fights you hear couples that work together have. It's been a pleasant surprise."

Amy laughed at Kara's skeptical expression. "I know it seems too good to be true but it works, so I've stopped wondering how it's possible."

"Lucky you."

Kara's comment sounded sarcastic but Amy took it at face value. "Yeah, it's great to do what you enjoy. This has worked out well for both of us. Andy started the company part-time. As demand increased we quit our jobs to devote more hours to the business. We work out

Bird of Paradise Drums Beating

of our home office and only have to commute to the city a few times a week. When we come for conferences we usually stay at my parents' house. Mom and dad go to Gimli to stay with our boys. How about you, what do you do to keep yourself out of trouble?"

Silence greeted Amy's comment.

Stealing a glance in Kara's direction, Amy was surprised by the dour expression on Kara's face. She'd bet money there was a story behind Kara's stony appearance.

Moments passed. Amy felt as if time had slowed. Their lighthearted conversation was replaced with a heavy cloud. If someone didn't say something soon the conversation would peter out. The awkwardness lengthened. Amy was surprised how her simple question had fallen so flat.

Out of the corner of her eye Amy noticed Kara twisting her hands in her lap. The gesture reminded Amy of someone she'd known who'd done the same thing when she was nervous or highly agitated. Could Amy's innocent question cause Kara to be so disturbed she was unable to continue a normal conversation?

Amy felt bad for Kara. Her mind raced as she thought of something, anything, to say. Amy wanted to cover the awkward silence that stretched before them like a blank slate begging to be filled.

"I miss my boys," Amy blurted. "Of course when we're in the city we get to visit Brittany but I like it better when the entire family is together."

Kara turned toward Amy, lips parted, an eager expression on her face. "How old are they?"

"The boys are eight and twelve. Brittany is eighteen. She just started university."

"I have two sons. They're ten and thirteen. No daughter though. Hey, our sons should meet one another since they're close in age."

Kara was suddenly eager to talk. "I never know what to say to them or my husband for that matter. Do you ever have that problem with your family?" Kara's tone was anxious.

Startled, Amy was speechless. How had their simple exchange veered in this direction? The raw longing in Kara's voice made Amy uncomfortable. Why had Kara broached such an intimate discussion? Kara seemed hopeful as she regarded Amy. It was obvious she expected an answer.

"Well, huh, um, I don't know if I have any trouble talking to them," Amy stammered. "They chatter a lot about what they do at school, homework, computer and video games, friends and the activities they're in. Then we talk about things we've done as a family or are going to do like camping, trips, movies and weekend activities. Brittany talks about boys a lot since she's boy crazy. Was that the sort of stuff you meant?"

Kara stared into Amy's eyes. It was like a silent exploration. She seemed to probe for something more than Amy had given her.

Amy shuddered as if something cold had tickled her spine. She waited, suddenly anxious.

"Maybe." Kara sounded disheartened.

Amy felt Kara's disappointment in her reply. She was saddened by the realization.

Then with an abruptness that seemed contradictory to her words, Kara stood as if to leave. After a moment's hesitation, Kara swept back to Amy. "Are you coming?" she demanded in a gruff voice. She didn't wait for an answer. Instead, Kara turned then walked away.

Amy was quick to join Kara.

They walked fast, not talking now.

The silence wasn't unpleasant. Amy sensed Kara wasn't interested in small talk.

"Would you like to see my house?"

Amy paused, thinking about Kara's question. Did Amy want to encourage a relationship by viewing Kara's home? She chewed her lip, deep in thought. Then she shrugged. After all, checking out someone's house didn't imply friendship. She'd do it to be sociable.

"Yes, I'd enjoy that."

Bird of Paradise Drums Beating

"My husband Morey should be home by now and you can meet my sons."

"What are their names?"

"Jason and Terrence, we call him Terry."

"Mine are Brittany, Eric and Sam."

They exited the park then walked down Scotia Street for a few blocks. As they neared Kara's home Amy gazed about with interest. A large house with two stories wasn't uncommon in this area but there appeared to be one section that jutted out along the water's edge. It stretched in an endless line like a long loping upside down L. The lengthy enclosed walkway seemed like a corridor more suited to a conservatory than a family dwelling.

Kara opened the door, indicating Amy should precede her.

The entryway made Amy feel at home with its warm and inviting atmosphere.

When they entered the living room Amy's eyes were drawn to a portrait gracing one of the walls. In the picture Kara sat on a chair in a plain black dress. Kara stared at her folded hands. Ordinary enough, but next to her in a gilded cage Amy saw the bird with the brilliant plumage. Amy turned to ask Kara about it but before she could voice her question a man entered the room.

"You've been out walking."

"Yes. Morey, I'd like you to meet Amy."

Morey turned then flashed Amy a dazzling smile.

"I'm always pleased to meet a friend of Kara's."

Amy felt Kara relax beside her. How strained was their relationship? Had Kara been afraid of Amy's reception?

Amy glanced toward the portrait again. She wondered at the significance of the bird. Again, before she could ask about it, Morey began to play host. He pointed to the view from the large picture windows that covered the length of the room.

"What do you think of that scene? Spectacular isn't it?" Morey threw his arms wide to indicate the view from the windows.

"It's breathtaking. Do you enjoy living beside the river?"

"Yes, I like it. Kara might have mentioned she built the house years ago, before we met."

"No, she hadn't."

"When we got married I sold my bachelor pad and moved in here. My view was skyscrapers not water. This is more peaceful and a lot quieter than living downtown."

Amy nodded. She had just opened her mouth to reply when a strident voice cut through the silence.

"Our friends think we're rich since we live in a huge house."

A young boy walked into the room. He glared at his father, his stare defiant.

"Jason, I'm sure we've gone over this before. The term rich is relative." Morey's voice held a note of annoyance.

Jason shrugged. He appeared bored with the answer. "Who are you?" he demanded.

"This is my friend Amy. Amy, my oldest son, Jason," Kara murmured.

Amy smiled then gave a brief nod in his direction.

Amy was rewarded with a disapproving sniff and a *'whatever.'*

So much for charm Amy reasoned. Youth could be disrespectful at times. Amy was sure Jason's behaviour embarrassed Kara as her colour rose at Jason's rude comment.

A younger version of Jason wandered into the room. He was greeted by an uncomfortable silence.

He flashed Amy an engaging smile as he said, "Hi."

"Amy, this is Terry. Amy is a new friend I just met," Kara said, by way of introduction.

"Do you have any kids?" Terry appeared eager to know.

"Yes, two boys and a girl."

"How old are they?"

"My boys are eight and twelve and my daughter is eighteen."

"Yeah, I'm ten and Jason's thirteen. Did you bring your sons with you?"

Bird of Paradise Drums Beating

Terry peered around the room as if he expected two boys to turn up in front of him.

"No, we left them at home. They had to go to school."

Amy held her hands out, apologetic, as Terry appeared disappointed. Young children's feelings were often mirrored on their face, exposed for all to see.

"Don't you live around here?"

"No, my husband and I are here for a conference. We live in Gimli."

"That's not far from here right? Do your sons stay with the servants?"

Amy laughed. The servants, perhaps this family was rich, as Jason suggested. "No, they're with my parents." Amy chuckled again.

"Oh, too bad they couldn't come." Terry appeared crestfallen for a moment. "Maybe they'll come tomorrow," he said. His face brightened at the possibility.

"No, not tomorrow, they'll join us on the weekend though."

"Great, I'd like to meet them," Terry replied.

"Maybe," Amy agreed, careful not to raise Terry's hopes too high at the possibility of a visit.

"Would you like a tour of the rest of the house?" Kara asked, interrupting Terry.

"Yes, I'd like that."

Amy nodded at the boys then followed Kara out of the room. As Jason had indicated, the house was large and it had been decorated in a tasteful manner. The warm and inviting colours made Amy feel at ease.

"Your home is welcoming. You've used many peaceful colours. I like your bathroom. It reminds me of a book I read about Morocco."

"It does, oh good. I used earthy colours and got these bathroom decorations when we went to Morocco. I'm glad I achieved the right effect."

Kara beamed.

"I had a question about the portrait over the fireplace in the living room."

Kara stopped. As she turned toward Amy her movements became slow and mechanical. She flashed Amy a sharp, questioning glance. Amy thought she saw fear, distrust and something like wariness flicker across Kara's features. Then Kara blinked. The moment passed.

"What about it?" Kara demanded.

"The bird beside you is the same one I noticed yesterday."

"Mm, hmm."

"Why is the bird beside you in the portrait? Do you know what kind of bird it is?"

"Yes, as I mentioned before it's a paradise tanager." Kara waved her hand as if to indicate the bird was of no importance.

"It looks like a tropical bird. Isn't it too cold for them to live here? I've never seen one in the park before." Amy hoped Kara would share her insights about the bird. She was eager to learn more.

"Yes, they typically live in tropical rainforests." Kara scrunched up her face. "I think they're found throughout most of the Amazon Basin. I could be wrong about that though. I'm no bird expert." She shrugged as if the topic bored her.

"Is it your bird?"

"Sort of...."

Amy stared at Kara. Why did Kara brush aside questions related to the bird?

"Does the bird live here?"

"Yes, it does."

Amy gave up. She was getting nowhere. Sighing, she glanced outside then noticed the approaching darkness. "I have to go. It's dusk and I'll have to walk fast to get to my parent's house before dark."

Kara led Amy down a hallway. "I'll take you out this way. There's a door at the other end you can use. It leads back to the road we arrived by. Where do your parents live?"

Bird of Paradise Drums Beating

"They're on Armstrong Avenue, right across from the park. I saw this section of the house when we walked here. It's like an upside down L."

"Yes, it's an indoor walkway."

"It's beautiful. You have gorgeous plants outside the glass enclosure. Combined with the plants and flowers inside it feels tropical. It reminds me of a conservatory."

"Yes, at first I had it built for exercise. I used to walk back and forth like I do now on the exterior paths. I use it more now in the winter when it's cold out. During the other seasons I go outdoors whenever possible. It wasn't always like that though. I never used to go outside."

"Never?" Amy tried to appear nonchalant yet was shocked by Kara's confession. Why would an able bodied woman remain indoors year round?

"No never. I was like a bird tethered to my gilded cage, free to roam the walls of my prison yet loath to go outside into the sunlight."

"Did your husband forbid you to go outdoors?"

"Morey. No, he wants me to get out more. Did you notice how happy he was I brought you home? I don't think I've ever done that before. I don't like strangers. I only walk on paths when there are very few people around. I'm a solitary person."

"Do you visit people, run errands, take the boys to activities, go out for coffee?"

Kara laughed. The sound reminded Amy of ice tinkling down a waterfall. The pitch was musical, the sound harmonious. It made Amy long to hear more, the laughter implied a hint of pleasant, sweet music.

"No, I don't do any of those. I told you I don't go out much. I'm a homebody."

"Do you sing?"

Kara's laughter had stirred a memory within Amy, something haunting, far off and fluttery.

After a long, drawn out pregnant pause, Kara answered in a firm voice, "No, not anymore."

The finality of her words gave Amy pause. She longed to ask why, yet sensed immense pain in Kara's sentence.

Amy knew it wasn't the time for further confidences.

"Will you come see me tomorrow?"

As Amy heard the raw longing in Kara's voice she agreed right away. Kara sounded so alone and in need. Like most mothers, Amy responded to the desperate tone.

"Of course, I'd love to. What time is good for you?"

"Whenever you like, I'm here all day. Remember, I don't go out except to walk and that's in the early evening."

"Great, I'll see you tomorrow afternoon sometime. Bye."

On the way back to her parent's house Amy regretted her hasty impulse. Why had Kara bonded with her? By her own admission Kara never talked to strangers. Amy quickened her stride, not quite ready to admit Kara intrigued her.

4

Amy's first thought upon wakening was of Kara. Why had she agreed to visit? She admitted curiosity had been one of the reasons, pity another. Kara seemed lonely. Was that enough to form a brief friendship?

Perhaps, after all they wouldn't be in Winnipeg for long. Amy might not see Kara much when they went home to Gimli. She should regard this as a positive thing. After all, she wasn't going for a root canal at the dentist. She was just dropping by Kara's for a quick visit.

Amy frowned. Thoughts of the dentist twigged something in her mind. Now what was it? Dentist, root canal, pain, ah, that was the connection.

"The pain and the bird song," Amy murmured aloud.

"What?" Andy muttered.

"Sorry, didn't mean to wake you."

Amy bent over to give him a kiss.

"That's all right. I don't mind being woken with a kiss, makes me feel like Prince Charming."

Amy gave him a playful swat.

"What were you saying?"

"I just thought of the odd occurrence that happened when I met Kara the other day. It was what triggered our introduction."

"Mm hmm, go on."

"Remember I mentioned when Kara and I passed one another on the path intense pain shot through my head. It started here at my temple." Amy indicated the spot with her fingertips.

"Yes, I remember."

"At the same time I thought I heard *'what about the pain?'* float by on the breeze. Just now when I thought of the word pain I recalled the melody the bird sang. I think it was a song about longing and regret. I wish I could remember the name of that song. Hmm, what is it?"

Amy sat up, then propped her hand on her chin while she thought.

"I see we're back to the bird," Andy pointed out.

"Yes, the bird, wait, the song had something to do with a bird. Now, how do those words go? If I can put the melody with the words ..." Leaning forward, Amy thought about songs with the word bird in it. This reminded her of a word association game. As it dawned on her she began to sing the tune for Andy.

"That's it, I remember. *'Why do birds suddenly appear? Every time you are near? Just like me they long to be, next to you.'* That's the song the mystery bird sang the other day."

Amy leaned back against her pillow with a satisfied smile.

"Yes," Andy replied. "It's a Carpenter song. Wasn't it popular in the seventies or eighties? Let's see if we can remember the title."

Andy propped himself up beside Amy.

"Something from the words, wasn't it?" Amy ventured.

"Yes, *'Next to you,'* no, that's not it. Close though."

"That's it, *'Close to you.'* That's the title." Amy clapped. "What a team, we can put together any old tunes at this rate."

"So why would a bird sing Carpenter tunes?"

"I don't know. Maybe I could ask Kara today. She might tell me. Then again, she might not. The woman doesn't seem to answer questions. She prefers to ask them."

"Don't we all?" Andy laughed. "It doesn't hurt to ask though. Kara and her bird sound fascinating. I can hardly wait to hear your stories tonight. This woman has given us something interesting to talk about besides the conference. Now I better hop in the shower then head off. Will you be able to man the booth for a while today?"

Andy leaned over to plant a quick kiss on Amy's lips then jumped out of bed.

"Sure. I want to check out a few workshop sessions but I'll be at the booth in between. I'll head over to Kara's later this afternoon."

"Great, why don't we meet back here around six and go out for supper?"

"Sounds wonderful."

⁓⁓

Brittany had gotten up early to go for a walk before her classes. She was still jazzed from yesterday. As she walked in the park she thought of her Biology class. It had been perfect. Of course she'd have to borrow notes from someone since Brittany hadn't been able to write down a single thing. No matter, she'd figure something out. Caitlin had been taking notes. She could most likely borrow hers.

Caitlin had been great yesterday. It was freaky about their timing. They had entered the theatre pretty much at the same time. They scanned for chairs as they walked down the stairs. The class was always packed so you had to get there early to get a seat. As they neared the middle of the room Caitlin had practically shouted, "Over there, quick."

Brittany had followed her since Caitlin had spied two empty seats. These weren't just any spot though. They were right beside Brad.

"Great, you saved us seats. How handy is that?" Caitlin high fived Brad as she greeted him. "What a handy lab partner you've turned out to be."

Then miracle of miracles Caitlin bounded past the chair right beside Brad and sat down in the far chair.

Brittany sat down, said hi to Brad then got out her notebook and pen.

Caitlin jabbered beside her, to both Brad and Brittany. Their conversation had been brief since the prof arrived a few minutes later.

Brittany's shoulder touched Brad's the entire time they were seated. She hadn't realized last night how broad his shoulders were. Did he work out?

She'd fantasized about Brad the entire class and carried on a silent conversation. She hadn't heard a word the prof said. Caitlin seemed diligent with note taking though so Brittany should be fine if she borrowed Caitlin's notes. Brad had taken notes too and appeared to be listening but she could hardly ask him for notes. That would be too forward.

Well, maybe not Brittany mused as she glanced around Kildonan Park. There weren't many walkers out at this time. She smiled as she thought about whether or not she'd ask Brad for his notes at their next class. After all, they'd gone for coffee and gotten to know one another.

Brittany grinned as she picked up her pace. Caitlin had arranged it of course, the coffee date.

As they packed up their stuff at the end of the class then headed toward the stairs Caitlin had announced, "I've gotta rush off, got another class. What about you two?"

"I've got a spare."

"Me too," Brad added.

"Wow, you guys are lucky. Why don't you go for coffee somewhere together? I would if I could but I gotta run. Hey, wait, we need to exchange cell phone numbers. You know, since we're lab partners and bio classmates and all. We'll need to arrange some study times and stuff."

Brittany had practically swooned. Wow, Caitlin was a godsend. First she mentioned Brittany and Brad should go for coffee and now they were getting one another's phone numbers. This was too good to be true.

They gave Caitlin their numbers first and she gave them hers then rushed off. They'd entered each other's into their respective cell phones.

"So, you game?" Brad asked as he did some sort of head bob toward the door.

"Sure."

"Let's go across the street to Stella's. I was there the other day and they have great coffee. I heard someone say breakfasts don't cost too much. Apparently they don't mind if you study there either if it's

Bird of Paradise Drums Beating

not too busy. They probably get pissed if you tie up a table at lunch time though."

"I didn't know this was even here," Brittany admitted as they crossed Portage Avenue. "Hmm, Stella's Cafe at Plug In, that's a different name. Hey, they have a take-out area. That's kind of handy if you need a snack or forgot your lunch."

"I've got a meal plan so I mostly eat at the university. How about you?"

"I eat breakfast at home then bring lunch. My mom and dad have been around this week so mom likes to make me lunch." Brittany shrugged. "I think it makes her feel useful or something."

"So you live in Winnipeg?"

"Well, I do now." Brittany gave a nervous laugh. Had that sounded odd? "I mean, obviously I live here now since we're going to university."

Brad stared at her.

"I'm from Gimli," Brittany rushed to explain. "My grandparents live in West Kildonan, near Kildonan Park so I live with them. My mom and dad are in the city a lot though. They happen to be at my grandparents this week. My parents and grandparents exchange houses a lot. My grandparents are thinking of buying a place in Gimli so they've been checking it out."

Brad nodded.

"How about you, are you from Winnipeg?"

"No, I'm from Beausejour. I've been to Gimli a few times. It's a real nice place. I like the beach and you have tons of restaurants there. We don't have many in Beausejour."

"I've been through Beausejour on the way to Lac du Bonnet. We have family friends that live there. We used to stop at that place on the highway for ice cream. It's always hard to choose a flavour since they have so many choices. One of my brothers takes forever to pick what he wants." Brittany laughed. "Little brothers can be a pain sometimes."

"I wouldn't know. I'm the little brother in our family. I have an older brother and sister. They've never called me a pain."

"Oh, sorry, I didn't mean, I mean, I," Brittany stammered.

Brad laughed, real hard and long.

He had a great laugh. Brittany smiled, just a bit. Then as Brad continued to laugh Brittany found herself joining in.

"I was kidding. You should have seen your face when I deadpanned how I've never been called a pain. I could almost read the words '*faux pax, retreat, back up*' on your forehead. That was so funny."

Brittany smiled at Brad. "So, I imagine you've been called a pain once or twice by one of your siblings."

"Oh yeah, more like a million times a day, especially by my sister. Of course I might have deserved it a few times like when I put frogs in her bed or dead bugs in her shoes." Brad laughed again. "Yeah, I'd have to agree with you. Little brothers can be a pain sometimes. How many do you have?"

"Two of them, they're not very old. Eric is twelve but Sam is only eight."

"And still a pain."

"Yeah," Brittany laughed, "sometimes."

They talked until they had to head back for a class. Brittany kept replaying the conversation over in her mind. It had been great to get to know Brad. He was in his second year of university and lived in residence so it was sheer luck he'd decided to take a first year Biology course. Well, not that much of a stretch really, maybe luck wasn't the word. There were probably quite a few people that took first year courses in their second or third year.

Brittany chuckled to herself as she recalled Brad's great sense of humour. When he led her on with that pain thing, it had been out and out hilarious. The guy was funny, cute and interesting. She could hardly wait to see him again. Even though Brad hadn't asked her out or anything they'd parted with encouraging words.

"My class is that way," Brittany had said as they entered Centennial Hall.

Bird of Paradise Drums Beating

"Okay, I'm going this way so see you at our next class. If you need any help with your Biology homework just text me. See ya," Brad said over his shoulder as he strode off toward his class.

"That's kind of encouraging I think," Brittany said aloud. Then she frowned. "Wait a minute, did Brad mention Biology homework? Damn, I didn't hear that. Oh man." She shook her head.

"Pardon me?"

Brittany stopped, turned toward the voice then ripped out her ear buds.

"Did you say something?" Brittany asked the girl who stood a few feet off the path.

"I said pardon me. You muttered something. I thought you might be talking to me since there's no one else around." The girl made a sweeping motion with her hand.

Brittany glanced behind her. The girl was right. They were the only two near the path. What a great time for a walk. Brittany noted the time since she liked having the park to herself.

"Oh, yeah, right. I didn't see you there. So, no, I wasn't addressing you." Brittany gave a self-conscious chuckle. "I guess I was talking to myself. Jeesh, I sound like some old person chatting to myself, how embarrassing."

"That's all right. I do that sometimes too. It's no big deal." The girl turned then walked to a nearby bench. "I was just out for some fresh air. I had to get away." The girl seemed uncomfortable. She glanced at Brittany once then away. She began to study her nails.

Brittany wasn't sure what to do. This girl was a stranger. Should she shrug, say something empathetic, then move on or did the girl expect more? Brittany began to chew on her lower lip. This was awkward.

Then the girl started to cry.

She didn't gnash her teeth and cry uncontrollably. Instead big, fat crocodile tears slid down her cheeks.

Brittany stared at her. She couldn't help it. The girl seemed so alone and sad, it was heartbreaking to watch. Before she knew it Brittany had moved toward the girl to sit beside her on the bench.

Brittany felt around in her pockets till she found a tissue. She checked it out, seemed clean enough. She held the tissue out towards the girl.

It hadn't seemed like a big deal. The girl took it though, wiped away her tears then turned to Brittany with a radiant smile on her face. Brittany was surprised at how beautiful the girl was when she smiled.

"Thank you so much," the girl gushed. "You don't know what this means to me."

Brittany was taken aback. What? All she'd done was hand the girl a tissue. There was no need to go over the top about it.

"You're the first person my age I've met since I got here. My name's Kara."

"Hi, I'm Brittany."

"Do you live nearby? I live right over there." The girl pointed down the path.

"Umm, yeah, I'm staying with my grandparents right now. Their house is across the park, on Armstrong." Brittany stopped. Why had she told this girl, what was her name again, Kara, why had she mentioned where she lived? What if she was some sort of stalker or something?

"I've been trapped inside for days. I almost felt like a prisoner."

Brittany was shocked. Had Kara been held captive? Is that why she was so emotional?

Kara must have seen something on Brittany's face. "Oh, no, it's nothing like that," she rushed to explain. "No one had me locked up or anything. I have trouble going outside sometimes. It's just one of those things. Then today I had this feeling." Kara stopped. "I shouldn't talk like this. It bothers some people." She smiled.

"Oh, right, well I was just out for a walk." Brittany glanced at her watch. "I've got to keep walking or I'll be late."

"What will you be late for? Do you mind if I walk with you a bit? I should get some exercise."

Brittany glanced down at Kara's shoes. She had on bright blue ballet slippers. Her eyes were drawn to Kara's clothes. She wore a short mini skirt in vivid colours of red, violet and yellow with a fancy green and black sweater. It wasn't an outfit one would wear for a fitness walk. Brittany glanced down at her own practical clothes. She wore running shoes, leggings and a long tee shirt, all black and grey. She felt drab beside this girl.

"Can I join you?"

Brittany wanted to say no but couldn't think of a reason to refuse Kara. "Uh, sure," she said aloud as she stood to continue her walk.

Kara talked nonstop as they walked around the park. Brittany had a hard time following at times. It didn't seem to faze Kara though as she kept up a running dialogue. Short, noncommittal answers seemed fine.

Kara was seventeen and went to a nearby high school. Brittany thought she had heard of it but wasn't sure. She didn't want to stop Kara's commentary to clarify where the school was.

"So can you?" Kara asked. "I'd really like you to."

Brittany shook her head. "Pardon?" It seemed Kara had asked a question.

"Come over, to my house. Not today of course since you have classes. You're so lucky to be at university. I can hardly wait till next year. Have you got time tomorrow during the day or after supper?"

"Uh, let me think," Brittany stalled. Wow, Kara moved fast. They'd just met and she already wanted to get together. Brittany wished Brad moved that fast. The thought of him brought another smile to her face.

Brittany had no idea her fate had been preordained. If Kara wanted her there, she'd be there. Kara's question wasn't really a question. It was already a statement of fact … .

5

When Amy arrived at Kara's house a manservant came to the door. He acted the part of a manservant anyway. Did people have manservants these days or was servant a title associated with the past? Were they called menservants or manservants? Amy shrugged. What did it matter? Her mind wandered a lot these days.

"Madame Kara is in the conservatory."

He must be a servant, otherwise why refer to Kara in that formal manner.

"Do you think I could wait for her? She asked me to drop by today for a visit."

The man stared at her. He seemed to consider the question of grave importance. After a long moment of silence he decided in Amy's favour.

"I'm sure she wouldn't mind if you walked down to meet her. Do you know the way?" he inquired in a pleasant manner.

"Yes, thank you."

Amy set off down the long runway. She gazed about with interest. The walkway was alive with flora and fauna both indoors and out. It was very humid. Amy imagined a rainforest would be like this. Small birds alighted here and there. Amy thought they were finches. She hadn't noticed them the previous night. Perhaps they'd been in another room she hadn't seen yet, or in cages.

When she neared the conservatory at the end of the corridor Amy paused to peer out the window at the river view. The setting reminded her of something out of a picture book. It was peaceful yet teemed with life. Sunlight reflected off the water and dappled the trees. Piercing light punctuated by dashes of subdued colours suggested there were a number of birds present.

Bird of Paradise Drums Beating

The activity outdoors surprised Amy. There seemed to be an unusual amount of birds in the area. Wildfowl including geese, ducks and swans were in evidence. Drawn to the area for some unknown reason, their beaks lifted upwards as if they searched for something in the air.

Then Amy heard what might have been the source of their inquiry.

Birdsong rose. It moved with intensity to pierce the serene atmosphere. It charged through the quiet, raising the anticipation level to a frenzied pitch. The tune, although unknown, roused the birds from their former stupor. They rose as one in answer to the song as it poured forth from the recesses of the room Amy had been about to enter.

A cacophony of noise exploded outdoors. The birds and wildfowl erupted, intent on drowning out their neighbour in song. The sound was something beyond this world, heavenly in timbre, the ultimate in sensory awareness. Amy closed her eyes then gave herself freely to the moment.

Amy wished the sensation emitted by the blissful sounds would extend forever. Her awareness was heightened to untold depths. Suspended in time, she held herself utterly still, poised on the edge of consciousness. Amy soaked up the notes like a sponge in water and felt a sense of wonder at the miracle pouring forth around her.

It ended, with an abruptness that caused Amy to sag against the window. Her limbs were a heavy weight. She leaned against the glass like a puppet whose puppeteer had forgotten to pull the strings. Her breath whooshed out, a helium balloon deflated.

Limp and drained, she was oddly refreshed by the incident. These weren't ordinary, everyday sounds she'd heard. The melody rose from a pinnacle of pain and longing, beyond anything from this world.

Amy waited to see if further harmony would happen. With a heavy sigh she acknowledged the performance had ended. What a stroke of luck to arrive at this opportune time. Perhaps a visit to Kara's hadn't been a bad idea after all. Could Amy hope for a similar scene next time she called?

In a better frame of mind Amy turned then entered the room. Again, she experienced sensory overload but of the visual kind this time. Fruit trees graced the room. Dappled sunlight coursed through, creating prisms of light that reflected off full, juicy specimens of fruit, ripe and luscious.

Amy imagined picking one from the overhang. She would open her mouth to its richness, juice flowing from her mouth, taste buds heightened to an unprecedented awareness. The sweet, savoury fruit would drip down her chin. Before Amy could act on her impulse, a sound from the back of the room caught her attention.

It was the shrill cry of a bird, possibly the one she'd heard singing its heavenly melody moments earlier. The bird in question perched high on a tree by an open window.

It was the paradise tanager Amy had seen on the path yesterday.

With cautious steps, Amy approached then gazed with wonder at the vision before her. The bird appeared to study her from its lofty perch. With an inquisitive toss of its head, beady black eyes stared intently at Amy.

No birdsong pierced the air. Instead, Amy heard the steady beat of drums. She gazed through the window eager to see if someone nearby was drumming. No one was in sight.

Amy's eyes alighted on the bird. If anything, the brilliance of the plumage appeared greater than before. Amy watched the bird with interest and noted the unusual blend of colours. It was definitely a tropical bird. Yet it lived here, or did it? Kara had been kind of vague on whether or not the bird was hers.

Thoughts of Kara brought Amy back to her initial reason for being here.

Where was Kara?

"Kara?"

Silence greeted her.

Bird of Paradise Drums Beating

The bird tilted its head toward Amy as if about to speak.

Forehead creased in thought, Amy turned to survey the rest of the room. Sunlight glistened off the tiled floor. Inviting chairs lined a bay window while tables and footstools were scattered throughout the room.

Amy walked to one of the tables, picked up a magazine then leafed through it. A book on a nearby chair caught her interest. It had been left open, with a bookmark beside it, like the reader had stood abruptly, abandoning the book. A stool stood a short distance away, ready to receive outstretched legs. Amy opened the book. She noted the reader had left in the middle of a passage, not at the end of a chapter.

"Have you read it?"

"What?" Amy shrieked, as she turned sharply. Shocked by the sudden appearance of Kara, Amy knocked the book to the floor. The distant sound of drumbeats ceased, broken off to be replaced by the clatter of the book.

Amy strained to hear the drums. She was greeted by silence. With a frown she turned back to Kara.

"The book, have you read it?" Kara stooped to pick up the fallen book.

Kara's cool blue eyes calmly regarded Amy.

Amy reached for the book. She turned to the book cover and recognized it right away.

"Yes, I like biographies and autobiographies. I just finished the book *'Flint & Feather'* written by Charlotte Grey about Pauline Johnson. Her Mohawk name was Tekahionwake. Have you heard of Pauline Johnson?"

Kara shrugged as if Amy's book list was of no importance. Amy frowned, about to pursue the topic further when Kara interrupted her thoughts.

"Do you think it's true?" Kara's voice held an anxious tone.

"What?"

"The book in your hand, do you think it's true?"

"I don't know. I guess I never thought about whether it was true."

Amy turned the book over then glanced at the back jacket before she opened the inside and began to flip through it.

"Take your time." Kara sat down in a seat nearby.

Amy sat in the wicker chair beside Kara. She was grateful to sink into the cushioned recesses, appreciative of the momentary lull. Her hand shook slightly as she leafed through the book. The novel provided a plausible excuse for silence.

Where had Kara come from?

One moment the room was empty then *'poof'* Kara appeared from nowhere. It was similar to yesterday when Kara turned up out of thin air beside the walkway. The drums had also ceased when Kara appeared. Were these events tied together?

"Where were you when I came into the room?"

Kara put down the magazine she'd been leafing through then turned toward Amy. "I was here."

Amy shook her head. "Where, I couldn't see you?"

"Sometimes we can't see what's in front of us. Our mind refuses to acknowledge the truth that stands before us."

"Ha, you sound like an ancient philosopher."

"Hmm, perhaps." Kara's tone was indifferent. "Do you think it's true?"

"What?"

"The book, what did you think of it?" Kara pointed at the book in Amy's hand.

"Oh, yes, the book." Amy checked out the cover again. She remembered parts of the book had been farfetched. *'Unbelievable'* had been the word that popped into Amy's mind on more than one occasion. Of course one never knew with the rich and famous.

"Well, I've never been wealthy or well-known. No one has ever hounded me for an autograph or tried to touch my hair or clothing. I can't relate to any of that. I found it farfetched. *'Unbelievable'* is the word I'd use if I was to review this book."

"Mm hmm."

"You know the main character, the woman. She seemed pleasant enough. Her brother treated her how siblings behave towards an annoying, often overindulged sister. Some parts seemed off somehow, I had trouble believing sections about her eating disorder."

Kara sat bolt upright. Alert now, she asked, "What do you know about eating disorders? Have you ever had one?"

Kara leaned forward, eyes trained on Amy while she waited.

"Uh, no, I haven't. I know very little about it."

Kara sat back heavily in her chair. "Hmm, too bad," she murmured.

Amy watched Kara cross her ankles then relax within the chair again.

"Who are you?"

"Ah, there is more to you than your initial reactions indicate. You show potential with that question. Maybe there's hope for you after all. I just might tell you one or two things about myself. We'll see."

Kara wagged her finger at Amy. She stood then walked over to the window to survey the water. The quiet was absolute.

Amy expected Kara to ignore her question. Startled, she realized Kara had spoken. She watched, fascinated, as words tumbled from Kara's mouth. Slow at first, they quickened then came in rapid succession. It reminded Amy of a locomotive chugging quietly along before shooting forward as it gathered steam.

"I've had," there was a long, pregnant pause. "An eating disorder ..... anorexia."

Kara shuddered. "That's why I asked if you knew anything about eating disorders. Doctors label it a disease. They're not exaggerating. It's not something you do consciously, it just happens."

Kara licked her lips. "Before you know it, this disorder has become part of your life. You can't help yourself. It's like you've been trapped by a wave. You watch it crash towards you, from a distance, dispassionate at first. You realize you're in the path of the wave and it'll consume you. You turn to run, but it's too late. You're swept away, trapped by the force of it. There's no turning back. It's all or nothing. You have to lick it like an alcoholic who gives up alcohol. The alternative is, it takes over and your life is no longer your own."

Kara stopped. With an abrupt movement she turned to stare at Amy.

"Did you lick it?" Amy put the book down, stood then walked over to join Kara by the window.

"No, it devoured me. I felt like the roaring flames of hell poured forth, harsh and relentless they consumed me."

Amy was surprised at the edge in Kara's voice.

"You make it sound so final."

"It was." Kara paused. Amy leaned forward, eager to hear the rest of her sentence. Kara uttered words that echoed through Amy's mind the rest of the day and into the evening.

"I died."

6

Kara wouldn't talk about it after she made her pronouncement. It seemed to be the end of the story.

Amy heard no more of the subject that day. It was frustrating but no matter how much she cajoled and begged, Kara refused to elaborate.

Amy longed for a more in-depth glimmer into Kara's intriguing world. If she'd been a fortune-teller with a crystal ball she would have gazed into the misty depths of Kara's life, witnessed the rising smoke, then watched the performance as a captive audience. For now though, Amy had to be patient. All she could do was hope Kara would continue her story.

Was it worth traveling on this journey with Kara, to learn more about her? Would Kara share further details or continue to throw out tantalizing imagery like streamers floating by on the breeze. Amy longed to grab hold of Kara's vague and filmy inferences and form them into concrete words. If only she knew the key to unlock Kara's reserve.

Amy paused. Was it up to her to unearth Kara's deep, dark secrets? What right did Amy have to interrogate Kara?

Amy didn't know what to say following Kara's confession. How do you react when someone announces they died of anorexia yet stands before you healthy and alive? It was a concrete contradiction. Plus, Kara refused to elaborate on the subject.

Amy decided to be patient. She refused to react to Kara's bizarre comment.

The silence lengthened while Kara stared into space. It fell to Amy to get them started on a new issue. Otherwise, she might as well leave.

Kara had mentioned something interesting the day they'd met, something about a gift. Amy wanted more clarity so she decided to broach the subject.

"Kara, about this gift you mentioned the other day. When we met, you said I had the gift but you haven't elaborated. I've asked questions yet gotten no answers. Honestly, I can't see any point in having conversations that go nowhere. So, about this gift…" Amy trailed off.

Amy was surprised by Kara's response.

"You are so refreshing." Kara laughed. Not just a chuckle, but big belly laughs. Kara doubled over as she laughed and laughed. She leaned against the window, unable to control herself.

What was this? Angered by Kara's laughter Amy turned then walked away. She headed toward the outside door. It was time to cut her losses and exit this nuthouse.

"Wait," Kara called out behind her. "I'm sorry, please, don't leave."

About to push the door open, Amy hesitated. Blood pounded in her ears. It drowned out some of Kara's laughter. She wanted to stalk out and never return. Yet she had to admit she was drawn to this woman. Turning on her heel, Amy whirled toward Kara.

"OK, I'll stay but only if you start answering my questions."

Amy crossed her arms. She didn't step back into the room. Instead, she waited for Kara to make the first move.

Kara's laughter died away. She strode over to Amy. With a welcoming smile she grasped Amy's elbow then led her back into the room. They walked to the chairs they'd vacated.

"Please sit," Kara urged.

Amy tried to contain her anger. As she threw herself into her chair she regarded Kara through narrowed eyes. Taking a deep breath she made a conscious effort to relax. Pettiness would get her nowhere.

Amy uncrossed her arms. She focused on a relaxation technique to center her. After a few calming breathes Amy felt better. Her anger ebbed away. She visualized her stress trickling away in a stream that

Bird of Paradise Drums Beating

led down the side of a scenic mountain. The image was one of peace and tranquility.

Amy felt better. Kara had made an effort, now she would. Amy settled further into her chair.

Kara flashed Amy a quick glance beneath her lashes then sat down.

"Ahem," Kara muttered as she cleared her throat.

Calm now, Amy turned toward Kara.

"I realize you have a number of questions."

Amy wanted to add, *'That's an understatement,'* but controlled herself.

"It's complicated," Kara admitted. Instead of elaborating she began to inspect the tips of her nails.

"Mm hmm."

"It all ties in with a person's spiritual beliefs."

"What does?"

"Well, everything in the universe, of course."

"Oh, all right then."

"The world is based on balance," Kara continued. "It's important to be aware of our surroundings and pay attention to our environment. We get our energy from within, as well as from earth's natural sources. You know the elements are fire, water, earth and air. Everything is important and connected. We need to respond to everyday occurrences and pay attention to what goes on around us. When we gather information we're like explorers on a fact finding expedition."

Kara smiled, "Does that make sense?"

"Yes, it's beginning to."

"Good. Children are prime examples of information gatherers. They do it in a natural manner. The more they find out, the more they want to know. Curiosity is more logical than we think. It's also necessary for growth."

Kara sat back in her chair then stretched her legs before her, arms crossed comfortably. "Now, as you know, individuals have come up with a variety of explanations for how people began to inhabit the earth. I'm not going to get into those since it would take forever to discuss evolution or summarize the religious beliefs of all cultures. Suffice it to say, there are differing opinions. Agreed?"

"Definitely." Amy was pleased to hear Kara talk, even if it was about evolution. What this had to do with Kara's confession about dying or Amy's so-called gift had become no clearer, but perhaps it would in time.

"Great. What I want to concentrate on now is our spiritual side. We experience events based on our consciousness. Yet we often don't take time to pay attention to our subconscious. Dreams, visions, daydreaming, meditation, these are all states we need to consider since they embrace our spiritual side. Amy, have you ever had anything out of the ordinary happen to you? Something you couldn't explain as a natural, everyday occurrence?"

"I don't think so. I mean, I can't recall anything offhand."

Kara focused on Amy. She appeared to search for something deep within her. Amy tried not to squirm. She imagined a bug felt this way while it was being examined under the lens of a microscope. Lucky she didn't have wings for Kara to rip off.

Amy sensed Kara's frustration. She felt like a reluctant student who wouldn't cooperate with her teacher.

Kara gave a slow shake of her head. In a serious, no nonsense voice she remarked sharply. "That's the point. You can't recall anything since you don't focus when it happens. You allow the obvious to pass you by. Do you ponder an unclear problem or situation for even a moment? Is it easier to blow everything off as that appears to be your initial inclination?"

Amy wanted to protest but had to admit she'd given a quick answer to Kara's question. Had Amy thought, even for a moment, her response would have been less trite.

"I'm sorry. I must have experienced something out of the ordinary at one time or another. I have trouble recalling it right now though."

Bird of Paradise Drums Beating

"Yes, well it's true there are occurrences that happen every moment of each day. Many have no concrete explanation. It's important for you to acknowledge they exist."

Amy nodded as Kara continued. "To reach our full potential as individuals we need to heighten our awareness of events. We should question what takes place around us. We shouldn't accept what others say as fact without investigating it on our own.

Think of this like a mini scientist. Read any materials you can get your hands on. It's important to experiment, interpret, delve, analyze and tune into nature and that which surrounds us. Life is a mystery, don't you think?"

"Oh yes, I agree wholeheartedly," Amy gushed. "I always tell my children to ask questions and discover the answers for themselves. It's the best way to learn."

Amy sat with her hands in her lap. Complacent, she was totally unaware of the direction Kara was headed.

"Yes. I like that. Oh, by the way, I'd like you to invite your daughter Brittany to join us in our conversations." She waited a beat. "Have you noticed anything different about me or the way we met?"

For an instant Amy wondered what this had to do with science and discovery. Why had Kara thrown out the offhand comment about Brittany? Was it a red herring? Amy sighed as she took a moment to consider Kara's question.

"I don't think so. Well, except for the fact I heard words float by. Yet there was no one around but you or I when we met on the path. Oh, and the pain I experienced. That was strange."

Content with her answer, Amy nodded at Kara.

"Uh huh." Kara arched her brows then nodded.

"That's it." Amy frowned. What more did Kara expect?

"What about when you came here today. Did you notice anything out of the ordinary?"

Amy sat up straight. She narrowed her eyes as she gazed about the room. There were a number of things she'd noted. She'd wondered where Kara had been when she arrived. The tropical bird was here with no sign of Kara. Come to think of it where was the bird now?

Amy stood then began to move about the room. She was quiet as she checked among the fruit trees for the bird. She couldn't find it. She returned to her chair then sat down.

"I have observed a few things now that you mention it."

Kara stifled a yawn.

Was she bored by the conversation?

Kara must have noticed Amy's expression, as she was quick to apologize, "Sorry, I didn't sleep well last night."

"Oh. Well, one thing I wondered is where you came from today? When I entered this room it was empty. Then *'poof'* you appeared out of nowhere. Yesterday and the day before you turned up out of thin air beside the walkway."

"Perhaps you're not aware of what takes place right before your eyes Amy. You might possess the gift. With proper training you could in time see what is in front of you." Kara words were mysterious, they held a mystic vibe.

"It's unfortunate though. From what I've seen, you're not a natural. It could require work. So much depends on you."

"What? Why can't you answer my question instead of spouting words that make no sense?"

Kara leaned forward. "They would make sense if you stopped to think about them. Are you willing to try something right now?"

"Like what?" Amy huffed as she crossed her arms.

Amy would have been surprised to find she had an obstinate, closed expression on her face. It didn't disturb Kara in the least though. She ignored Amy's stubbornness and apparent irritation.

"I want you to close your eyes. Think what happened around you yesterday and the day before when you saw me on the path. Then I want you to imagine how this room was today when you entered it.

What occurred before you came into the room? What do you remember? Feel free to accept any ideas that enter your head. Talk aloud while you replay your experiences. Can you try that Amy?"

"Hmm, I don't know. Well, maybe." Amy was unwilling to embrace the notion fully.

"Through an awareness of your surroundings you'll become more in tune with yourself and others. Then we'll see if you have the gift or merely stumbled upon something. Don't worry. I'll be here. You're safe."

"All right, I guess I have nothing to lose."

"Great, close your eyes and start from wherever you feel comfortable."

Amy squirmed in her seat. She closed her eyes then took calming breaths. She placed her hands in her lap. Then she visualized what she'd seen today.

"It wasn't so much what I saw that caught my attention. It was what I heard." Amy's voice was calm, measured. "The sweet poignant sounds of a song bird greeted me. I wanted the melody to continue forever. It captured my attention, made me want more. When it ended I felt sad. I longed for it to continue." She chuckled. "I hope to catch a repeat performance tomorrow."

Amy fidgeted in her seat. "The smell in the room overpowered me. The fruit on the trees was enticing. I wanted to reach up and eat one. I imagined juice running down my chin."

A smile lit up Amy's face. "I saw the bird. I thought it had been singing. It was the tropical bird I noticed the other day on the path. I've glimpsed it three times now. Well, four, if you count the portrait over your fireplace."

"When were the three times?" Kara whispered.

"Hmm, let me get it straight in my head. Today, I saw the bird after I smelled fruit on the trees. I'd been searching for you. You were nowhere in sight. I spotted the bird then."

Amy smoothed her brow with her hand. "I saw the bird after we met. You'd just left. I turned to say good-bye since I didn't want to appear rude. I'd snubbed you earlier and felt bad about my lack of manners. You'd disappeared though. I thought it odd how you vanished into thin air. That was the first time I noticed the bird. It was on the path. Oh, there's one other thing too."

"What's that?"

"Each time I've seen the bird I've heard a drum beat in the background. It fades away or stops when you appear."

Amy stiffened, "Wait a minute. I've just thought of something else. The colours of the bird are unusual. The combination twigged something in my mind. I couldn't recall what. I've just thought of it now."

Amy turned to Kara. "The colours of the bird were the same as the ones you wore that day. I took note of your outfit since it struck me as eccentric. The colours blended, yet didn't."

Amy's eyes widened as she took in what Kara wore. "You're wearing them again," she shrieked. "I can't believe it. You've got a red bow in your hair and those outrageous yellow high top sneakers on your feet. Your skirt is blue and green and your top is violet and black. Your earrings have a bird of paradise on them. Do you always wear that colour combination? That's too freaky!"

Kara smiled, yet said nothing.

As if in a trance, Amy sat back in her chair. She spoke in a slow, calm voice. "I remember the second time I saw the bird. It was in the same spot, on the path where I'd seen it the evening before. The song intrigued me. I felt uplifted yet sensed immense pain. It emanated from the bird. I was drawn to it. I wanted to approach yet simultaneously flee from it. I was emotional, caught between two choices. I stumbled about the path. Should I get closer to the bird or free myself while I still had the chance?"

Amy turned slowly toward Kara then pointed her finger. "Then you appeared out of nowhere and the bird disappeared. I felt bereft at the loss of the bird, overpowered by my conflicting emotions.

You were matter of fact though. You described what type of bird it was, gave me details. I wondered at the time if there was a connection since you mysteriously appeared at the same spot more than once. I didn't think about it until now though. There's one more thing. Every time you appear, the drum fades away."

Amy paused. "Is this why you wanted me to visualize everything that's happened? Is there a connection between you and the bird? What about the drum?"

Kara nodded.

Amy willingly shared her next thoughts. "My husband Andy thought you were related to the bird somehow. Besides the fact it lives here. Andy thought you mentioned my hidden gift as an invitation to ask questions or help you solve a puzzle. Was he correct?"

Again, nothing, Kara merely smiled. It reminded Amy of a cat who'd been fed cream and was content to just sit now.

"Are you going to tell me about the link or make me guess?"

"What do you think?" Kara's tone was pleasant, easygoing.

Amy groaned.

"No matter, it will come to you when you're ready. You've made wonderful progress today. Don't give it a second thought."

Something nagged at Amy as she stared at Kara. It was filmy and vague, like a thought whispering. She closed her eyes to open her mind to the notion that flitted about.

Ah, that was it, the pain.

Amy's eyes flew open. "There's something else I remembered about the pain. When I heard the tropical bird sing the first time it was a Carpenter song. Remember that group? Andy and I figured out the name of the tune. It was *Close to You*." Amy hummed the tune.

Kara leaned forward in her chair, eyes closed, mouth slightly ajar, ear cocked toward Amy.

"What do you think it meant?" Amy asked as she finished the chorus.

Sitting bolt upright in her chair, Kara opened her eyes. Like an outfielder she lobbed a mysterious, noncommittal answer into the air. It was up to Amy to catch then interpret as she wished. "You'll learn in time if it was meant to be."

Kara stood then walked to one of the fruit trees.

What kind of cryptic remark was that? Amy shook her head. Kara was certainly an odd duck. First she refused to respond to questions. Then she spouted off ideas like a water fountain spurting a stream into a pond. One moment she reeled off information like a professor lecturing an eager student. Then she'd clam up and hoard answers as if they were of tantamount importance. It was confusing.

Chewing her bottom lip, Amy stared at Kara's back.

Kara turned her head then returned Amy's stare. She gave a slight smile almost as if she read Amy's mind.

"I should go."

"Of course." Kara sounded indifferent. "Come again tomorrow if you like. Oh, and bring your daughter Brittany with you. I'd like her here for our conversation tomorrow."

Kara turned back to her fruit trees.

As Amy left, she heard the melodious sounds of a songbird.

7

Against her better judgment, Amy returned to Kara's house the next day. Brittany accompanied her.

That had been weird in itself. When Brittany got home from her classes Amy mentioned meeting Kara.

Brittany riffled through her purse. "Oh, you've met her on the path too?"

Amy was flustered. "Well, yes, why? Do you know her?"

"Yes, we met when I went for a walk this morning."

"I went over to Kara's house today and I'll be going back for another visit tomorrow. She wants you to come with me."

Brittany shrugged. "Yeah, maybe, what time are you going?"

Amy hid her surprise. They'd discussed a time convenient for both of them then agreed to go over to Kara's together.

Kara started out with a question when Amy and Brittany walked in. No *'hello'* or *'how are you today?'*

"What do you think about reincarnation Amy?"

"I don't know, I never thought about it." Amy glanced at Brittany.

Brittany was checking out the room, her eyes bright with interest.

Where did Kara think of her questions? An image came to Amy's mind of Kara throwing subjects at Amy like a pitcher in the minor leagues. Some topics were like a wild pitch while others were a strike. Andy loved baseball and had tried to familiarize Amy with it. Amy found baseball confusing and some of Kara's conversations baffled her as well.

"Do you believe in it?" Kara persisted.

"What? Um, I don't know anything about reincarnation so I'm not sure what I think about it." Amy glanced at Brittany. Brittany's gaze was fixed on Kara.

"There's something different about you," Brittany blurted as she glared at Kara. "Yesterday you seemed insecure and ill at ease. Now today you're assertive and, you know, sort of demanding. I found it rude how you didn't welcome us when we came in. What's up with that? Did we come at a bad time?"

Kara seemed confused for a moment. Then with an abruptness that was startling, she laughed.

Amy and Brittany didn't join in the laughter. Instead, they exchanged a puzzled look. Brittany shrugged as Kara's laughter died down.

"What a refreshing child you are. Do you always interrupt conversations to express your opinion? No, you did not come at a bad time. I'm just not used to social pleasantries. I find them tedious."

"Why would you call me a child? I thought you were a year younger than me?"

"Yes, you're right. I am different today. I hope to explain why to you and your mother. Not right this instant though. Clarity can only be achieved after one has walked through a maze of confusion." Kara smiled. "Consider this part, your maze of confusion."

Brittany opened her mouth to reply.

Kara held her hand up. "Stop, don't say anything. Just listen, that's your task for today. Can you handle that Brittany?"

Brittany narrowed her eyes at Kara. "I can handle anything you dish out Kara," she answered in a snide tone.

"Hmm, we'll see."

Kara turned to Amy. "You were about to ask me something, weren't you?"

Amy shook her head. Then she remembered the previous subject. "Right, I wondered if you could tell us more about reincarnation?"

Bird of Paradise Drums Beating

"What do you want to know specifically?" Kara's tone was eager.

Amy felt as if she were on the edge of something. Kara wanted her to make a specific request. She didn't want to mess it up.

"I want to know how it relates to you."

Amy held her breath, eager to see if Kara would answer.

Amy might have hesitated longer had she known what she'd asked. A door was about to be opened. Amy and Brittany were poised on the edge of knowledge. Their introduction to age-old wisdom would span time. This present course of action would take them down a path they'd never known existed.

The awareness and understanding Amy and Brittany would collect along the way would provide them with wealth unparalleled by mere dollars. Amy was blissfully unaware of any of this when she asked her question.

A key to the past was about to be unlocked ...

Amy and Brittany would be the lucky recipients of untold riches....

Kara sat down in a wicker chair between Amy and Brittany. With no fanfare whatsoever she began her mysterious tale.

Amy leaned forward. She found herself caught immediately in the web of language woven effortlessly by Kara.

The story Kara embarked upon was one of eternity.

As the journey of discovery unfolded it became clear this was no low level drama. It had elements of truth, courage, pain, love and fortitude. Like every great storyteller, Kara wove her elements skillfully together. She was quick to capture Amy and Brittany's interest.

Amy was enthralled. She realized immediately Kara was no ordinary female. Kara's words flowed as she spoke of reincarnation. Amy sat on the edge of her seat, eager and attentive.

"Reincarnation is defined as the rebirth of one's soul in a new body. It's a system of belief some live by, while others disdain. Depends on your religion of course and the period you were born in."

Amy leaned forward, closer to Kara.

"Throughout the ages, reincarnation, or rebirth as some call it, has been a state many people believe in. In Aztec mythology warriors were reborn as hummingbirds. In Greek mythology there was a river of forgetfulness, situated in the underworld and a place known as Elysium. It was a land of perfect peace and happiness where great heroes were made immortal. Then there's the Utopian vision of harmony and progress. Quite the variety of views, don't you agree Brittany?"

"Yeah, sure."

"There's more. Christianity believes in the immortal soul. Through faith, a person may be granted God's presence in the afterlife. Eastern religions state once you've been caught in the cycle of reincarnation the human soul must achieve the highest level of purification and knowledge. Only then will one achieve the ultimate reality. Can you guess what that is, Amy?"

"Umm, well, no, I can't."

"That's all right." Kara chuckled. "How about you Brittany, care to guess?"

"Hmm, no, I have no idea either."

"Most people aren't aware of this knowledge unless they've studied the subject. No matter, I'll fill you in quite adequately I'm sure. Enlightenment, a higher state of consciousness, involves death and rebirth."

"Ah," Amy murmured as if the word had been on the tip of her tongue.

She was rewarded with a slight smile and nod. Amy felt as if Kara had read her mind and found her mildly amusing.

"According to Buddha, we need to attain four virtuous attitudes in life. They are loving-kindness, compassion, sympathetic joy and serenity. To be enlightened we need to overcome greed, hatred and ignorance. As we experience rebirth we hope to move towards betterment. The only way to do this is to fulfill one's duties towards society.

This means we must perform acts of charity and observe the moral code of Buddha. One cannot steal, kill, engage in harmful language, sexual misbehaviour or use intoxicants. When we observe these five guidelines we overcome the three roots of evil, lust, hatred and delusion. Any questions so far?"

"Mind if I take notes?" Brittany began to rummage in her purse. "I can use some of this stuff for a paper I have to do. No wonder you don't have time for friends, you must have read a ton of stuff and been on the Internet for days to figure all this out. You're a great storyteller."

Brittany beamed at Kara.

Kara ignored her praise. "What about you?" she asked Amy.

Amy shook her head. "No, your explanations are clear. Although, I don't think lust should be a root of evil. I think it's good for your spouse or significant other to exhibit lust. It is healthy for a relationship."

Kara frowned.

Amy rushed on. "What a fascinating topic though. Did you study it out of personal interest? Are you working towards a degree in some area related to reincarnation or religion?"

"Hardly." Kara sighed as if Amy's question and Brittany's praise barely warranted the effort it took to reply.

"I think Buddha meant lust as in wanting something that doesn't belong to you. If you lust after a man who is someone else's, then set your sights to get him, you exhibit the roots of evil."

"Ah, like coveting your neighbour or friends' possessions."

"Precisely, if I may continue, all religions speak of reincarnation in one form or another. It depends on how you interpret what they say with what your faith is. Of course, if you believe in Buddhism you also have the threat of transmigration hanging over you. That's where you come back at a lower level. It's often something repulsive like an animal or bug. Of course that only happens when you've been extremely unpleasant."

Kara made a face.

Amy laughed. "A bug," she repeated as she chuckled at the image.

"Yes, a bug or an animal. You don't get to choose of course. What one tries to achieve through reincarnation is face challenges presented to us. As we learn to overcome life's little problems and rise above petty differences, we grow to be a better person. Our spirit becomes more enlightened. Thus it progresses to the next level of consciousness. This raises the question posed throughout the ages. Is there life after death?"

Kara paused then glanced at Amy.

Amy was about to blurt out some half-formulated sentence when Kara forged ahead. "I don't pretend to know the answer to that age-old question. I can tell you about my personal experiences and what happened to me though.

Whether this occurs on a universal or individual basis I can't say. If you wish, I can relate my story. Then you can grapple with the moral questions presented. How's that for a deal? I promise to raise your awareness but can't guarantee enlightenment on your part. That's for the two of you to determine."

"Sure, sounds great." Amy had no clue what Kara meant.

Brittany shrugged as she continued to take notes.

Amy glanced at Brittany then smiled. Brit had always had a weird habit of taking notes. Amy thought it was an endearing trait but odd nonetheless.

With her mysterious statement delivered, Kara began to narrate her story. It was a tale unbelievable at times, yet poignant in the startling simplicity of the telling.

Amy and Brittany were enthralled. Not once were they tempted to leave Kara's house. The door to enlightenment, to borrow one of Kara's words, had been left slightly ajar.

Would Amy and Brittany dare enter through it?

8

"I remember bits and pieces of my lives. It is odd how parts have been erased from my mind," Kara murmured, her tone thoughtful.

Amy gave a quick nod, unsure of what Kara referred to.

"I don't think I'll go in order or anything. I'm sure I'll bounce around at times. It's not as if I'm doing a chronological life history and you're recording it. If you were a reporter, historian or writer I might tell my story in a different way. For now though, I'll just talk about whatever pops into my head. How's that sound?"

Kara waved her arm at Brittany.

Brittany shrugged. "It's your story. Tell it however you want."

Kara frowned then glanced at Amy.

"Uh great, yeah sure, tell us whatever you want. Oh, by the way..." Amy trailed off.

Kara raised her eyebrows, impatient for Amy to continue.

"I'm a writer. In my spare time I mean. More, recreational..." Amy trailed off again at Kara's expression.

Kara measured Amy through narrowed eyes.

Amy squirmed then perched on the edge of her seat, eager to hear about these '*lives*' Kara referred to.

Perhaps Kara thought she was a cat with nine lives. These stories might provide some scenes for a new book. At the very least, Kara's tales would provide topics Brittany and her could share. Amy smiled.

Noting Amy's smile, Kara seemed to take it as acknowledgement to begin her narrative.

"My recollection involves stairs."

Penny Ross

Kara stared into the distance mesmerized by something only she could see.

"There were at least fifty stairs. I was glad there were so many. Each step took my breath away. It was part of my last moment on earth. You see, I knew it was the end of my life and everything I'd experienced up to this moment was precious. I was a virgin. About to be sacrificed to one of the agricultural gods. The rain god or corn god, I'm not sure which one now. I can't remember. No matter, I must have been about fourteen, I'd guess."

"Wait, back up a minute. I think I missed something. I'm confused," Amy interrupted.

With a dismissive toss of her hair Kara ignored the unwelcome intrusion.

"My locks were raven black. They hung down past my waist. I wore an elaborate hair dress with a tiara on top of my head. You know, now that I think about it my hair has always been dark. It's been chestnut brown, copper, black, dark brown or reddish gold. I don't remember ever being a blond. I wonder why?"

Amy shrugged, confused by Kara's remarks. Who cared about hair colour?

"Blonde hair would be strange on you. I don't think it would go with your skin tone. Just saying." Brittany frowned then bent over her notes.

As if unaware of their presence, Kara continued her narrative. Like a person in a trance she was immersed in her tale.

"My body was covered with tattoos, made up of elaborate, intricate designs. They were on my arms and entire upper body. I wore simple clothing. A blouse made of woven cotton and a skirt. Both articles had embroidery on them. I probably sewed them myself. I was a commoner you see, not an aristocrat or noble."

"Where were you and who were you?" Amy demanded.

Kara paused then spoke in a slow, hesitant manner, almost as if she had to sift through her thoughts. "This is an earlier recollection. You must understand there have been many of them. I can't be sure of dates every time. I think this was during the Mayan Civilization. It would have been around 300 or 400 A.D. It's the region now known as southeast Mexico, Guatemala, Belize, the Honduras and El Salvador."

"Kind of strange how you talk in the first person all the time," Brittany noted. "When we write essays it's usually in the third person. Is that something your teachers like at your school?"

Kara narrowed her eyes at Brittany.

Amy had heard of the Mayan Civilization but wished she knew more about it. She raised her hand then leaned toward Kara like a keen schoolgirl eager for her teacher's attention. When there was no response, Amy gave a vigorous wave. Kara ignored Amy just as she'd brushed aside Brittany's question. She plowed on with her story.

"I don't remember my name. It might be difficult to say in English anyway. It doesn't matter since I wasn't anyone famous. Later I'll tell you about someone legendary and you can guess my identity. That should be fun, don't you think?"

"Whatever." Brittany sniffed then shook her head.

Amy pasted a silly smile on her face. Was Kara serious? She imagined she'd been a famous person. Who did that?

"There I was, walking up these steps. They were made of stone, carved into the shape of a pyramid."

"Hmm," Amy murmured. One had to give Kara credit for extensive research into the subject as she narrated her make-believe story.

"The entire village was composed of stone pyramids, temples, stone houses for noble persons and of course the immense palace where the ruler lived." Kara shrugged. "We lived in a humble home. We were fortunate though since we didn't have to perform menial tasks like the slaves in the village. They were often sacrificed when their owners died. Then they could continue to be slaves and serve their owners in the afterlife. At least when I died I didn't have to work for anyone."

Amy nodded as if that made sense.

"My spirit was free to roam about. For some time anyway until I was reincarnated as another person. I'm not sure who decided I'd come back or why they chose me to be someone famous. No matter, I think I had an impact in that life. I'll tell you about that one later."

Amy glanced at Brittany. She longed to ask if Brit was as confused as she was. Why did Kara refer to other memorable lives? It was hard to follow Kara's narrative when she didn't stay on topic. This reincarnation business was trickier than one would think.

"When one is sacrificed it's supposed to be an honour since it appeases a god. At the time I didn't feel privileged though." Kara shuddered. "I was scared as I walked toward the priest. He stood on an altar on top of the pyramid. It was a mound made of rubble. Imagine being sacrificed on top of a great pile of garbage. Seems rather undignified doesn't it?"

Kara laughed.

"Yes, when you put it that way it does," Amy agreed. The image Kara portrayed was amusing.

Kara sobered quickly. "I remember my senses were heightened. Children cried softly while mothers consoled them. The soulful song of a bird was off in the distance. I've always had a soft spot for birds.

In some of my lives I had a cat. You know, as my familiar, but most times it's been a bird. I express myself more freely as a bird. Ah, I see I've confused you again."

Brittany frowned at Kara while Amy stared wide-eyed.

"A familiar," Amy yelped. "What are you talking about?"

Kara waved her hand as if the distraction was of no consequence. "No matter I'll explain later. Where was I?"

Brittany jumped in. "You had a cat as a familiar in some lives but you prefer a bird. Before that you mentioned a priest and a pile of garbage."

"Right, thanks Brittany. My mother stood off to the side. I watched tears slide down her cheeks unheeded. She was focused on my ascent to the top of that rubble.

My younger brothers and sisters were grouped around my father, intent on my last steps. They hardly dared to breathe. I imagined little sighs escaped unbidden from their lips. They were eager to know if they were next in line for this honourable ritual. The sky was brilliant. The sun was merciless. It hurt my eyes as it beat down like a great round star. It radiated warmth and radiance at this final, crucial time."

Amy was appalled by Kara's description. How could Kara have a cavalier attitude toward death? Who cared if the sun resembled a great round star for heaven's sake? Now was not the time to wax poetic.

"I'd always heard your life flashes before you at the definitive time. I don't recall that happened."

Kara frowned. "Perhaps I was too young or the occasion generated something deeper. For me, it was a critical point. I sensed why this had happened and what my future held. Of course, I didn't know what reincarnation was at the time, or how it would affect my life. I knew I was destined for greatness though, even then."

Kara laughed as she shook back her hair. "You know, it seems odd now that I relay this aloud. It's hard to explain. I realize my reality was altered at that exact second in time. At that last instant I had a brief glimpse into my future. I knew I'd be faced with great challenges. Change had come for me. My soul would soon become part of the higher good."

Kara's face was grim. "I had no idea my soul would be lost as I became part of the universe." She sounded sad as she added. "The person I'd been ceased to exist. I became a chattel. It doesn't matter whose property I am. Suffice it to say the ability to govern my thoughts, control my actions, lead my life on the path I choose, disappeared at that moment."

Kara shuddered. "I lost my freedom. I am enslaved by an idea borne upon wings of chance. Restrictions forced upon me at that instant govern the lives I've led since."

Kara hung her head. In a soft voice she whispered, "The only time I'm free to express myself is when I'm unhindered by human form. Only then, am I able to pour forth my thoughts and emotions.

With unbridled passion and longing I yearn for that which I cannot have."

Amy watched in amazement as tears poured from Kara's eyes. They cascaded down her cheeks, a flood unleashed with relentless fury. In that instant, Amy made her decision. Kara's state of mind was irrelevant. Kara believed she'd told Amy and Brittany the truth. Her hold on reality was fragile.

Kara thought she'd lived in the Mayan civilization. She felt the pain of her knowledge. As she gathered Kara into her arms, Amy soothed her the way she would one of her children. She rocked gently to and fro as she hummed a quiet tune of comfort.

Brittany was quiet as Kara cried into Amy's shoulder.

"Thank you," Kara hiccupped moments later. "I didn't realize this outpouring would be so emotional. I've always imagined I'd tell someone my story. I thought I'd feel good about it, happy to share what I experienced.

The feelings I've generated and these emotions caught me off guard. I feel stripped before you, naked, like a newborn baby birthed before an audience. Before I can tell you the truth about my destiny though, I need time to myself. It will do me good to sort through the twisty path of knowledge I've stumbled upon. I have to regroup, to decide what course to take down this wordy passage. Perhaps we could continue our chat again tomorrow? I'll see the two of you then."

Kara managed a shaky half smile as she stood. She swayed slightly then grasped the chair for support.

Amy stood then reached out to squeeze Kara's shoulder. She hoped the affection would help steady Kara in the process.

"I can hardly wait," Amy murmured.

Kara turned then left without a backward glance.

Amy sat back in the chair she'd just vacated.

What had just happened? Kara's revelation was preposterous. Amy was convinced it was an elaborate tale contrived for their benefit. Yet Kara's reaction had been real. Her distress was not manufactured.

"What do you think?" Amy turned to Brittany.

Bird of Paradise Drums Beating

Brittany took her time. She capped her pen, closed her notebook, leaned down to get her purse then placed both items inside.

"Well, her story seems to span centuries since this part took place in 300 or 400 AD. It's 2012 right now. I'm interested to see how she gets back to this time. Will she claim to be some sort of time traveller maybe?" Brittany shrugged. "Whatever, let's go, I have a class tonight. We can talk as we walk home."

As they walked out the door Amy commented. "I guess it's not fair to judge Kara as crazy until we listen to more of her story. I wonder what lives Kara will pretend she's survived through? She talks about reincarnation as a familiar state. I guess we shouldn't judge her though."

"Yeah, she's certainly interesting. It's odd how she invited you and I separately then asked you to bring me along today. I wondered what a seventeen year old would have to say to my mother but she has no problem keeping us both amused."

"What do you mean Brittany? Who's seventeen?"

"Kara is."

"No, she's not. She has two sons and a husband. She's gotta be in her late thirties for sure."

"Mom, didn't you check her out? You must be confused. Maybe you met her mom and dad and those are her brothers."

Amy shook her head. "No, it was definitely her husband and sons. She introduced them to me."

Brittany huffed.

Amy didn't want Brittany to be mad. There must be a logical explanation about the discrepancy in Kara's age. They just had to figure out what it was.

"Let's think about this Brittany. We think Kara is a different age. She can't be a teenager and a woman in her thirties. That's impossible, isn't it?" Amy paused. Was it impossible? Her eyes met Brittany's.

"She just told us some fantastic story about reincarnation mom. Maybe her age has something to do with it. I mean, really, what kind

Penny Ross

of woman wears that strange colour combination? What about her shoes? Come on, who would wear those? We'd laugh if you walked around like that. She has to be a teen."

"Yeah, you've got a point there. She dresses weird even for a teen."

They laughed as they neared the house.

"You know Brittany we could learn something about women and history. Kara has a natural flair as a storyteller."

"Yeah, maybe you can write your next book about her."

"I thought the same thing. This could be a perfect research opportunity. Obviously the book would be fictional though."

"Yeah, imagine if it was a bestseller. When you get on some famous talk show you can tell this story about how we thought Kara was seventeen and thirty-some simultaneously. That would peak people's interest. Don't you think?"

"Me on a famous talk show, wow, imagine."

"You've always told us to dream big mom, then turn your dreams into reality. Who knows, maybe this is part of your reality."

Brittany leaned over to kiss Amy on the cheek.

"I've gotta get my stuff."

"Thanks honey. Want a sandwich to take with you?"

"That would be great. Thanks mom."

As Amy went in the kitchen she saw a message from Andy. A client wanted to take them out to dinner. Great, she'd change then walk to the restaurant nearby.

Amy called out to her daughter. "Brittany can I borrow your red shawl? I need something to take to the restaurant in case the air conditioner is still on."

"Sure, I'll bring it down with me."

Amy thought it was great they could borrow clothes from one another. Even though Brittany was a few inches taller and a size eight while Amy was size ten and only five foot six they still managed to fit quite a few of the same clothes. They both wore size seven shoes so that was a bonus when it came to shoe shopping.

As she stepped outside awhile later, Amy was pleased the evening was still warm. She thought of Kara as she walked. Tomorrow held promise of another exciting day. This could be a fantastic experience Amy and Brittany were privileged to share. It was the perfect mother-daughter bonding adventure.

9

Brittany was headed toward the door when she heard someone call her name.

"Brittany, Brittany, hey, wait."

She turned around to see Brad hurrying toward her. Brittany grinned. How excellent was this, she hadn't seen Brad in days.

"Did you have a night class?"

"Yeah, we just finished, how about you?"

"I was hanging out with a friend downstairs." Brad moved away from the door back into the hallway as a few students approached. He gently pulled Brittany out of their way.

"Oh, thanks," she acknowledged as she leaned against the wall. "What's downstairs? I've never gone there."

"You're kidding. You must have. Here let me show you." Brad moved further into the hall then leaned forward over the railing. "You can see right to the bottom from here. Brandon and I sat on those couches."

Brittany followed Brad then glanced down. "Hmm, definitely haven't been down there. This place is bigger than I thought."

"Guess you haven't checked for used books yet."

"There's a book store down there, where?"

Brad laughed. "Want to grab a coffee or drink then wander down there? I can show you around. The couches are sort of comfortable. Have you got time?"

"Yeah, that sounds great. I thought everything was closed by now though."

"We have to go outside. They have drinks and stuff over at Extreme Pita. It's still open."

"Makes sense. I mean that we have to go outside to a restaurant. The night was perfect for a walk when I came to class. Still seems nice out."

Brad told her about the friend he'd bumped into. They'd gone to high school together and played volleyball, basketball and badminton together.

"So this is the first time you've bumped into him?"

"Yeah, Brandon works part-time, so his schedule is different from mine. He just happened to be here because he'd dropped by the used book store after a shift at work."

"Are you going to meet up again?"

"I got his cell number and we thought we'd go to a movie or something on the weekend. We always got along. You know how jocks are." Brad chuckled.

"Yeah, one of my brothers is a jock. He sweats a lot, that's what I remember. Phew, what a smell." Brittany fanned her face as if batting away something unpleasant.

A strange expression crossed Brad's face as if he wasn't sure about her comment.

"Hah, got you." Brittany laughed then linked her arm through his in a playful manner. "I was kidding, there's more to jocks than sweaty socks."

"Funny, hardy, har, you're hilarious and yeah some of us do have sweaty socks."

Brad made a fist then flexed his muscles for her. "Check this out. Jocks have more than stinky feet."

"Whoa, impressive." Brittany gamely felt his bulging bicep.

He laughed then grabbed her hand and squeezed it gently. He wrapped his fingers around hers then pulled her closer to his side.

Brittany liked it. She made sure to breathe normally so Brad wouldn't feel her excitement. They were holding hands, how cool was that!

They got to Extreme Pita far too soon. Brittany scanned the menu to see what kind of drinks they had. It was too late for coffee.

She didn't want to be awake all night. "Smoothies and juices are over there." Brad nodded toward the far side of the room. "Want a pita?"

"Sure, I could eat." Brittany realized she was hungry. She'd only eaten a sandwich and that had been hours ago.

"I didn't know Booster Juice was in here," Brittany commented as they wandered over to check out the menu.

"You've missed a lot haven't you?" Brad teased. "You didn't know about the basement with couches and a book store and now you claim you've missed the Booster Juice, Extreme Pita restaurant combo."

"Yeah, I kind of feel like I've been living under a rock now that you mention it. You had to show me Stella's too. Yum, Maui Juice, I think I'll order that."

"Good choice, I'm going to splurge and get a smoothie. I'm craving some major protein right now. You know us jocks."

Brittany giggled as Brad ordered food. After Brad paid he turned to Brittany. "Shall we?" He grabbed the bag, opened the door then motioned for her to go ahead.

What a gentleman. No one besides her dad and old guys ever held the door open for her. It was a nice change.

Brad transferred the bag to his other hand then grabbed hers again.

Brittany wanted to sigh with contentment as she wrapped her fingers around his.

They chatted about classes as they headed back to the university. Then Brad led her down a few flights of stairs to the lower level.

"I'll show you where the used books store is in case you ever want to check it out. I come here all the time. Some of the profs want you to order new textbooks every year but if you get the same one and it's just one edition older there's hardly any changes."

"Petrified Sole Used Bookstore. Sounds like the name of a shoe store."

"There you go with your shoe comments again. Do you have a shoe fetish?" Brad teased.

Bird of Paradise Drums Beating

"Ha, ha, funny guy." Brittany playfully swatted his arm as they passed a few offices on their way back to the couches. "I do like shoe sales though, I gotta admit I'm a girl through and through."

Brad grabbed her hand then pulled her closer to him. He leaned toward her then stroked her cheek. "Mm, you're right, you smell good, just like a girl."

Brittany held her breath. Was he going to kiss her?

He gave her a devilish smile as if he'd read her mind. "Later," he promised. "First, let's eat."

Brittany let her breath out slow and steady. Get a grip she thought. It's no big deal, really, what was the rush?

Brad sat on one of the couches then pulled her down beside him.

The couch was a bit saggy but not too bad. Brittany took her coat off then took the drink Brad held out to her.

"Oh, I should call my mom and let her know I'm still here. She'll worry if I don't come home at my usual time." Brittany reached into her purse to grab her phone.

"Good idea, don't want a worried mom after me." Brad grinned as he reached into the bag to retrieve their pitas.

Brittany called her mom, put her phone away then began to eat her pita.

Brad had already eaten half of his. He didn't talk while he ate intent on his food. Brittany watched him out of the corner of her eye as she took another bite. He seemed to enjoy his food. He didn't wolf it down like one of her brothers.

When Brad finished he took a napkin then wiped his mouth and hands. He glanced at Brittany who was halfway done. "That was great. I love pitas." He flashed her a quick smile.

"Same here, I'm getting full though. Want the rest of mine?"

"You sure?"

"Yeah, take it." She held it out to him even though she could have finished it off. Sharing was nicer.

"Kay, yum, this is a good one too."

Brittany smiled as she watched Brad. She could get used to this.

10

"Oh, you're here."

Kara sounded despondent, not happy Amy and Brittany had showed up.

"Would you like us to leave?" Amy was quick to ask.

There was a lengthy silence.

Amy was sure they'd be asked to go.

Then without warning, Kara broke the uncomfortable hush with a witty remark.

"Not at all, this can't be nearly as bad as the guillotine or being burned at the stake as a witch, now can it?"

Kara's harsh laughter echoed off the walls.

"No, I imagine it can't be. Are you saying...."

Amy broke off at the expression on Kara's face.

"Now, now, let me tell this at my pace." Kara wagged her fingers at Amy. "Some stories are more interesting than others. I've been slaughtered so many ways I'm sure I could write a book about it, of the shake and bake variety." Kara chuckled, this time with more amusement.

"No, the reason I was unhappy when you arrived is I've noticed I've put on a few pounds this week. I can't understand it. I walk and never overindulge. It seems odd."

"Perhaps the scale is off."

"You should power walk," Brittany suggested. "You have to get your heart rate up and make sure to sweat. You'll lose more calories that way."

Brittany smiled as the sweaty comment reminded her of her conversation last night with Brad. They were going to meet up after class tomorrow. She could hardly wait.

Bird of Paradise Drums Beating

"Hmm, yes, well, perhaps." Kara frowned at Brittany.

Brittany wiped the smile off her face at Kara's expression. Oops, she'd better concentrate on this conversation and think about Brad later. She didn't want to upset Kara.

Doubt made Kara's tone edgy. "It's unfortunate our fairer sex is so preoccupied with weight. Don't you think?" She turned back to Amy.

"Well, yes, I guess so. I've never thought about it a lot."

Amy cringed at Kara's skepticism.

"I have a high metabolism and don't overindulge. I've never gone on a diet so I'm not the person you should ask about weight."

"Mm, good for you. If more women shared your attitude there'd be fewer problems. So, let me get this straight. Have you never been ashamed of your body?"

Amy met Kara's frank appraisal head on.

"Well, no, I can't say that. I never think about my weight, that's all. I do wear makeup and pay attention to my personal hygiene. I like to buy clothes that flatter my figure. I enjoy favourable comments about my appearance. I guess that relates to my self-confidence. I know my weight is average for my size. I'm a size ten so I've never tried to lose more. I feel comfortable with myself."

"I like that." Kara nodded then turned to Brittany. "How about you, ever been preoccupied with your weight? Do you think men help perpetuate an unrealistic image for women? I think they encourage us to put unbelievable strain on ourselves based on appearance. What for, them or us?"

Kara didn't wait for Brittany's answer, eager to jump on her soapbox. "If we're happy with our body then what's it to them anyway? I've never told my husband, or any man for that matter he needed to lose a few pounds. Believe me some of them should drop tons of weight. I mean tons. Get it?" Kara chuckled.

Amy and Brittany joined in.

Serious again, Kara asked. "So why do men feel compelled to tell us it's time to slim down? I think they like to exert power over us. Do you realize women are taught shame at an early age while men aren't? No wonder so many women have low self-esteem."

Kara stopped as if her battery had run down. "I need a drink. Would you like juice, water or a soft drink? Oh, and I think there's iced tea."

"Iced tea sounds good."

Kara glanced at Amy who nodded in agreement. Then she wandered over to an intercom on the wall. She gave her order to someone at the other end, her manservant Amy assumed.

Kara wandered back then sat down. They were silent while they waited. Brittany rummaged in her bag for her notebook and pen. Before long, Amy heard the approach of footsteps down the corridor.

A man appeared with a tray. Besides iced tea he had a bowl of nuts and some biscuits.

"Thank you Carl. This is my friend Amy and her daughter Brittany."

They nodded at one another then Carl took his leave.

"See." Kara pointed at the snacks. "I ordered iced tea only. Not nuts or biscuits. Yet he felt compelled to add something to the tray. Now why is that?"

"Well, maybe it's something people who serve you do. If a woman had waited on us she probably would have added something as well. I don't think Carl did it because he's a man," Amy pointed out.

"Hmm, maybe you're right. I tend to get carried away about the topic of weight. I guess I overreact at times. I think I mentioned I had an eating disorder in one of my lives, didn't I?"

"Yes, you mentioned anorexia."

They paused to sip from their glasses.

Amy was reluctant to eat any of the snacks after Kara's monologue about body image and power. She waited to see if Kara took any food but Kara didn't.

Brittany didn't share Amy's qualms as she grabbed a handful of nuts then began to toss them one at a time into her mouth.

"Do you want to tell us more about it?" Amy asked.

Bird of Paradise Drums Beating

Kara toyed with her iced tea while she considered the question. She ignored Brittany who'd taken another handful of nuts. "Yes, maybe if I talk about it I won't feel so hostile. I was powerless to stop the disease. I don't think I've healed from the experience yet. It was more recent than some of my lives. The memories are fresh and the pain is still raw. Talking might help. Thanks for asking."

"No problem."

"You can't guess who this person was though."

"What?"

"I don't want you to tell me who this person was. Don't say her name out loud even if you think you know who it is. I don't want to hurt her family since they're still alive."

"Oh, all right, that makes sense."

Kara glanced at Brittany.

"Yeah, sure, whatever you want. These are great nuts." Brittany reached for another handful.

It seemed Kara was still under the illusion she'd lived other people's lives. This must be one of her *'famous people.'* Amy shifted a bit in her chair, as she got more comfortable. She smiled at Kara, prepared for another captivating adventure.

"I think it started out natural enough. My weight loss I mean. It wasn't a conscious decision to lose any set number of pounds. I traveled a great deal and I don't like restaurant food. When people cook with quantities of grease and fat it turns me off. I hate all that oil."

Kara shuddered. "Combine that with the imagery of a stranger who prepares the food you're about to swallow. The thought of their hands poking about my food as they spread assorted germs. Ugh." Kara's shudder echoed her words. The descriptive image conveyed her immense dislike.

Kara's depiction made Amy a bit squeamish. She'd never thought about restaurant food preparation before. It sounded disgusting now that Kara mentioned it.

"When you put it like that eating at a restaurant doesn't sound glamorous or pleasurable. I've always associated going out as an adventure. I think of it as an opportunity to try new delights beyond my cooking abilities. Of course, presentation is everything. I agree, greasy french fries aren't appetizing. They taste good though if you're in the mood for them."

"I like sweet potato fries. Those are great. I think they might be healthier than regular fries," Brittany added.

"Yuck, I don't recall ever being in the mood for greasy anything, especially french fries. I've never had sweet fries, they sound disgusting as well." Kara made a face then shuddered again. "Spare me the imagery, please."

"Sorry," Amy apologized.

Brittany shrugged then took a biscuit from the tray and began to munch away.

"That's OK. It's not your fault. Now where was I?"

"You didn't set out to lose weight," Amy prompted.

"Ah, yes. When I think back on it I guess I had the profile of a *'typical'* anorexic. I was a high achiever and extremely self disciplined. When I exercised two or three times a day I didn't think anything of it. I thought I needed to work out since it helped put things in perspective. I had absolute control over my body. It made me feel better about my life."

Kara held her hands out as she implored them to understand. "I had a strict daily regime. Someone else scheduled almost every moment of my day. When I insisted on exercise, they had to include that as part of my routine. I bent them to my will instead of the other way around. I was intoxicated by my power."

Kara grimaced. "Of course, that was the beginning of the end. I didn't stop there. I refused to eat restaurant food, anything I deemed unhealthy. My mother brought in a chef and he traveled with us. There was a little kitchen set up in the back of the bus. It was more like a large motor home. He tried to cook healthy food for me. On a typical day I didn't eat any of it. I pretended to eat then slipped the food into a napkin in my lap. Later, I emptied the food into the garbage in the bathroom."

Kara stared at Amy, her expression sly. "I knew my family would disapprove of my refusal to eat especially since they'd brought in a fancy cook for me. I craved my family's approval. Much of what I did was done to please them. That's how I began to sing. It made them happy, so I did it. I was a famous singer, someone people read about. You might have owned one of our records you know. The famous brother and sister singing duo, how droll is that?"

Kara laughed.

The sound was brittle and hollow to Amy's ears.

"Now remember, you promised not to guess who I was," Kara teased. She wagged her fingers at Amy.

Amy nodded while Kara flashed a broad smile.

"I'm not going to guess," Brittany chimed in. "If my mom knows who these singers are I'm pretty much guaranteed not to. I'm not sure how she'd know some teen brother and sister group though. You listen to CD's with woman singers and you have a lot on your iPod mom. I've never seen any teen brother and sister groups. You must have been real young when you listened to those."

Kara ignored Brittany's comments. "I was triumphant there for a while. I guess I never appreciated or saw it for what it was though."

Her voice dropped. "I always wanted more, to be thinner and prettier. I longed to sing as well as my brother. I wanted to compose songs people would die to hear. I felt inadequate and overshadowed by my sibling. I was out of my depth," she murmured.

"I felt a constant need to tread water just to keep afloat. My life wasn't mine to order and I felt depressed much of the time. I had low self-esteem and was unable to stand up for myself." Kara's voice broke off.

Amy slid her eyes away to give Kara time to compose herself.

"You know, many of the times I've been reincarnated I haven't been aware of my other lives. I lived in the present and knew nothing of my past or future. I'm not even sure what I achieved in some lives, particularly when I died young. Then again, some lives are vivid. They've been stored in my memory, like they happened yesterday."

Kara trailed off.

It was interesting how Kara talked in the present when she referred to past lives. Even if it was a charade, Kara thought her stories were true.

"All around me was this noise. People demanded things of me. It was constant."

Kara's voice rose. "They expected so much. They surrounded me, crushed me with their thoughts. It was as if they repressed my individuality. They attempted to make me into something I wasn't."

Angry now, Kara ranted. "I was told how to dress, what amount of makeup was healthy, what image I would present to the public, even how to wear my hair. I had no control or power over anything, ever. They had no right!"

Kara grabbed her iced tea then banged it down after she took a big gulp. Some of the liquid splashed onto the table.

"So, I quit eating. It made them pay attention to me. I did what I wanted."

Kara slashed the air for emphasis. "When I didn't eat, I asserted my independence. I was able to dictate when and where I'd allow nourishment to be ingested into my body." Her eyes flashed.

"I remember I felt out of control so often my head seemed to float free of my body. It wasn't related to me in any way whatsoever. When I performed on stage I saw myself as an image presented to the mass public for their consumption. The more they took from me, the less I gave back to myself."

Kara held her hands out as she implored them to listen. "It was like they ingested me. They took me into their sphere. They made me powerless while they sapped my energy then drained me of the ability to exert my own force. I only asserted myself when I didn't eat. That was the only thing I manipulated one hundred percent. It became my identity. Anorexia overtook my life and described who I was.

You see it made me unique and special. Everyone took great pains to help me on my '*road to recovery.*" Kara made quotation marks with her fingers. "That's their phrase, not mine. I was sent to a therapist to make me feel better about myself. It was supposed to improve my psychological growth and physical health."

Kara stood then moved to the window where she gazed outdoors. Her movements were jerky.

"Did she help you?" Amy asked.

"No."

Kara turned back. "I guess for a time she did. I began to eat a little bit. My main reason was to keep everyone content. I didn't feel happier though. I guess my self-esteem was so battered it would have taken countless positive affirmations to help me feel better about myself. '*Positive affirmations*' are when you say something good about yourself." Kara made quotation marks again with her fingers.

"I had to do it every day. Whenever I said or thought something negative about myself I had to counteract it with a positive statement. You know something like '*I'm a thoughtful person*' or '*I'm a good daughter.*'

The problem was, I didn't think I was thoughtful or a good daughter. After all, I caused a great deal of grief and pain. How kind is that? As I said it was difficult and I never did get the hang of it. Another failure I had to live up to."

Kara moved from the window then returned to her chair, her face like a thundercloud.

Amy wanted to say something kind, to boost Kara's confidence. Even if everything was in her mind, just an illusion, Kara was disturbed by these memories, real or contrived.

"I'm sure what you thought at the time was distorted as you ate less." Amy made sure to adopt a warm and friendly tone. "You sounded like a wonderful person. You were confused by your feelings and unable to express yourself. Most teenagers feel that way. It was just more pronounced in your case."

Penny Ross

Kara met Amy's eyes. Tears formed at the corner of her eyelids. As teardrops leaked onto her cheeks it was like a well began to overflow from an abundance of rain.

"It's all right," Amy soothed. "Cry if you need to."

"I know I should." Kara wiped her tears on her sleeve. "When you mentioned confusion and how teenagers feel that way it made me sad, that's all."

"Why?"

"I was a grown woman and I acted like a petulant teen," Kara wailed.

Amy's brows rose, she didn't know what to say.

"At least you weren't into drugs and alcohol. Tons of singers die from that or go to rehab like a million times," Brittany commented. "That's gotta count for something. I read about singers like that all the time. It's almost normal for famous people to at least have an eating disorder. That's acceptable in some circles you know."

"Not in any circles you hang around in I hope Brittany."

"Mom, come on, I'm not famous."

"Thanks. I still feel petty though." Kara shook her head. "What a waste. I could have had a real life. Cut down on my performances, formed a lasting relationship, had a family and children of my own.

Instead, I wanted a perfect world. I tried to live up to high standards that were impossible to achieve. I created constant stress for myself. The mirror I held up was so distorted it failed to show the real me. In my mind's eye I was fat and grotesque. In reality, I was a scarecrow ready to blow away in the slightest breeze. Our image of ourselves is often derogatory. It's tragic. Don't you think?" Kara's voice held a note of desperation.

"It's harder when you're a celebrity. Everyone watches your every move then tweets about you. Remember when Amy Winehouse died? The press had a field day. She never had a chance. Michael Jackson, wow, people went nuts! Women pretend famous guys like Justin Bieber got them pregnant. When women confess to an eating disorder the media either shrug it off as inconsequential or make it sound like the person might be lying. Like Alanis Morissette, she was in the paper alluding to an eating disorder. I didn't like the tone of that article. Man, no one has a chance if they're famous. Don't be so hard on yourself."

"Brittany's right. I mean it's sad when people are critical of themselves," Amy pointed out. "When you're famous the media watch your every move. They like to find fault with celebrities. You have to counteract that with the positive. I don't think everyone has low self-esteem. Many people see themselves for who they are. They're able to appreciate their outer and inner qualities.

I agree. It's harder for women, especially if you're famous. In our society, appearance is important. In every culture, worldwide, females have been brought up to uphold a certain image."

"Yes, you're right it's all about the impression we make," Kara agreed. "Think for a moment of the woman, or man for that matter, so attractive you want to be near them at any cost. It's as if they glitter with gorgeousness. You want to soak them up in your sights, embrace their sexiness, most of all, you long for their touch. Beautiful people get anything they want. Their personality is inconsequential. It's all about the flash."

Kara's animation returned. "Once you've been caught in their web it doesn't matter if you want to escape. You made the mistake when you entered their personal domain. When they've caught you, they'll use you for their own end. You're like a fly in a spider's web."

Kara spat out the words. "What was your downfall? It's obvious isn't it? It was the godlike image, flawless skin and arresting eyes. Blend in the right clothes, make-up, hair and you have an irresistible combination, the total package. Once you see this person it's impossible to settle for less. You must be around them. It's all or nothing. It's all about image." Kara laughed, the sound dry and brittle. "Of course if you have enough money most of the package is phony."

Amy was mesmerized. This sounded personal. Amy decided to inject cultural context into the subject.

"There is that take on the topic. When you mentioned image I referred to cultural expectations. That has a lot to do with how people think."

"What?" Kara shook her head as if confused by Amy's comment.

"The word image brings to mind expectations. I've read women are pressured to be beautiful. You said you felt in control when you refused to eat. Think of all the women who count calories."

Amy's voice was grim. "Imagine all the little girls who are told how to dress and what to eat or given fancy little doodads to wear in their hair. Girls are instructed from birth how to act and what image to present. We're programmed like puppets and it's hard to break out of the mold.

Women present the image they're most comfortable with. A striking appearance may help us accomplish a goal. That's why people equate beauty with power and control. I have a theory Kara. I think women use beauty to get what we want when it achieves something we desire. That's where the word charm originated from."

Amy laughed. She stopped mid laugh as she noticed Kara's frosty air.

"Ahem." Amy coughed. "Kara, if we use personal appeal to bring something about isn't that projecting a certain image?"

Disapproval flashed from Kara's eyes.

"Helplessness, think how many women use that one or portray the poor me or dumb blonde. You've seen women use these. Come on, admit it."

Brittany's laugh was muffled. "Sorry, don't mind me. You sound so into this mom."

"Well, it's true. Come on, both of you have seen this happen. Kara, can you honestly say you've never used any of these ploys just one teeny tiny time? Have you ever portrayed a romantic image or sex kitten? Fess up, you've used at least one of these to your advantage. I know you have. We all have. Even you Brittany."

"OK, you're right. You've guessed my deep, dark secret, I'm human." Kara sounded cross. "I guess I got carried away when I referred to image. People might start out naïve and innocent before their actions turn into something ugly. Image is a word that conveys many things."

"Yes, and as women we can use our image for good or evil. We can portray ourselves in a positive, realistic manner or control others. It's a misuse of power to flash a dazzling smile at every gullible soul that walks by."

"Only works if you're beautiful. Ugly swans don't have much power I'd wager," Kara quipped.

"Yes, well there is that."

They chuckled.

Kara reached for her iced tea. "When you mentioned culture I had a thought."

"Mm hmm."

"What culture are you?"

"Me?"

"Yes, you. What's your culture?"

"Well, I'm Métis on my dad's side and German on my mom's."

"What does that mean to you?"

"Well, Métis means people of First Nations and European ancestry. My ancestors were Cree, Métis, and Scottish on my dad's side. Some of my people came from the original Red River Settlers here in Manitoba."

Kara made a face. "Thanks for the definition. That's not what I asked. What does being Métis mean to you personally?"

11

"Let me think." Amy tapped her brow. "I've started to figure out what being Métis means to me now that I'm older. I've asked my relatives questions and I read a lot. I've researched Aboriginal cultures and attended some ceremonies and events. It's still a question mark though. I don't live my life in the traditional way. I have certain beliefs and follow my conscience so that's part of my culture and who I am.

I've listened to Elders and heard their stories. I wish my grandma were still alive because she could help me figure it out. At least I could ask her more specific questions than I did when I was young."

"Hmm, we always regret things when they're gone don't we? So tell me Amy, what are your beliefs? I'm interested to know, have you passed these on to your children?"

They glanced at Brittany bent over her notebook taking notes.

"Well, I think it's important to be honest and straightforward. I respect others and expect the same of them. Common courtesy is important. I think many people have forgotten to instill those values in their children. Our society flounders as youth show nothing but contempt for others and the earth."

Amy began to warm to her subject. "I believe goodness and kindness are essential parts of our self. Without them, people don't have a soul or conscience. We come into this world in the purest form. We should have faith that our parents and Elders will guide us as we learn right from wrong. That's why it's important to have at least one person in our life that helps teach us values, or virtues.

I think the earth and environment should be treated with respect, not disdain. I regard the living world around me and quietly appreciate what surrounds us. Trees, sky, flowers and soil, they're gifts

Bird of Paradise Drums Beating

from Creator. We need to treat them with respect or one day we'll lose them.

Family is of the utmost importance to me. As I mentioned, we need at least one significant person in our life when we're young. When we grow up we form a bond with our partner. Then we branch off to begin our own family. If we have children we should raise them in the proper way. It's better to be kind and gentle than mean and tough. Goodness is highly underrated. Those are values I've always tried to teach my children."

Amy reached for her iced tea. "In many ways children are similar to a tree, they need roots to survive and flourish. Roots are the gift a caregiver can give when infants start out in life. We help form our children from the first day they're born. If you shower them with kindness, respect and honesty, most children grow up to be good.

Children are short people who grow taller. I've always talked to my kids like they were little adults. I've explained ideas and words to them in detail, yet at a level they understood. As they got older the message remains the same yet specifics become more suited to their maturity. Humour is of utmost importance in our home. I think laughter can get you through most anything, the good and the bad times."

Amy put her glass down then added, "Those are the things I believe in. I give daily thanks for those who surround me with goodness. I seek positive people. I try to show patience yet I confess it's hard to be around people who are negative. I'm not comfortable around mean spirited people nor do I count them as my friends."

"You sound like you know yourself well. Being Métis is a part of who you are. It's not separate from you. It doesn't take great effort on your part to figure out how it fits in your life. Your beliefs fit well within the Aboriginal culture. Even though you're not traditional it doesn't mean you're less native. You're just you."

"Thanks Kara."

Brittany glanced up. "I've never heard you talk like that about your beliefs mom. I've heard bits and pieces but I guess I never paid much attention. It's great to hear this since it is part of my culture too."

"Thanks Brit. I guess I should explain myself when I say I'm still figuring out the Métis part of me. When I was young, I didn't know I was Aboriginal. My family didn't acknowledge it so I never asked questions till I was older. As a child, I never knew anything about my culture or heritage. I didn't understand or appreciate it."

Amy crossed her arms. "Raised as a Canadian I never questioned anything else. It didn't seem relevant to my life. Children have different needs than adults and teens. They like to play, pure and simple. I liked to have fun and hang around with friends. When the phone or doorbell rang I welcomed the friend at the other end with a big grin and we were off for a fun time.

How do we become aware we're different from those around us? When does the unknown become important?" Amy shrugged. "For me it came from an annoying bully. It was a guy I didn't acknowledge. He preyed on the weak and powerless and pounced when he saw a chance. You did not want to be caught in this guy's radar. He was relentless."

Amy shook her head. '*You're not the same as us*,' I remember this guy announced one day. I was in the eighth grade and popular enough. It was quiet when his strident voice made this damning declaration. Shocked and puzzled I asked, '*Why not?*'

'*You're a goddamn Indian, that's why!*'

Amy hung her head. "It seemed like a death toll. My world changed. Prejudice reared its ugly head and entered our classroom. I got caught in the middle of a timeless battle."

She sighed, gathered her hair back then shook it out. "The question for me was how to escape from the taunting, cruel jibes of others intent on creating a hostile, hurtful atmosphere. We all know the playground provides an opportunity for troublemakers to excel. Survival of the fittest is a fact of life. Bullies are king of the jungle.

If you're smart and don't panic you know it's only a matter of time until the crowd moves along to someone else. You have to get the focus off you though, no matter what. You're at their mercy for the short term but you do not want to be at their mercy indefinitely. So what do you do?"

Amy shrugged. "I'm not proud of what I did. The answer stared me right in the face. I didn't see any options. Well, I did. I could have thrown a more naive, defenseless classmate into the crowd to be torn apart. Fortunately, I'm not like that. I'm a quick thinker, calm under pressure and have good instincts. So I made a choice I was comfortable with at the time. It was simple and it worked."

Kara and Brittany leaned forward.

"What was it?" Brittany urged.

Amy couldn't meet Brittany's eyes. "It was denial, plain and simple," she confessed. "As I said, I'm not proud of it. When I was thirteen I didn't see any upside to being native. I shrugged it off as inconsequential."

Amy finally met Brittany's direct gaze. "Of course I didn't have time to think about what I'd done. As I said, in the schoolyard, survival of the fittest demands a quick reaction or you've had it." Amy snapped her fingers. "Just like that, one can lose their friends, be taunted and become the joke of the class. It's lonely when you're on the outside. I couldn't let that happen to me. I'd watched it happen to others and it was not a pretty sight." Amy shuddered.

Brittany nodded. "I know we've all been there." She patted her mom on the shoulder.

"We know what the preferred choice is, don't we?"

They nodded at one another.

"It's preferable to hang with your cozy band of friends and maintain the status quo. What do you think most people at that age choose? It's sink or swim and self-preservation tips into high gear. There are only a few brave individuals who have the courage to stand up for themselves and fewer still that stand up for others. It's a hard age."

Amy took a deep breath. "The scene is etched in my mind like it happened yesterday. It was a defining moment in my life. *'No, I'm not,*' I loudly proclaimed to the class. '*I don't know what you're talking about.*' Then I walked away, in a huff, you know, like preteens do. I hoped my classmates believed me."

Amy cupped her chin in her hand. "The truth is I didn't know what I was. It had never been an issue before. That's odd now that I think about it. You and your brothers brought home a family tree assignment. We listed your ancestors on it. I never did that as part of my schoolwork. How did I get to grade eight and was never faced with the question of who I was and who my people were?"

"You're right," Kara agreed. "We've done a few family trees. Sounds like you didn't do them when you were in school."

"I don't know." Amy shrugged. "I thought about who my people were after class settled down. The vultures, my classmates, circled and watched me warily as they searched for signs of my '*native ness.*' No, let me restate that, it would have been for my '*Indian ness*' or '*squaw ness*' since native and Aboriginal weren't terms people used in the late seventies, early eighties. Not in my neighbourhood at any rate."

Amy chuckled. "It's interesting, you mentioned definitions before. It reminded me of the meaning of Aboriginal people. Indian, or the correct word, First Nations, doesn't refer to Métis people. We have our own definition. We have our own culture, heritage, traditions and spiritual practices. I'm not an Indian. I find it offensive when people use the word in a derogatory manner to describe me or someone else."

She smiled. "So, had I known this when I was young it would have helped. If someone scoffed and called me an Indian it wouldn't have bothered me so much. I'm Métis. It reminds me of bigots that call a person they think is Ukrainian a Bo hunk and that person is Polish, not Ukrainian. People are derogatory, offensive and hurtful when they call you names. When it comes to prejudice and intolerance I doubt that bully at my school would have been interested in a little history lesson."

"You can tell me. I'm interested."

"Me too," Brittany added. "This is fascinating mom."

Bird of Paradise Drums Beating

"All right. I've done considerable research over the years. Métis refers to people who are of mixed First Nations and European ancestry as compared to First Nation, Inuit or non-Aboriginal people. My ancestors were Cree, Métis and Scottish on my father's side. My paternal grandmother was Cree and then on my paternal grandfather's side his mom was Cree. If you go back to 1700 I have a great, great grandmother I'm not sure how many greats, who was Ojibwe. That's why I'm Métis. I had my family tree done at the St. Boniface Historical Society here in Winnipeg years ago and it has tons of fascinating information in it."

"Hey, you showed me that before mom. I didn't really pay much attention to it though. Do you think you could show me again? I'm interested now."

"Sure, I'd love to Brit."

"So, why do you use the term Indian sometimes and First Nations at others, are they interchangeable?" Kara wondered.

"Oh, First Nations is the term that started in the seventies to replace the word Indian. Believe it or not many people find the word Indian to be offensive."

Kara grinned. "No kidding. They must be hypersensitive or something. Like you maybe?"

"Yeah right, so when that guy called me a '*goddamn Indian*' I could have launched into a discourse about First Nations people as compared to Métis people. That would have blown my class away. After all, it was the early eighties. People should have been aware of the term. Unfortunately though, they weren't."

"Are they now?" Kara asked.

"Some are, but not many," Amy admitted. "I think it's taught more in schools. First Nations has become a more common term and I know my children are familiar with it."

"That's because you use it constantly mom. We're used to it."

"Yeah, that's true. I've noticed it in textbooks though so it's being used more. Just like the word Eskimo, that's not as common as it used to be."

Penny Ross

"So, you mentioned the word for Eskimo is Inuit right?" Kara clarified.

"Yes, Inuit refers to people who live above the tree line in Northwest Territories and Nunavut. I think some Inuit people live in Labrador too and maybe Northern Quebec. If I recall correctly Inuit means *'the people'* in their native language of Inuktitut. Eskimo means raw meat eaters. Eskimo is a derogatory term just like Indian. So when you take our three groups, First Nations, Métis and Inuit we comprise Aboriginal people of Canada."

"Wow, that's something to be proud of." Kara leaned forward in her chair.

"Yeah, it is."

"Right on mom, we have something to be proud of for sure. Our ancestors were part of the original people of Canada. That's super cool."

"Hey, I just thought of something." Kara cupped her chin in her hand. "When you mentioned your ancestors what mix or percentage are you? I mean how much Scottish as compared to Cree?"

"Well, it's interesting you should ask. I thought I was more Scottish than Cree but that's not true. My husband and I figured it out one day and I'm 7/16ths Cree, 1/16th Scottish and 8/16ths German. Those are approximate, we couldn't be sure we were exact."

"Why do you base it on sixteenths?"

"I don't know exactly. From what I've been able to figure out and this has to do with my dad's side, we trace everything back to how we're descendants of Roderick Ross. Roderick's father was Scottish and he came from Scotland. Then he married a woman named Marie Delorme. She was Métis so I've got First Nations and Métis on that branch also. That's where the Ojibwe comes in. Another one of my greats also married an Ojibwe woman so that shows up a few times in the family tree. Then as I said my paternal great-grandmother was Cree and my paternal grandmother was Cree."

"Why don't you include Ojibwe as part of your equation?" Kara asked.

Bird of Paradise Drums Beating

"Good question. I guess we didn't know how to include that so we left it out. I know we decided the sixteenths have to do with what generation you are. When we figured out my dad's genealogy we based it on eighths so I'm based on sixteenths. I guess my children would be based on thirty-seconds. When you go far back, their ancestors start getting watered down since we have to add in Icelandic and German on my husband's side. I think that's how you figure it out anyway. It's our best guess."

"Well, it's fascinating however you've done it. I wish I could trace my ancestors back like you have, but I don't even know who I am."

Amy smiled. "Yeah, I'm lucky. Reminiscing brings an image of my grandparents to mind. They resembled First Nations people in modern picture books or on the computer. They didn't wear a headdress or have feathers in their hair. It wasn't overt or anything. First Nations people don't dress that way on a daily basis anyhow. They do for powwows and ceremonies. For school or work they dress the same as everyone else.

My grandparents had dark skin tone, brown eyes, dark hair and high cheekbones. I never saw them suntan. They worked in the garden so they would have been out in the sun then. They never went to the beach though.

My grandfather wore long sleeved shirts and long pants. My grandmother wore a skirt no matter what time of year it was. In the winter they never went on a cruise or vacationed in hot spots."

Amy rolled her head to stretch her neck. "When I was young, I never thought about my grandparents skin tone or features. I never wondered why they looked like they did. Over the years I never asked who my grandparents were or questioned anything about them. I loved to listen to their stories though."

She paused, "I think in our society there's a great deal of ignorance when it comes to culture and heritage."

"What do you mean by that?" Brittany wondered.

Penny Ross

"I'd say relative to prejudice and bigotry. By that I mean if you're not the *'right'* culture you're often punished for it. I mean stereotypes. For example, how many of us squirm when we hear a loud individual who drank too many drinks start their tirade of racist jokes. They might put down the stupid Ukrainian Bo hunk, the lazy well-endowed Negro, the fat, slovenly Indian squaw, the slant eyed Chink, or the goddamned rag head Hindus who own all the real estate. No matter what culture one is, everyone is the same inside. It hurts when people target others for their appearance."

Amy's voice rose. "Why do those blankety, blank good for nothings live here? They don't belong in this country. That's the general gist of some conversations isn't it? I've heard those comments since I was young."

She crossed her arms. "So why are Aboriginal people inferior to others in some circles? We lived in North America ages before anyone else. Did you know there were about 2.4 million First Nations people who lived in North America before the first arrival of explorers and settlers? It doesn't make sense. People need to take time to learn more about Canadian history and the importance of Aboriginal people and their rightful place in our current society. Then perhaps people won't put us down for who we are."

Amy shook her head. "I know racism, prejudice and bigotry never cross the chasm of logic. Some cultures are rarely made fun of. Off the top of my head I can think of Germans, Swedes and people from New Zealand. You rarely hear disrespectful jokes about them unless it's some reference to *'down under'* which is not as derogatory as *'why don't ya go drink some lighter fluid ya squaw.'* That's not amusing, it's hurtful."

Amy lowered her voice. "I think that's why I was raised like I was, to deny myself, my father, grandparents and ancestors. I was taught to ignore my own people and to hide from the truth. I wasn't encouraged to be proud of who I am or to share the truth with my classmates."

Brittany jumped up then gave Amy a fierce hug. "I'm proud of who you are mom. I'm grateful you've shared your story with us. I'm honoured to be your daughter and be part of this story."

"Thank you darling. That's kind of you to say. I appreciate it."

"So where did you live when you were in grade eight?"

"Regina, Saskatchewan."

"I thought lots of native people live there."

"They do. The prairies have a large Aboriginal population. The neighbourhood we lived in was a typical white, middle-class area. I don't remember any natives who lived near us. I saw them downtown but I never knew any of them. I should rephrase that, I might have known native people but never realized it."

"What do you mean?"

"Well, a few things. I wasn't aware Métis people are Aboriginal so some of my friends and classmates might have been Aboriginal and I didn't know that. We don't have a label to identify us on our foreheads."

Brittany chuckled. "Hah, funny one mom, imagine having a name tag blazoned on your forehead, ouch."

"Yeah, that doesn't sound pleasant now that you mention it Brittany. I've noticed as I've gotten older my Aboriginal ties are more real and by that I mean more meaningful. As a young adult I asked my grandma to tell me stories about the old days and our culture. She was a great storyteller, her memory was incredible." Amy smiled.

"I wanted to know the good things our people did. I was tired of hearing negative stereotypes and the typical put-downs. My grandma told me about her mother and half brothers. She never talked about her father though. No one seems to know anything about him."

Amy shrugged. "I hung out with two sisters in grade eight who were native. Well, one of the sisters was anyway. Since I'd become more aware of cultural differences I could tell their mom was First Nations and their cousins were too. One of the sisters had blonde hair, blue eyes and white skin though. That confused me but I didn't ask questions. I'm not sure why. Often, it's hard to remember why we did things when we were young."

Kara nodded, "Yes, youth is a confusing time."

"I'll say. I wanted to know things but was afraid to ask. My dad could have explained how I wasn't an Indian. He could have mentioned the word Métis. That would have cleared things up. When I was in my twenties I found out my grandma lost her treaty rights when she married my grandpa. Even though she was Cree he was Scottish Métis so she lost her status and band membership rights. She got them back in 1985 when Bill C-31 was passed so men and women were treated equally."

Amy sighed. "My grandma was First Nations but my grandpa was Métis. That was never explained to us. I'm not sure why. It's hard enough to figure out who you are at that age and maintain your sense of identity without being confused about your culture. I tried to hide my culture yet never really knew what it was. I'm not First Nations or Indian since I have many other mixes in my blood."

Brittany glanced up from her notes. "Hey, did you know Indian is a term the Europeans came up with when Christopher Columbus came to America?"

Amy nodded but Kara had to admit she didn't know that.

"You should explain it to Kara," Amy urged.

"Sure, when he discovered North America over five hundred years ago Columbus thought he was in the Indies. He miscalculated how large the world is and was on his way to Asia. When he mistakenly landed in North America, he called the people he met Indians.

It had nothing to do with what the people called themselves though. They already had names. So, Indian is purely a European term and mostly used in a derogatory manner. Imagine that, Indian people were named by some bonehead who was lost and the term stuck for centuries." Brittany made a face.

"Really, that doesn't seem right."

"Yeah," Amy piped in. "I guess that's how the term First Nations came about. Aboriginal people, who are descendants of the

Bird of Paradise Drums Beating

original inhabitants of North America, got tired of being called something they never were. First Nations makes sense since they were the first people in this nation. It's a good term."

"Yeah, better than Indian, that's for sure," Brittany agreed.

"This talk of culture reminds me of another story. When we moved to Gimli, Manitoba I was fifteen. I thought it was the end of the world to move to a small town. I noticed tons of people had names that ended in '*son*.'"

"Why's that?"

"Gimli is an Icelandic community. Everyone there is extremely proud to be Icelandic. When I got there I met people who had strange last names and liked to brag about their ancestors. I found this weird. They were teens and I didn't think they should care about their culture but they did. It was often the guys who bragged about '*Vikings*' and how they were known for rape and pillage. I guess that could be expected of pea-brained male boys."

They chuckled.

"Don't tell your brothers I implied they have tiny brains," Amy warned as she wagged her finger at Brittany.

"I wouldn't dream of it."

"That's when I realized in a small community when most people are of one ethnic group they have bragging rights and pride in who they are. I didn't hear others in the community proclaim their ancestry since they weren't Icelandic. So I kept quiet about my heritage since Métis and German weren't the '*in culture.*' At fifteen, I wasn't familiar with the term First Nations so I never mentioned that either."

"So you kept it a secret," Kara mused.

"Yes unfortunately. When I went to university I thought there were grants, scholarships and bursaries I could have applied for since I was native. Of course, now I've realized there isn't much money for Métis people. You can apply for funding when you're First Nations and live on a reserve. I never lived on a reserve though."

"There's no free money mom. You told me that when I started university."

"Yeah, I know that now. When I was young though and needed money I thought it was an avenue to pursue. I'd learned how my grandmother was Cree and my grandfather was Scottish Métis. It was a surprise when I realized not only was my father Aboriginal, he was mostly First Nations."

"Ah, yes the percentage. You began to figure it out," Kara commented.

"Yeah, who would have thought? My dad refused to sign papers associated with money for Aboriginal people. He said it was taking advantage of something we had no right to claim. He was right of course. One shouldn't apply for funding when you've never lived the traditional way."

Amy shrugged then lifted her hands up as if in surrender. "I scraped through university. My parents helped the first year then I paid for the rest. I graduated with a student loan like everyone else. I grew up in a white man's middle class world. I denied my culture and buried it beneath a cloak of invisibility unaware it would rise out of the ashes one day."

"What a theatrical statement," Kara commented with raised brows.

Amy smiled then gave a little bow for her impromptu speech.

Brittany glanced up, shook her head then smirked at her mother.

12

"We can't ignore facts forever...."

"Why do you say that?" Kara wondered.

"Our ancestors catch up with us eventually. There's a book by David Bouchard called, *'The Elders are Watching.'* It's true, our ancestors are there, to watch over us, keep us safe and guide us on our journey. We need to acknowledge them and listen to their words of wisdom."

"Ah."

"When I lived in Yellowknife there were many Aboriginal people in the community. I admitted I was native to a few coworkers. It was beneficial since our work boasted mainly white Anglo Saxons. I helped boost statistics."

"I assume your boyfriend, or spouse knew you were native by then?"

"Oh yes. Andy, my husband, is one of the Icelanders I mentioned from Gimli. I told him about my grandparents when we dated. I don't remember when exactly. It wasn't an issue, merely a topic of conversation."

"So the one person who means a great deal to you didn't react negatively when you mentioned your native heritage."

"No."

Brittany glanced up.

Amy smiled at her daughter.

"Hmm, perhaps it wasn't as bad as you'd built up in your mind."

"Perhaps Kara. I guess since I didn't talk about culture and didn't attend ceremonial events or anything it wasn't something we dwelt on. We rarely mentioned it."

Kara nodded, "Hmm, good theory. Go ahead. Continue with your Yellowknife story."

Penny Ross

"All right, I remember an event that stands out in my mind. It was a turning point for me. I was a youth representative at a conference in Toronto. There was a person from each province and one from the North West Territories. This was before Nunavut became a territory. We were the Canadian delegates. There were also representatives from each State since it was a North American conference."

"You never mentioned this before mom. That's impressive you were a youth representative at an International conference."

"I attended many fascinating events and did tons of training in Yellowknife. The YWCA is an incredible organization. I'm forever grateful for the opportunities I received when it came to training, leadership and skills. I worked at the YWCA in Winnipeg and then in Yellowknife. I have countless fond YW memories."

"You'll have to tell me more about it mom."

"Deal," Amy agreed.

They grinned at one another.

"You were about to tell us something specific that happened to you at the conference weren't you?" Kara reminded Amy.

"Right, I remember a lot of discomfort when the Quebec delegate accused us of not being representative of Canada. She pointed at me and said, 'Check out who they sent from the NWT, she's not even native.'

Amy made a face. "Of course the logical reply would have been to proclaim I was Aboriginal. At twenty-three though, I wasn't that quick on my feet. I'd been raised to deny who I was so I let the moment pass. I never admitted to the other nine young women what I thought was my shameful secret."

Amy lowered her eyes. "I was plagued by guilt the rest of the day."

"Oh mom, don't be so hard on yourself."

"Yeah well, that evening I confessed to one of the other women I was native. It was coincidental, that's not why I'd been sent. We spoke of prejudice and intolerance. It was a subject of great debate back in those days, still is. Prejudice and racism seem to cross decades with little progress."

"Why do you think you denied it that time?"

"Habit, I guess." Amy shrugged. "Up to that point it had been drilled into me I wasn't native. I lived the life of a middle class white female. My ancestry had been treated like a secret."

"Secrets have a way of catching up with us."

"Yeah, they do. I remember a lot of confusion and guilt when I admitted to being native. It had been in the back of my mind for a long time. I'd been unwilling to address it in an honest, forthright manner though. When it came down to it, I found myself unable to admit my ancestry to that group of women."

"Did they ever find out?" Brittany whispered.

Amy laughed. The sound was edgy with a hint of nervousness. "Yes, they did, the next day. The girl taunted me again for not being native and I blurted it out. My friend backed me up. The Quebec girl quit being a pain in the butt. She'd proclaimed she was a lesbian and French. She felt none of the rest of us represented the melting pot of Canada. Those were her words, not mine. She said the U.S. delegates would get a biased viewpoint of Canada based on who'd been sent to the conference."

"Why did it matter?" Kara wondered

"I don't know. We had come early to prepare a Canadian presentation for the other delegates. The Quebec girl wanted us to be true ambassadors of our country."

Amy rubbed her knee. "In the end it barely made a difference. Most of the questions were directed at me since I was from the North. They asked about the lights in the sky, Eskimos and polar bears. I knew about Aurora Borealis, the northern lights, and had seen them dance on many winter nights. I was able to tell them the proper name for Eskimo, which is Inuit. I knew a few amusing northern anecdotes so it kept everyone entertained.

Our Canadian presentation was a hit and I was a bit of a celebrity. They didn't care if I was native or not. Had I been Inuit I could have increased my status especially if I would have let them call me '*Eskimo girl!*' They didn't know who Métis people were. It wasn't something they asked questions about. Culture wasn't an issue. They regarded us as Canadians, nothing more, nothing less."

"Did you start to acknowledge yourself as an Aboriginal woman after that?" Kara leaned forward, attentive.

Brittany focused on Amy as well.

"Hmm, interesting question." Amy gave it some consideration. "I guess I did in my own way. It seemed a natural progression after that. When people asked, I said I was Métis. It was no big deal. I questioned my grandma more and paid rapt attention to her stories about the past. I wrote down information she told me so I'd have a written record. I also researched my ancestors as I got older."

She sighed. "I only wish I'd asked my grandma about her life earlier and recorded her stories when she was younger. By the time I thought of making notes she was very old and her memory had begun to be sketchy. She also lived in Saskatchewan while we live in Manitoba so I didn't see her that often. She died when she was ninety-nine years old, just a few months short of her hundredth birthday."

"Whoa, does longevity run in your family?"

"Yes, I guess so. My grandpa was eighty. My grandfather and grandmother on my mother's side were in their eighties when they died. Now that you've asked these questions I realize I'm happy with whom I am. So yes, I can honestly say I'm proud to be Métis. I've become more vocal about Aboriginal issues. I research and read about the Métis, First Nations and Inuit people on a regular basis since I enjoy it."

"What sort of things have you learned?"

"Well, for one, I know the difference between the three groups of Aboriginal people. I realize we have diverse ancestral origins. I can explain distinctions between the groupings. I think it's important to use proper terms when people ask for clarification."

Amy warmed to her subject. "As I mentioned before, many individuals don't even know there are three groups of Aboriginal people, let alone how distinct they are. Each of the three groups has unique heritage, language, cultural practices and spiritual beliefs. Consider

First Nations for instance, there are distinct differences between each band. Most people don't realize this. As I've taken the time to research and ask questions I've become more knowledgeable about Aboriginal people. I find it fascinating."

"I'm glad you've made the effort mom," Brittany praised. "Now you can teach me more about our culture."

"Yes, that would be fun. You know what else I've noticed?

"What?" Brittany wondered.

"I've begun to stand up for myself in my own quiet way. If someone tells a racial joke in my presence I say it offends me personally. That's something I never would have done ten or twenty years ago. It's a big step. You know, there's still a great deal of racism and intolerance in our society. It's amazing, but not in a good way. It almost seems ingrained in some people. That's not something to be proud of."

"Yes, I agree," Kara stated.

Brittany nodded.

"I remember years ago a young woman from Revenue Canada came to fill out some special form with me. I'd checked the Aboriginal box on my tax form. I think that was where she was from. Maybe it was one of the forms used for voting in the Federal election. No matter, it was a woman from one of the Federal government offices."

"So, what was the big deal?" Brittany wondered.

"It should have been straightforward. I wouldn't mention it except this young woman pissed me off because of her attitude."

"I don't follow," Kara commented.

"I'll explain. She made an appointment to come to our house. I was at home with Brittany and my oldest son he would have been around one so you were seven. She acted as if I pretended to be Aboriginal. It was weird."

"Pretended?" Kara clarified

"Yeah, both my sons had dirty blonde hair when they were young, like their father. Brittany's hair is more similar to mine it's darker. I guess I have the appearance of a Métis person if you search for it. My dad, siblings and I aren't automatically pegged as Aboriginal people. This girl went over my father's lineage and questioned me endlessly. She thought I'd exaggerated my ancestry. I had it all on paper though so she had to accept it."

Amy paused then wiped her forehead. "It made me mad. She implied I had a nice home and had set myself up well for a Métis woman. I guess since I didn't fit the stereotype she had in her head she felt compelled to examine my form more closely. It was odd and I resented her implications. It seemed to bother her I had a charming home. We also managed our money well so I only worked part-time when Brittany and the boys were young."

She shook her head. "I don't know why we care what other people think about us. This woman was a stranger. Her opinion shouldn't have concerned me, yet it did."

"It's hard to stand up for something you believe in. We want everyone to like us for who we are. We don't want them to question our income, background, values or culture."

Amy grinned. "That's true. Sounds like something my dad would say. He's very philosophical about people and racism. He has many amusing stories and sad ones too but he has a way of telling them that are non-offensive. Now that I'm older we talk about native culture, customs and beliefs quite a bit. Maybe when I was young I didn't ask the right questions. He's quite knowledgeable about First Nations bands in Canada including some of their customs, traditions and culture. I never knew that about him."

"Yeah, grandpa likes to tell stories," Brittany noted.

"Maybe he's more comfortable with who he is now that you've become more vocal about the culture you share. As you increase your knowledge and are more secure with your heritage it allows him to tell stories and show off to some extent. The two of you have found something in common."

"Yeah, we have Kara. We can talk for hours." Amy laughed. "I always have fun with my dad and his siblings. They're a riot. We used to go to a lot of family weddings when I was first married since I have so many cousins. My aunties like to dance and attend social events and they would drag their brothers and husbands around to everything."

"Mom's right about the aunties." Brittany turned to Kara. "They have a lot of energy and a zest for life. The uncles are way more laid back." Brittany grinned. "Well, except for grandpa. He can keep up with the aunties."

"That's for sure," Amy agreed with a fond smile. "At weddings, dances and anniversaries it was pretty common to see the aunties jigging and dancing up a storm. Grandpa is always in the center of the pack. We had a family reunion in Saskatchewan years ago and even though everyone was older they held their own on the dance floor."

"I remember that. They had a pig roast and we played softball. Then the old people danced to some sort of country music and you drove us back to our place. We stayed in a log cabin in Katepwa, right by the beach. It was a fun trip. Weren't we there for a week or so?"

"Yes, I wanted you to see the Qu'Appelle Valley and places nearby."

Brittany's face lit up. "We walked up to the top of those hills and pretended we were the Von Trapp Family from *'The Sound of Music.'*"

Amy and Brittany began to giggle. "I thought the boys were going to die of embarrassment when you and I started to sing, *'The hills are alive with the sound of music.'* Brittany snorted. "You were so funny mom." She turned to Kara. "My mom is the worst singer but it never stops her when the mood hits."

Amy chuckled. "Yes, you and the boys used to beg me to stop when you were little."

"We'd cover our ears then say, *'Mommy, please stop, you're hurting our ears,'* " Brittany agreed. "It was too funny. Now that I think about it mom your relatives at that reunion were playful just like you and grandpa. It must run in the family."

"Yeah, they've got quite the sense of humour and do enjoy joking around." Amy fiddled with her hair. "I hope I'm similar to my aunties when I'm in my seventies and eighties. They take good care of themselves. None are overweight, they're in good health, their hair is always done just so, they have beautiful clothes and shoes. They wear the right amount of make-up. There's a lot to say about one's lineage when your older relatives are in good health."

Amy giggled, "I certainly don't want to be one of those little old ladies who pack rouge on their cheeks. Imagine wearing curlers to the grocery store. I'd be mortified walking out of the house like that."

Kara shrugged. "To each his own they always say."

Brittany laughed. "I've never even seen you in curlers mom. I can't imagine you walking down to Super A with curlers in your hair. Unless you were doing it as a lark of course."

"Yeah, I'm sure I'd get some odd looks if I walked around town like that."

Kara leaned forward. "Thanks for sharing your private thoughts with us Amy. I feel closer to you now that you've given so freely of yourself."

"Yeah mom, way to go."

Amy grinned. "Yeah, I guess I monopolized the conversation there for a while. Thanks for listening. When I began to reminisce I forgot you and Brittany were here."

"I guess it's easier to tell our innermost secrets when we're not focused on who's in the room. I'm glad you're comfortable around me."

"Yeah mom, now I know some of your deep, dark secrets to hold over you," Brittany teased.

"Right," Amy agreed as they all laughed. "As if I don't have any juicy tidbits I could share about you."

13

"So, are you up for another one of my stories?" Kara asked abruptly, interrupting the merriment. She smiled sweetly in Amy's direction.

Grinning, Amy agreed, yes, it was time for another story.

"Yeah, I love your stories," Brittany agreed.

"Great." Kara clapped her hands and seemed truly delighted Amy and Brittany wanted to hear another tale.

"Have you ever seen a truly beautiful woman? Someone you had to gaze at, paint a portrait of or capture her essence in a medium you can view at your leisure?" Kara's tone was expectant.

"Yes, I think I know what you mean. I watched a woman in a restaurant not too long ago. When she walked in the room everyone stopped what they were doing. There was a hush while we watched her move towards her table. Her skin reminded me of porcelain, clear, smooth and translucent."

Amy clasped her hands. "I loved her hair. It was thick and luxurious. I wanted to stroke it. It reminded me of silk and I'm sure the colour was natural. This woman was more than striking. She had grace and poise. I found her truly beautiful."

"Mm hmm, as I mentioned before, a woman like that commands power. You said everyone, including you, watched her movements. Were you eager to meet her?"

"I would have been thrilled to get close and talk to her. Yes, I did want to meet her. I always wonder if exceptionally beautiful women are intelligent as well. Are they good conversationalists? What kind of fascinating life do they lead? Do they have hobbies, a career or family? Would we talk about shared interests?"

Amy smiled. "I know this is a generalization but the dumb blonde image instantly comes to mind. I know quite a few brunettes and redheads that can't hold their end up in a decent conversation though."

"Beauty doesn't detract or add to your intelligence." Kara's voice was measured. "Although I think image goes a long way towards how we treat people."

Kara tapped her index finger on her lip. "How's this for a theory. We imagine beautiful women are less intelligent than the average person. They have nothing to say and their only talent is their favorable appearance. So we treat them in a manner that shouts *'you are beautiful but stupid,'* or *'your ideas count for nothing.'* Naturally these women act accordingly. Extremely beautiful women often lack self-confidence. They bow down to popular opinion and behave in the manner expected of them."

"That's a sad commentary on our society," Amy exclaimed.

"Often true though."

"Oh I agree. After all, I just questioned the intelligence level of beautiful women and I'm a woman. I feel bad but have to admit we often disregard the possibility a striking woman can exhibit a high level of intelligence or creativity."

"That's your generation mom. I'm not sure if I agree my generation does that."

"I don't know Brittany. Remember some of the cliques at high school. You've mentioned how awkward it was when another girl gave you dirty looks when they thought you were more attractive than them."

"Yeah, well, OK, I guess that's true. You're right. We're a sorry bunch when it comes to being magnanimous to gorgeous people. I'm glad I'm pretty average."

"I think you're beautiful Brittany."

"Yeah, thanks mom. We're talking about a ravishing, outrageously attractive breed of women though. Not the girls whose moms and grandmas think they're pretty."

Bird of Paradise Drums Beating

"OK, I give up." Amy raised her hands in surrender then gave a hearty laugh. "I think ravishing women get a bad rap and are often thought of as bitchy as well. It's a double-edged sword. Who wants to be gracious and charming when people approach you because you're gorgeous?

I resisted going near the woman I mentioned in the restaurant. I noticed a number of people dropped by the table though. They didn't appear to be friends. They didn't stay long and the couple didn't show signs of recognition or affection towards them. It must be rough having others hassle you simply because you're attractive. Glad I've never had the problem."

Amy tossed her hair over her shoulder.

"Yes, I wish I could say the same." Kara's tone was wistful.

Amy and Brittany exchanged a quick glance. Amy turned back to Kara who returned her gaze with raised brows.

"I don't mean now of course. That's obvious. Although I am pretty, I'm not truly beautiful. I refer to another time. I'd like to tell you a story about beauty and power."

"Yes, do tell." Were they about to get a glimpse into Kara's life? Amy caught her breath then sat back obediently.

Amy and Brittany were taken back in time to a place Amy was sure no one in her lifetime had heard of. Fascinated by Kara's tale, Amy paid rapt attention. She was determined to guess the identity of this woman before Kara told her. Brittany continued with her notes.

"I was born in 69 B.C., in Alexandria, Egypt. Although I don't remember the early years, people told me I was intelligent. I had an aptitude for the sciences, you know subjects like astronomy, arithmetic, geometry and medicine.

I was well rounded and enjoyed the Greek classics. I liked to draw, sing and play a seven-stringed lyre. Of course I was a superb horsewoman and danced like an angel. I liked challenges and was fluent in a number of languages."

Kara smiled, as if the recollection reminded her of a happy time. "My father liked to show me off. He was proud of my gifts. I often was paraded around to say a few words to foreign ambassadors. I must have been quite young at the time. My first impression begins in my early teens. When I feared for my life," Kara whispered.

Good effect, Amy thought. As a storyteller, Kara had dramatic flair.

"Oh, have I mentioned I was a princess and then a queen?"

Amy shook her head. Brittany glanced up, frowned then bent back to her page.

"I must have forgotten. Silly me, how could I overlook that? I had numerous privileges bestowed upon me due to my exalted position. I had my own quarters, servants, horses and even a little sailboat to sail around our private royal harbour. Yes, I enjoyed being pampered. My father adored me. I was his favourite so I imagine I had more liberties than my siblings."

Amy thought she'd burst. She had to interrupt Kara. "I know who this is," she blurted.

"Well, go ahead then. Now that you've disrupted the flow of my story you might as well jump in and throw out a name." Kara's voice was indifferent. She shook her head as if bored by the interruption.

Amy burst out. "Is it possible you were Cleopatra, Queen of Egypt?"

Could Kara have been this powerful person? Cleopatra was one of the most famous women in history. Impatient for more, Amy leaned forward in her chair.

Brittany put her pen down then turned toward Kara. She leaned forward as well, with an expectant air.

Kara took her time. She checked her nails, flicked an imaginary speck from her sweater then ran her fingers through her hair. With a smug expression she acknowledged Amy's theory with a slow nod.

"Yes, are you saying yes?" Amy squealed as she bounced in her chair.

"No way," Brittany murmured, "Awesome."

Bird of Paradise Drums Beating

"Mm, hmm," Kara concurred.

"Wow, I never imagined." Amy reached out to touch Kara's shoulder. Yes, Kara was definitely flesh and blood. More important, she'd just claimed she'd been reincarnated as Cleopatra, Queen of Egypt. This was too good to be true.

Amy grinned at Kara. She felt like an idiot yet couldn't control herself. It was ridiculous to fawn over Kara. She couldn't help it though. She rubbed her hands so she wouldn't cave in to her impulse to touch Kara again. Amy wiggled in her chair. She wanted to stand up and hop around like an eager schoolgirl as she waited for a treat.

Brittany appeared to be giving Kara's announcement the same amount of consideration. She stared transfixed at Kara, with wide eyes and her mouth slightly open in a little 'o.'

Out of the blue, a thought came unbidden to Amy's mind. It shot out of nowhere, like a shooting star that streaked across the twinkling sky. Amy didn't realize she'd spoken the words aloud until Kara turned toward her with an icy stare.

Hostility had replaced Kara's earlier smile.

"How could you be Cleopatra in 69 B.C. when your first reincarnation happened around 300 or 400 A.D? The dates don't add up."

"Do you doubt me?" Kara roared. Her words dripped with venom.

Brittany recoiled from the hatred in Kara's voice. If anything, her eyes got even wider.

Amy widened her eyes at Brittany then turned back to Kara. "No, of course not. I merely wondered how you went back to that time. It's an ancient period. I didn't mean to question you. It was just an idle thought, that's all."

"What are you talking about?" Kara shouted. "Do you doubt my stories? You shared an insightful moment with me. I thought I would repay the favour. Are you implying I made everything up? Why would I do that, for my enjoyment, or your confusion?"

Brittany shrunk back into her chair as if she wished to be invisible as Kara jumped up then stalked past her. Kara strode to the window, crossed her arms, shook her head then turned away while she pointedly ignored them. Brittany gave Amy *'the look,'* shook her head then lifted her hands up in a silent entreaty.

Amy shrugged then wordlessly tried to convey deep regret for what she'd inadvertently done. She hated when Brittany gave her *'the look'*. It was almost worse than Kara's anger.

Kara watched the birds outside. With a furious gesture she slashed the air. The birds began to screech and shriek. Amy was filled with guilt. Their earlier jovial conversation had just died a fiery death.

The cacophony of noise distracted Amy for a moment. She couldn't figure out what had set the birds off. With a quick motion she jumped up then moved to stand beside Kara. Brittany joined her. They watched what the birds were doing with considerable interest.

One of the birds quieted down. Then the rest followed suit. One by one they swiveled their heads towards the window where Kara, Amy and Brittany stood.

Amy turned to Kara to question the bizarre action. She hesitated as something in Kara's stance made her stop.

Kara's face was tilted forward, nose lifted high toward the glass. Her eyes were fixed intently on the scene laid before her like a frozen tableau.

The birds were motionless.

Amy watched Kara nod. She blinked her eyes once then raised her palms slightly towards the sky.

The birds rose as if on command. They hovered for a moment in front of the window then scattered to the four winds.

The stillness was absolute.

Moments later, a few birds alighted on a tree outside the picture window. They twittered and chirped in a quiet manner as if subdued.

Kara gave a complacent nod. Then she turned toward Amy and Brittany with a satisfied smile.

Amy stared while her mind swam with questions. What had happened out there? Had Kara done that? If she had, how had she done it? Why did the birds listen to her? Did she control them?

Bird of Paradise Drums Beating

Kara reminded Amy of a conductor whose every motion the musicians followed with absolute intent. Her power seemed absolute.

Amy stifled her questions. She sensed Kara would ignore her. She was also loath to be given *'the look'* again by either Kara or Brittany. Nor did she want to be greeted by Kara's stony silence. If Kara wanted to share anything about the birds she would, in her own time. Amy had learned patience was something Kara valued.

"Now where were we?" Kara asked, as if nothing had happened.

"You were about to elaborate on Cleopatra." Brittany sat down, crossed her legs beneath her then reached for her notebook and pen.

Kara nodded toward Brittany. Then she turned to Amy, raised her eyebrows and waited with arms crossed.

Amy realized she needed to win Kara over. The regal tilt of Kara's head reminded Amy of a woman used to getting her way. She certainly had the temperament of a ruler.

Empathy, maybe groveling, was in order. Amy hoped Kara would forgive her thoughtless comment then continue her story. She took a deep breath then went for the plunge.

"I can't imagine how lonely you were as the daughter of a king. I read about that time in history. Weren't siblings rivals rather than friends since they vied for the throne?" Amy chattered non-stop. It was a nervous habit. "How many siblings did you have? What about your mother, you haven't mentioned her yet. Of course with my rude interruption perhaps you were at that part of your story. I sincerely apologize for my comments. We'd like you to continue."

Amy peeked at Brittany. Brittany's eyes were glued to her notebook. Smart girl, Amy thought before she rushed to add, "I got carried away. I find this so exciting. I've read so much about Cleopatra. I know her patron goddess was Isis. While she reigned it was believed Cleopatra was the reincarnation and embodiment of the goddess of wisdom." Amy clasped her hands. "I'd love to hear stories about Cleopatra. Please go on."

Penny Ross

Absolute silence greeted Amy's apology. The saying, *'you could hear a pin drop'* applied here. Amy glanced beneath her lashes at Kara, careful not to stare or irritate her further.

Kara took her time before she answered. She stretched her arms, did a few head rolls, shrugged her shoulders. To Amy, it appeared Kara wanted to shake off negative energy. At least Amy hoped that was her intent.

"All right, if you insist."

Amy sighed. What a relief. The storm had passed ….for now.

14

"I was fascinated with ancient Egypt even though my heritage was Greek," Kara began. "With an intense curiosity, fired by the need to know more about my country, subjects, languages and the state, I was ambitious. I acquainted myself with all things necessary to prepare me for the crown I might receive one day. There was one quality I craved and admired most. I wanted what average women don't even dream of. It was the one thing that would make my subjects follow me willingly and enemies fear me. Above all else I desired that which would make me whole and absolute.... I wanted power."

Kara's expression was triumphant.

Amy nodded.

"Can you understand that?" Kara demanded. With arms folded she tossed her hair, defiant.

"It was the absolute need to have something, the yearning and the dream to fulfill your destiny. I knew with all my being I would reign one day. To be the absolute ruler I needed power to protect myself from those who would vow to kill me. Enemies surrounded me. I needed to safeguard myself from those who wished to harm me. Power would shield me and provide permanence. It would help realize my dreams for myself, and Egypt."

Wide-eyed Amy nodded again, afraid to stop the flow of words.

"I was fortunate to live to be queen. I was Cleopatra VII. I was young when my father fled from Alexandria, around nine years old. My life was filled with peril and dread as my two older sisters vied for the crown. One of my sisters, Cleopatra VI disappeared mysteriously one day, which made my second sister Berenice IV the queen. It was rumored Berenice had her killed."

Kara grimaced. "I lived in constant fear of being strangled, poisoned or hastened to my death in a convenient manner. Fortunately, my youth probably saved me. Berenice had other matters to deal with and left me to my own devices. I don't remember much of those days," Kara admitted.

"Berenice married but made a fatal mistake. She failed to seek approval from Rome for a union with her new spouse. When our father, Auletes had fled Egypt he went to Rome since he had ample protection there. My father was intent on being restored to the crown. With the help of his Roman friends he found a governor named Gabinius worthy of leading an army. With the promise of great wealth, Gabinius and the army overtook Alexandria. They restored my father to his throne."

Amy jumped in with questions.

"Why do you talk about your life when you were young as if someone else told you stories about it? Do you remember growing up in Alexandria?"

"No. I don't recall exact details from my youth. It's rather foggy and indistinct. I vividly remember when my father returned though."

"How old were you?"

Kara furrowed her brow, as if lost in thought.

Amy could almost see her calculate years and her probable age.

"I would have been fourteen," Kara estimated.

"Hmm, interesting."

"Would you like me to continue or did you need anything else clarified?"

"No, go on. I had a thought but we can discuss it another day. Oh wait, what happened to the sister, Berenice?"

Kara settled more comfortably in her chair. "Interesting you should ask. As a traitor she was executed of course, beheaded."

Kara shrugged. "No matter, it was expected."

Amy was shocked at Kara's cavalier attitude.

Brittany glanced up from her notebook, met Amy's eyes for a brief moment then quickly returned to her notes.

Bird of Paradise Drums Beating

"What do you mean killed? How did you feel about that?"

"What? Oh, I don't remember."

Kara waved her hand as if to dismiss the question. Then, she hesitated and with furrowed brow turned toward Amy.

"I guess I might have been relieved," Kara admitted. "After all, as I got older she would have killed me as a possible rival. With her gone I was next in line as the eldest surviving child. Knowing the throne would be mine one day after aspiring to it, would have replaced any feelings of regret my sister had been killed."

Could Kara be that heartless? Then Amy recalled what she'd read about ancient times. Kara had repeated something considered natural in those days. Royalty were raised to be ruthless, to kill or be killed, to live among traitors, to crave power. These were qualities they were expected to have to survive. With this in mind, Amy settled back to listen to Kara's tale. After all, it was more likely make believe.

"My father, who had a reputation among the people as a weakling and a buffoon, decided to show his subjects how important they were to him." Kara grinned. "He erected new buildings then restored temples that had crumbled to ruin. Unfortunately, his days were limited. When he was barely into his fifties my father's health failed. He passed from this world to the next."

Kara sounded gloomy but quickly recovered. "In his will he decreed the crown of Egypt would pass to my ten-year-old brother Ptolemy XIII and me. I jointly inherited the kingdom with my brother when I was eighteen."

"Whew, you were both young to rule a kingdom weren't you?"

"Yes, indeed."

"Imagine ruling a kingdom at your age Brittany."

Brittany smiled. "I can't even get a mental image in my head. I haven't lived on my own yet or bought a car. I wouldn't know where to start."

"Yes, well I tried my best to keep my subjects happy. I admit it was hard though. One reason people didn't like the ruling class was because of the cultural gulf that separated us. Egypt had two cultures, one indigenous and one Greek. Our distinctions were heightened by religion, ancient customs and beliefs. On the other hand, religion enabled the monarchy to survive.

Kings and queens replaced the native pharaohs who linked earth to heaven. Pharaohs, who were considered gods themselves, were the go-betweens among gods and mortals. Now that we no longer had pharaohs, even though we were Greek, the monarch replaced the pharaohs in the minds of common native subjects. That's why my father was intent on bringing the temples back to their former glory. It won him affection among the Egyptians. It probably helped with my popularity as well."

"Wow, sounds complicated," Brittany noted. "This is fascinating Kara."

"Thanks," Kara acknowledged with a gracious nod. "Yes. It was complicated. Once you realized what was expected of you it became easier. It was hard to be yourself. I always felt as if I had to please someone or needed to put on a show. I was on display most of the time."

"Couldn't exactly relax and read a magazine or anything," Amy agreed.

Kara chuckled. "There weren't magazines or books back then. What a silly notion. Even if there had been I couldn't imagine having time to curl up with a good novel or sit and listen to my favourite CD. It seems ludicrous now that you mention it. My life back then was full of pomp and ceremony. People surrounded me constantly. I don't remember any privacy. I had no friends to share experiences with." Kara's voice was grim.

"I associated myself with the native gods. I was hailed as Isis incarnate, a goddess on earth. Do you know anything about Isis?"

"Yes, Cleopatra's patron goddess was Isis. While she reigned it was believed Cleopatra was the reincarnation and embodiment of the goddess of wisdom."

"I've never heard of her," Brittany noted. "Was she famous?"

"Yes, she was one of the major figures of worship."

Bird of Paradise Drums Beating

"So when I read about this it sounded like you pretended to be this goddess. How did you do that? Why?" Amy wondered.

"I didn't imitate her. It was more the idea of being hailed as a goddess. A great number of priests were at ceremonies. I would represent Isis. I was like a goddess on earth to the people. Isis, a compassionate and virtuous goddess, together with her brother whom she married, ruled Egypt. They were closely associated with royalty. Statues of Isis always show her with a throne since the people linked her to the sovereign. I found her appealing and liked the connection people made between the two of us. It was an honour to be equated with her name."

"Oh, all right, that makes sense. I'm beginning to get the picture. That time seems so foreign compared to now. Why were brothers and sisters married to one another? We call it incest. Wasn't there any taboo associated with it?"

"I don't know."

"Eew, you married your brother. Gross." Brittany shuddered.

Kara ignored her. "From what I remember, royal incest wasn't an accepted thing back then either. It scandalized the Greeks and Rome wasn't fond of it. For the Ptolemaic family who were my descendants, it was tradition. We had practical reasons too. No one could dispute any order of succession so it simplified matters when siblings married. Also, since gods wedded their goddesses who were brother and sister, and I was associated with the goddess Isis, it was natural I marry my younger brother.

Well, maybe not natural. It was expected in my family though. By marrying, we maintained the idea of divine, hereditary kingship. You have to remember gods and goddesses were heavenly and magical. The divinity got away with things mere mortals never could. In my world, royalty were connected to the gods so it was a practice we adopted."

Amy was shocked by Kara's confession of voluntarily living in an incestuous relationship. She tried not to judge Kara though for something she'd had little or no control over. Besides, this was made up so it was pure fantasy anyway.

Kara had fabricated a tale about incest with her brother, a royal family, gods and goddesses. Was this part of a made for TV movie, a history special or more suitable for a trip to Freud's couch? The topic might have been a ringer for a talk show. Amy grinned. There she went again, fantasizing about being a guest on a talk show.

"Did you and your brother get along?" Brittany's comment brought Amy back to the present.

"It wasn't a question of getting along. You have to understand he was eight years my junior. We didn't rule together since he was far too young. He had a regency council who represented him. I was supposed to cooperate with them but I couldn't stand the leader, Ptolemy's tutor. Pothinus, was horrid and wore disgusting make-up."

Kara shuddered. "It made him look no better than an Egyptian prostitute. He was a eunuch. I tried to ignore him and Ptolemy as often as I could.

I didn't like my brother though. He was weak, spoiled and I never had an intelligent conversation with him. Overlooking him was my undoing, however. Pothinus and the regency council manipulated those who hated me. I began to fear for my life. After three years on the throne I fled from Alexandria with only a few trusted servants."

"Oh no, you must have been devastated."

"Yes, I was. It's good of you to recognize that."

Amy reached out to lay her hand on Kara's shoulder but hesitated an instant too long. The moment passed.

"I was considered willful and headstrong. I guess those traits held me in good stead though. I certainly wasn't going to remain in exile forever."

"Oh, where did you go and what did you do?" Amy leaned forward in her chair, eager for Kara's answer.

"I went to Upper Egypt for a while. It wasn't safe for me there so I went to a city-state called Ashkelon, between Egypt and Palestine. My grandfather saved Ashkelon years before from being taken over by

Judea. The people in the city loved him so they welcomed me with open arms. It was wonderful to be appreciated. My people judged me harshly. Being a woman didn't help. They'd never respected my father so I had to fight for the right to rule."

"Isn't that something people admire though? Those are traits associated with men. Guys are supposed to be tough. When they threaten to wage war and flout their power words like forceful, commanding and a natural leader spring to one's mind. I guess it's considered admirable in men but less important for women. Wasn't Cleopatra regarded as a great ruler? I always thought history books portrayed her in a positive light."

"Yes, that's true. Of course they probably liked the fact I was associated with the great Julius Caesar and Mark Anthony."

"That was undoubtedly part of it. I'm sure an element of the mystique was due to the fact Cleopatra was a woman ruler though," Amy pointed out. "There are only so many queens in history that garnered respect and were described in a flattering way in chronicles. Think how many of them have been denigrated by the written word. It seems to me, queens are often thought of as weak and disagreeable, or greedy and power hungry."

"Tell me about it," Kara agreed, grinning. "Besides Cleopatra, every other time I've been a queen I've had to fight tooth and nail to maintain my power. If I wasn't being exiled I thought I'd be beheaded or sent to the tower for goodness sake."

"Wait a minute, you've been other queens?"

"Of course, didn't I mention that before?"

Kara flashed Amy a haughty stare, worthy of a queen.

"No, I'm sure I would have remembered."

Amy glanced at Brittany. Their eyes locked then Brittany confirmed what her mother had just said.

"You definitely never mentioned other queens."

"Oh, well we can talk about them later." Kara waved her hand in an offhand manner. "I'll let you pick a century and tell you if I was a queen or princess. What fun that would be, don't you think?"

Kara almost clapped her hands with glee. The thought that Amy and Brittany would enjoy a guess the queen and princess game obviously pleased her.

"Have you ever hung out with vampires or werewolves?" Brittany wondered. "They've been around for centuries."

"Like that girl in the Twilight book?"

"Yes, like Bella."

Kara sniffed. "She's a made up character, clearly not real like I am."

"Well, yeah, but still, have you?"

"Of course."

"Wow, can you tell us a story about that later? How cool. Were you ever bitten?"

"Do you want me to continue this story?" Kara interrupted. "Clearly it's infinitely more interesting history wise than vamps and werewolves."

"Sure, why not? I'll remind you about the vampire story another day." Brittany glanced at her watch then jumped up. "Whoa, look at the time. I gotta run. I've got a class soon. Mom can I use your car? Otherwise I'll be late. Wow, I didn't think we were here that long." Brittany scrambled about, grabbing things.

"What, you're leaving? I'm in the middle of a story. You can't go," Kara griped as she stood.

"I better take off too. I could drive you to your class then I should run down to the booth for a while. I've been ignoring my duties," Amy confessed as she jumped up to join Brittany.

"You have to leave too Amy? What about Cleopatra? I thought you were excited to hear more. So much for enthusiasm," Kara muttered as she crossed her arms then frowned at them.

Amy paused at the door, her hand on the doorknob. She threw Kara an apologetic look. "Sorry, it's just, well, you know, we have to go." She looked to Brittany for help.

Bird of Paradise Drums Beating

Brittany sighed as she glanced back at Kara. Something about Kara must have made her pause. "Yeah, um, hey, maybe we could head back later," Brittany suggested as she turned back to her mother.

Amy smiled. Brittany was such a considerate girl she thought with pride.

"What a wonderful idea Brittany. What do you think Kara? Would that work for you?"

Kara tapped her foot for a moment as she considered the idea. She smiled then acknowledged, "Yes, I'd like that."

They discussed a time then made their way outside.

As they walked double time toward the house Brittany brought up the bird scene they'd witnessed earlier.

"Mom, what do you think happened to those birds outside Kara's house? Did you hear how much noise they made when Kara was mad at you? When they watched Kara they got real quiet. It was freaky."

"Yes, I did notice that. I wanted to ask Kara about it but I'd already made her angry when I questioned her Cleopatra reincarnation."

"No kidding, she was hopping mad. Talk about awkward."

"Yeah, it was. I got the impression Kara controlled those birds. They seemed to stare right at her. It definitely was odd."

"Did you see how she stood, like a statue and the birds imitated her."

"That's right. After that I saw Kara nod, blink her eyes once then raise her palms toward the sky. That's when the birds rose up, right in front of us."

"When they hovered there in front of the window I noticed their eyes were glued to Kara's. She must control them or something mom. Kara calmed down when the birds flew off. She seemed real satisfied after that. Like she'd done something to be proud of. I was glad she wasn't mad at you anymore. It was odd though."

"I had the same impression Brittany, and you're right, it was a relief when her anger passed. The birds seemed to calm her. You should have heard the incredible birdsong I heard the first time I went to Kara's on my own. This reminded me of it."

"How so?"

"I thought it was unusual how many birds were right outside Kara's window. I've never noticed such a variety of wildfowl either."

"Ooh, fancy word mom, wildfowl."

Amy laughed. "Yeah, well, there were swans, ducks, geese and all the birds we saw today. The pitch of the noise was unbelievable."

"Hmm, I wonder why?"

"Well, I thought it was the birdsong I heard from the conservatory."

Amy stopped midstride. "Brittany, you should have heard it. The melody this bird sang was otherworldly. It was blissful yet intense. I felt as if I'd been lifted up to heaven. I was at peace yet my senses were heightened to this incredible level." Amy turned away, embarrassed. She began to walk, faster than before.

Brittany was quick to reassure her. "It's all right mom, there's no need to be uncomfortable around me. You've shared a lot of your feelings lately. There's nothing to be self-conscious about."

Amy gave her daughter a grateful smile. "You always know what to say Brittany," she praised as she stopped to give her a quick hug.

As they neared the house Brittany said, "I'll just grab my stuff. Do you have to do much or can we take off right away?"

"I'm good to go in about five minutes."

"Great, we can talk about Kara more when we're in the car."

As they drove off they resumed their earlier conversation.

"The birdsong I heard at Kara's that day, it was unbelievable. When it ended I felt drained yet oddly refreshed. I must admit that's why I went back. I hoped for a repeat performance." Amy chuckled.

"Today was the first glimpse I've gotten of any birds in the area but it was nowhere near that first time. The atmosphere was charged like today though when Kara was near the window. It was as if the birds outside reacted to the solo birdsong within the house. They were quiet at first then they erupted into song."

Amy smiled at the memory. "I had the impression the outdoor birds and wildfowl were intent on drowning out the main singer. They were like a chorus gone amuck as their sounds rose to an unimaginable height. Yet they were in perfect harmony with the lead bird." Amy sighed then shook her head. "This wasn't everyday birdsong. The melody seemed to rise from a pinnacle of pain and longing."

"I wish I could have heard it."

"Yes, it was extraordinary. I hope you get the chance to hear it Brit. When the song ended I waited for more but there was none forthcoming. The birds outside settled down so I entered the conservatory."

Amy cleared her throat. "I was caught off guard by the shrill cry of a bird. I was shocked to see it was the bird of paradise I'd seen the day before on one of the paths in Kildonan Park. Kara calls it a paradise tanager."

"What? Did you say it looked like a bird of paradise, like Kissakee?" Brittany shrieked.

"Brittany." Amy was about to scold her daughter as the shrill cry was amplified in the close confines of the car. She stopped though as Brittany's words penetrated her brain. "Did you say Kissakee, I mean Kiskadee?"

"Yeah, right, that's what they were called." Brittany waved her hand. "That's the kind of bird I saw the other day on a path. I told you and dad that."

"Well, yes, I remember the conversation. You started to describe the bird but then you realized you had to leave so you rushed off."

"Right, so anyway, the bird I saw had all these wild colours, even more than Kissakee." Brittany paused as her mother glanced her way, "I mean Kiskadee," she corrected. "It reminded me of a bird of paradise. You said Kara calls it a paradise tanager. Hmm, I'll have to look that name up on the Internet. So you saw the same bird on the path and in Kara's house? How weird is that?"

Penny Ross

As Amy turned into the entrance of the roundabout where she always dropped Brittany off at university she echoed Brittany's words, "Yes, how weird is that?"

"Thanks mom, we gotta talk about this more later, it's wild, gotta go, bye." Brittany grabbed her stuff, pushed the door open then rushed out of the car.

Yes, Amy thought as she drove away, they certainly needed to talk about it more. The bird might provide some clue to Kara's mysterious persona.

15

"Do you like to read?" Brittany blew on her Chai tea to cool it off. They'd popped into a local coffee shop after class.

"Yeah, who doesn't? I mean, it would be kind of awkward to be at university if you weren't a reader, wouldn't it?"

Brittany gazed at Brad. His comment sounded logical yet was it necessarily true? "Hmm, yeah, well it would certainly help. I guess it depends on the courses you're in. Some have more reading requirements than others. There must be some allowances for people that don't like to read. What I mean is, you know, people that just read because they have to, not because they love to."

Brad nodded.

"What I meant is, do you like to read in your spare time? Like is it something you do for enjoyment?"

"Gotcha, yeah I see the difference." Brad cupped his hands around his drink.

"I love graphic novels, sci-fi, astronomy and books about sports. I mean any and all kinds of sports. I'll read a biography by an athlete or a how-to sports book. I read this book not too long ago about this runner that ran in his bare feet. He liked to run across country. He ran really far. So, yeah, I like to read. I guess you could say I love to read."

Brad flashed her a wide smile.

Brittany smiled back then took a deep calming breath. She felt like one of those heroines in an old time Victorian novel, about to swoon with adoration at the hunky male character. What was wrong with her? Man, listening to Kara must be rubbing off in the wrong way. She wasn't the melodramatic type so what was up with these weirdo thoughts?

"What kind of books do you like to read?" Brad leaned toward her.

Brittany gulped. Man he was good-looking. She could hardly concentrate on his question when he fixed her with that impish grin and gave her his undivided attention.

"Me, books, yeah, I love to read," she gushed. Man, what was that? She barely sounded coherent.

"I mean, let's see I read all kinds of books. Right now I'm into historical fiction and I've been checking out fantasy books. I don't like romance novels, I used to read them when I was a teen but fortunately I got over that phase." She gave a sheepish smile. "I've read a few sci-fi books. I like Orson Scott Card. I read 'Ender's Game' and 'Speaker for the Dead' but then I read another author, Isaac Asimov and his stuff was way too heavy for me."

Brad nodded. "Yeah, the thing with sci-fi is there are so many books out there on it. You can read about robots, an alternate universe, the future, space or really heavy topics from science. There's a lot of variety and not every author appeals to everyone."

"I guess you could say that for most genres though."

"Yeah, I've never read romance though so I'm not too sure how much variety there is in that type of novel," Brad teased. "I mean isn't it basically nerdy girl meets hunky guy who's going out with her model type, hot best friend? Then nerdy girl gets rid of braces, takes the braid out of her hair, clears up her skin, wears revealing clothes and bam hunky guy falls for her. Instant love, lots of kissing and making out and they ride off into the sunset. Oh, and it usually takes place in some exotic city or country."

Brittany couldn't help it. She burst out laughing. Brad was bang on the money with his description.

"I'm glad I wasn't drinking my tea," she sputtered after her laughter died down. She grinned at Brad. "Admit it, you snitched one of your sister's romance books when you were a little kid didn't you? That's the formula for most romance novels. You must have read at least one to know that."

Bird of Paradise Drums Beating

It was Brad's turn to laugh. "Guilty as charged," he admitted, hands raised. "I nicked a few of her books when I was young. It really got under her skin when I quoted juicy parts at the dinner table. She always got into trouble. My parents chewed her out for reading that crap. Then they'd accuse her of leading me down the path of debauchery since she let me read them and I was too young to know any better. It drove her crazy."

Brad flashed her a brilliant smile. It was worthy of a bratty younger brother caught in the act yet able to bluster his way past his parents to get his sister in hot water.

"You beast," Brittany accused. "Your sister must have hated you. Of course she did add to your vocabulary since you learned words like debauchery."

"Those words were actually from her Harold Robbins phase. He had a lot of immoral behaviour and sinful scenes from what I recall."

Brittany blushed. "Yeah, I read him for awhile," she confessed. She didn't elaborate or add she'd read at least a dozen of his books when she'd been into him as an author. How embarrassing to acknowledge that.

Brad gave her a penetrating stare. "You're blushing." He took a healthy slug of his drink. "Admit it, you've read your fair share of Harold Robbins and romance novels. Man, I just shared my huge confession. Come on Brittany, fess up."

Brittany blanched. Was he serious? She began to shake her head then reconsidered and gave a nervous giggle instead. "OK, OK, yeah, you got it out of me. I was a closet romance reader then graduated to Harold Robbins and read a bunch of trashy novels. I can't even remember all the author names. I used to take out half a dozen at once and consume them like junk food."

"I knew it. Had you pegged from the very start." He flashed another smile.

Brittany took a sip of her tea. Brad's smiles were making her stomach do fluttery things. Maybe it was time to switch the talk from romance and trashy novels to something that reminded her less of smut and passion. She didn't want to make a fool of herself and look like some sort of nympho.

"One thing I can't stand though is when they take an amazing book and turn it into something barely recognizable onscreen. I typically prefer movies where I haven't read the book."

Brittany smiled. Now that was a safe subject to change the topic to. She silently congratulated herself for the smooth segue. It was still about books yet referred to movies.

"Yeah, I can relate. I guess it's great for an author though when they base a movie on their novel. Look at J.K. Rowling. I doubt if she's too upset with the way they changed her books onscreen. She's made big bucks. Every novel got made into a blockbuster movie and her books have been bestsellers all over the world."

"That's true. I guess exposure is great for authors. I like to imagine the characters and settings in my mind though. It bugs me when they're nothing like what I pictured. I get caught up with my image and don't want to see something that's radically different onscreen."

Brittany shrugged. "It must run in the family. My mom loves to tell the story about how she saw 'Tess of the D'Urbervilles' with my dad when they were my age."

Brittany took a sip of tea. "I guess it pissed her off how the movie was so different from the book. My dad always agrees with her when she complains about how wrong the movie was. There's this scene at Stonehenge. I guess my mom got so angry she almost walked out of the theatre when that part was shown. My dad says he remembers it because she kept hissing stuff like, *'This is nothing like the book. It's horrible. I hate it. They've ruined the whole story.'*"

Brittany smiled. "It's this old classic by Thomas Hardy. I read it last year and she's right. It's brilliant and has all the ingredients of a fantastic novel. There's sex, love, betrayal, guilt, a murder." She shook her head. "I guess it's the ultimate romance novel. I loved Tess just like my mom did. She's one of those characters you never forget."

Her eyes met Brad's.

"Yeah, I know what you mean," he whispered. He reached over to put his hand on top of hers.

Brittany sneaked a peek at their hands. The gesture was tender yet sexy at the same time. Brad began to rub his thumb along the inside of her hand. She gulped. Shivers ran up her spine, the good kind where you knew something great was about to happen. Brittany took a deep breath. She felt as if the anticipation of what might take place could jeopardize what would occur if she screwed this up.

Careful to appear nonchalant as if guys did this all the time in coffee bars Brittany smiled at Brad then raised one eyebrow just slightly.

Brad winked then gave her a bratty grin. "Come on Miss Romance and Smutty Book Lover, let's hit the road." He jumped up then captured her hand in his as he began to weave his way around the tables. Brittany barely had time to grab her purse before she was propelled toward the door.

As soon as they got outside Brad pulled her over to a nearby bench. He plopped down then pulled her into his lap. "Sorry," he breathed into her ear as he held her close. "I couldn't stand it. I had to get out of there and get you alone. I need to do this."

He looked into her eyes for a moment as if searching for a silent answer. Brittany gave a slight nod.

When their lips met Brittany felt like the heroine in a Victorian novel. She was glad they were sitting down or she would have swooned. She didn't even mind that she sounded like a love struck girl eager for the hunky guys' kisses. So what if it was a cliché? Brad was a fantastic kisser. Yum, that's all that mattered to her.

∽∽

Amy and Brittany didn't get to discuss the bird of paradise that evening. Brittany jumped on the bus then headed home as soon as her and Brad parted. Amy had driven home alone, made a quick supper then went for a brisk walk before she headed over to Kara's.

Brittany arrived moments after Amy, out of breath and flustered.

Amy greeted her daughter. She opened her mouth to comment on Brittany's flushed cheeks. Radiant, Brittany flashed her mother a warm smile. Kara interrupted them and the moment passed.

"Perfect, you're both here. May I begin?"

"Sure, do you think we could get a snack though," Brittany asked. "I didn't have time for supper."

"No problem." Kara jumped up then went over to the intercom to talk to Carl.

"Did you ever lead an army?" Brittany dug in her purse for her notebook and pen.

"Interesting you should ask." Kara arched her brows at Brittany. "As I mentioned before, I certainly wasn't going to remain in exile forever. I took ample money and jewels with me when I left Alexandria. After all, it would have been foolhardy to leave empty-handed. I was a queen you know."

As she spoke Kara sat tall and proud. As she watched Kara in action, Amy could imagine her as a queen. She certainly had the right attitude. If a haughty demeanor were any indication, Kara was a ringer. She had no problem exhibiting the traits and stance equated with self-important royalty.

"As a ruler, it's obvious you had the forethought to think ahead. That's why I asked about the army. You had to get your throne back somehow and I imagine war was the likeliest choice." Brittany hunched over her notebook as she waited for Kara's answer.

Kara gave a regal nod. "You're right. I managed to raise a mercenary army to face Ptolomy's forces. We were at a standstill for days. It was like a face off with no takers, neither side was willing to make the first move. It was that damn Caesar."

Abruptly Kara stopped. She appeared to be far away. Her lips were curved in a secretive smile.

"Were you in love with him?" Amy prompted.

Kara turned towards Amy. Her movements were slow, like a reluctant sleeper awakened from deep slumber.

"What?"

Bird of Paradise Drums Beating

"I wondered if you were in love with Caesar."

"Of course I loved him. He was brilliant, powerful, handsome, and experienced with women. I had never been bedded so I approached him with some trepidation." Kara gazed coyly at Amy from beneath her lashes. "He was a lot older than me, more than thirty years. Considered a brilliant strategist in war, his men worshipped him. I agonized over how to approach a general who could help me get my throne back."

"What do you mean you'd never been bedded? How could you be a virgin when you were married to your brother?"

Kara was shocked. "Haven't you been listening? He was a child, ten years old when we began to rule. Who sleeps with a ten year old, particularly their brother? Eew, what do you take me for?"

Kara couldn't hide the disgust in her voice. Eyes boring into Amy's she waited as if she expected a soothing remark.

Brittany saved Amy. "Wow, that's a relief. We were confused there for a minute about the whole marrying your brother thing. Glad you cleared that up for us." Brittany smiled as if everything was settled.

"I'm sorry. I didn't mean to imply you did anything offensive. As Brittany said we were caught off guard by your earlier comments. I apologize for interrupting. Please continue," Amy urged.

"As I was saying before I was rudely interrupted," Kara scoffed, "I had to come up with a plan."

Kara leaned forward, eager to share her idea. "It was while I sat in my tent with my army, ready to attack. I came up with an ingenious strategy to approach Caesar. I must say I outdid myself."

Kara preened like a peacock, feathers open to an appreciative audience.

"What did you do?" Brittany coaxed.

"Well, Caesar was in Alexandria as I suspected. He was at the palace. Who wouldn't stay there? It was luxurious, sophisticated, there were ample baths to relax in and servants were available for every need you could imagine. He called Ptolemy and me back from the battlefield. I guess it was up to him to end what he likely imagined was a petty argument. Ptolemy, the little weasel, scampered back to the palace like an eager dog attempting to please his master."

Kara was scornful as she recalled that day.

"I, on the other hand, could not merely walk into Alexandria and expect to be presented to Caesar."

"Why not?"

Kara glared at Amy. "I swear you don't pay attention. I realize you can't be expected to understand the intricacies of royalty, but come on Amy."

Amy wondered if she'd be taken to task for her error. Should she hang her head like an errant school child?

"My life was in danger." Kara spoke slowly, as if Amy was a bit dim. "Assassins waited to kill me. They lurked around every corner in Alexandria. I couldn't expect to waltz back to the palace and have people welcome me with open arms. Ptolemy, and that horrid eunuch Pothinus, poisoned my subjects towards me, remember."

"Yes, yes of course I do. Silly me, sometimes I swear I'd forget my head if it wasn't screwed on." Amy's laugh was nervous.

Brittany glanced up, pursed her lips then shook her head at her mother.

"What? You too, come on, it wasn't that obvious."

Kara gave a gracious nod toward Brittany. Mollified, she resumed her story. "Since I was in mortal danger, I had to approach the palace unseen. Not an easy task as you can imagine."

Kara glanced at Amy, measuring her ability to picture this feat. "Well, pretend you can anyway." Kara sighed as if aware this was way beyond Amy's ability.

Amy nodded quick, eager to appear worthy of Kara's trust.

Brittany smirked at the exchange.

"Oh Carl, yes, do come in," Kara commanded as Carl hesitated nearby. "The sandwich is for Brittany. You can put the fruit on the table here."

Carl did as he was told, nodded then left.

Bird of Paradise Drums Beating

Brittany chomped on her sandwich then reached across the table to grab some grapes. "Yum, this is awesome. Thanks Kara. Mom can you please pour me some iced tea."

"Sure." Amy poured then passed a glass to her daughter. "Kara, do you want some?"

"No, I'm fine."

Amy poured herself a glass of iced tea.

"We're ready for the rest of the story. I'll take notes when I'm done this." Brittany waved her sandwich.

"I went with one of my most trusted servants by boat to the palace. It was evening so we had a greater chance to approach the stronghold undetected. Then I had Apollodorus, my manservant, roll me into a bedspread."

Kara chuckled. "He tied it up and carried it to Caesar's apartment. It appeared to be a rug slung over his shoulder. We were admitted and when he unrolled the gift I tumbled out. I was practically at Caesar's feet." Kara laughed, pleased at the memory.

"How clever you were," Amy praised. She clapped her hands appreciatively.

Brittany nodded in agreement.

"Yes, I was, wasn't I?"

Kara flashed a wide smile. It was obvious she relished the memory of Caesar's surprise at her unexpected entrance.

"He found it amusing. Caesar was impressed with my creativity and boldness. So he persuaded my brother Ptolemy to share the throne with me. Of course, after Caesar and I became lovers, I realized Caesar had the power to help me achieve all I'd dreamed of."

Kara idly touched her cheek then began to caress her face. "He thought I was beautiful," Kara whispered.

"I've heard Cleopatra described as an unconventional beauty," Amy agreed.

"I love Cleopatra's hair. The bangs are awesome," Brittany raved. "I noticed some celebrities have copied it."

"Really, after all these years? I had more than one hairstyle you know Brittany. I wore at least three that were popular. I particularly liked the regal one I wore with my royal headdress. I had a rearing cobra made of precious metal for that hairstyle.

My appearance was original, eccentric even for those times. Most women had a fair complexion while mine was dark. As Brittany noted my hair was glorious, flowing and luxurious with copper highlights. Caesar loved to run his fingers through it. He considered me truly beautiful. What more could a woman ask for?"

Kara paused, then added, "Well, besides power of course."

She chuckled at Amy's frown.

"Don't be so naïve, my friend. Caesar was a genius and knew the importance of power. He protected me. I felt Caesar was my equal in every sense of the word. So, I was willing to rule with my worthless brother if it pleased him.

You've probably forgotten Caesar came from Rome. He was in Alexandria to enforce the terms of my father's will. From a political viewpoint it was imperative I agree to Caesar's conditions. Otherwise, I'd have to remain in exile for the rest of my days. Since I wanted to rule Egypt my only recourse was to take on my brother Ptolemy as my colleague. I had to share the throne." Kara shrugged. "I swallowed my pride and agreed to Caesar's terms."

Amy was startled by Kara's abrupt laugh. It sounded more like a snort than a chuckle.

"What's so amusing?"

"I'll never forget what happened when Caesar invited Ptolemy to join us the night after I arrived at the palace."

Kara's laugh turned to merriment. "Ptolemy was ready to explode. His face got bright red, like a tomato. He threw a temper tantrum. Can you imagine thirteen years old and still having fits? It was unseemly for a monarch." Kara chuckled then shook her head.

Amy and Brittany joined in Kara's laughter.

Amy imagined a young teenager strutting around in a fit of temper with a room full of attendants. It did seem inappropriate.

"Ptolemy was very dramatic. He yelled then urged everyone to take his side against Caesar and me. He called Caesar rude names then cursed him as my lover."

Kara flashed Amy a sly glance.

"When Ptolemy ran outside and put down Caesar publicly he was dragged back inside the palace by Caesar's soldiers. Just like the naughty boy he was. Caesar promised to make a great announcement in the next few days to please the angry mob. He held a banquet then made a speech where Caesar declared Ptolemy and I were reconciled. He stressed how we were prepared to rule Egypt jointly as our father had wished. It was very moving."

Kara grinned. "Caesar could be very magnanimous. He gave the island of Cyprus to my younger brother and sister to rule as king and queen. It kept everyone happy and restored peace. Unfortunately, my brother and sister remained at the palace instead of leaving immediately."

Kara shuddered. "I hated them. They were horrid to me."

"Did things get better after that?"

"No, unfortunately they didn't. It was that swine Pothinus. Remember, he was Ptolemy's tutor. He secretly ordered Ptolemy's army who were encamped on Egypt's eastern border to march towards Alexandria and declare war on Caesar."

Kara shook her head. "It was terribly unsporting of Ptolemy and Pothinus. My brother always was a stupid ruler. He never thought things through." As Kara smiled she reminded Amy of a Cheshire cat. "Caesar put Ptolemy under house arrest. I was gratified by his thoughtfulness."

"I don't understand. Why did he do that?"

"Oh, Ptolemy would have rallied my enemies to his side. Then he would have attacked both of us within the palace. He knew his army was on their way so he would have had reinforcements. If they would have made it in time that is. As I mentioned, his actions were ill-advised."

"Hmm, I see what you mean. I guess your entire life was based on political maneuvers."

"Yes, that and preservation," Kara agreed. "One wrong move and I would have been killed by one of my siblings." She made a slashing motion across her throat. "They were a blood thirsty lot."

"And you weren't?" Amy couldn't resist teasing.

"Yes, I was." Kara chuckled. "I don't know how much more I should tell you though," she teased as she wagged her finger at Amy.

"Oh please, don't stop now," Amy pleaded.

"How about you Brittany, still game to hear more about Cleopatra or are you more interested in vamps and werewolves?"

Brittany appeared to give the question some consideration before she answered. "I like the Cleopatra story. I'd like to hear about your connection to vampires and werewolves though another day. Is that doable?"

"Hmm, well, all right, I think that could work. When Ptolemy's army arrived they declared war. Caesar thought the war would be short. Fortunately he was victorious in the end. At times I felt my heart would burst when I thought how fragile our lives were. I would have died without him championing my cause. I depended on his triumph. Men are better warriors than women you know. Although I tried to be tough and powerful, in the end I needed to lean on a man to achieve my ends."

Kara shook her head. "The best part of the war was my brother's tutor Pothinus was killed. After five months of fighting, Caesar triumphed as the official winner. My brother fled the Nile. He tried to escape by boat but drowned with the other escapees."

"That must have pleased you. Now you could rule alone."

"No, unfortunately that's not how it works. I had to rule with my eleven year old brother to maintain peace. Ptolemy XIV was easy to get around though. In practicality I ruled alone. It wasn't so bad."

Kara shrugged, philosophical to the end. "The worst part was dealing with the ancient legend."

"What ancient legend?"

"Ptolemy drowned in the Nile. According to legend, it meant he would have instant rebirth and immortality. My enemies came out in droves. They claimed to be Ptolemy reincarnated. It became quite tedious."

"Did they challenge you or attempt to harm you in any way?"

"Oh, people questioned my power daily," Kara admitted. "This was nothing new. Caesar was not a patient man though. The constant badgering wore him down. He had the Nile dredged and retrieved my brother's body."

"What? That sounds so, so overboard."

"Great pun Amy." Kara grinned. "It was necessary though. When Caesar showed the King's golden armour to the people the war was officially declared over. You can imagine my relief."

"Yes, I'm sure you enjoyed the reprieve."

"Oh, it was more than that." Kara clapped her hands then leaned forward, eager to share this part of her tale. "I had a secret to share with Caesar."

16

"What was it?" Amy leaned forward, eager to know the secret.
"I was pregnant. I was sure it would be a boy."
"Ooh, how exciting. Was it a boy?"
"Of course." Kara flashed Amy a triumphant smile.
"Before I had my son Caesar and I journeyed up the Nile on my state barge. I'll never forget that trip." Kara gazed off, eyes brimming with tears.
"Did something happen to make you sad?" Amy ventured.
"Oh no, quite the contrary." Kara wiped away a tear. "The trip was glorious. It was like the honeymoon we never had. We considered it a victory celebration. Caesar had won the war and the people of Egypt could see the alliance between Caesar and me. That made it political as well, but I didn't mind.

It was wonderful having Caesar by my side. We took in all the sights of Egypt. I wish that trip could have lasted forever. Alas, like all good things it ended when we reached Aswan. That's at the southernmost part of Egypt," Kara added, for Amy and Brittany's benefit.

"When you say it was like a honeymoon do you mean Caesar acknowledged you as his wife? I thought you were married to your brother?"

Kara shrugged. "I was, and Caesar had a wife back in Rome but that was of no consequence."

"He did? You never mentioned a spouse."

"Of course he had one." Kara waved her hand in the air as if it was not important. "Roman law would never have acknowledged us as husband and wife since I was a foreigner. In Egypt, my people accepted us as married since we were publicly together. I loved Caesar and carried his child. It was essential my subjects see us as a couple. Of

Bird of Paradise Drums Beating

course, in my naivety I also carried the hope my son would ultimately rule both Egypt and Rome one day. You know how focused a mother's dreams can be."

"Yes, I do."

"I thought even if ultimate power could never be mine it might be my son's," Kara reasoned. "Have you ever noticed women are happy to relieve themselves of control? We're pleased when we know a man we love, like a spouse, lover or son will retain power instead. We're so gullible."

"You weren't like that with your brothers, but yes, I agree that typically happens."

"My brothers were imbeciles. I was glad when they died." Kara's voice was harsh.

Amy was shocked by the vehemence of Kara's statement.

Brittany looked up, obviously surprised by Kara's hostile tone.

"I think as mothers we allow others to maintain power since we're peacemakers. Most of us desire security rather than upheaval. War and fighting don't jive with reconciling quarrels. Most women strive for happiness and a comforting environment. The less likelihood of hostility the better."

"Perhaps you're right," Kara allowed. "That happened to me when I had my son Ptolemy Caesar. His nickname was Caesarion. It means *'Caesar's son'* or *'Little Caesar.'*"

"How adorable."

"Yes, wasn't it? What you said about mothers makes sense since I know I fell in love with Caesarion the moment he was born. I would have moved mountains to see that little smile light up his face. I wanted to lay the world at his feet. To ensure he had the power and privilege that should be accorded to him. Caesarion became my life."

"I know what you mean," Amy agreed. "A mother has the special task of offering the best for her children. I've always nurtured and loved my children and provided a safe, encouraging atmosphere. I hope they'll grow up to be happy, contented, well-balanced individuals. When other people describe your kids as positive, or a joy to be around, your heart swells as a mother."

Brittany smiled at Amy then leaned close for a quick hug.

Amy hugged Brittany tighter. "Our life is so entwined with theirs. Even though Brittany has moved to the city we still see her often. The boys are young so we have a houseful of kids around when you include all their friends. The empty nest syndrome isn't something to laugh about or treat lightly. I'm not looking forward to it."

Amy crossed her legs. "It must be hard when you grow older. We have to find something meaningful to fill up the days when we're used to satisfying the needs of others. We constantly place their desires before ours. If mothers were more selfish, perhaps we'd adjust better to the immeasurable loss of our children growing up."

"Isn't that one of the reasons we have grandchildren?"

"What do you mean?"

"It's part of the cycle of life. We crave others who need us. It fulfills some inner drive or passion women have. When our children grow up we encourage, no, I think nag is the word." Kara laughed, the sound was melodic.

"We nag our kids to start a family. It ensures we, as mothers, have a new role in life. We become grandmothers. You know how bossy and demanding grandmothers can be. It becomes our right as women to be as unreasonable as we please. Since we've sacrificed for our children now they get to pay us back in spades by procreating."

Kara smiled. "This allows us to fulfill our primary function. Now we can be involved as doting caregivers again. Who doesn't want to be the loving granny who spoils her grandkids rotten? It's rather neat and tidy, don't you think?"

"Well, yes, it is, when you describe it like that. I'm sure women wouldn't necessarily be so black and white about it though. You lay it out in a logical, sequential manner. You make women sound a bit resentful don't you think?"

"More like martyrs I'd say." Kara sounded indifferent. "You're right though. We are resentful. We have every right to be. We give of

Bird of Paradise Drums Beating

ourselves without any regard to our personal welfare or mental health. Think of women today who put their career before children. How would you describe them Amy?"

"I guess career women fall into three basic categories. The unmarried ones who don't have a family life, the married ones who don't have any children or women who have children but put career before family. There are a variety of groupings within those but that would be the main three. As to descriptions, I don't know. I guess it depends on the women."

Kara sighed, crossed her arms then rolled her eyes. "Come on Amy. Can't you broad brush for once? I know it requires making assumptions, something you aren't willing to do. Do me a favour though and try."

Kara fixed Amy with one of her piercing stares.

"All right, let me think."

Kara tapped her fingers impatiently on the chair of her arm.

"If I have to make a sweeping generalization I'd say career women are described as selfish, egotistical, aggressive, domineering, controlling, power hungry, tough, demanding and money motivated. How's that?"

Kara beamed at Amy. "Excellent. Amy you have just described a man."

"That's hilarious," Brittany chuckled.

Amy and Kara joined in the laughter.

"I'm serious," Kara was quick to add. "Women who choose a career are labeled with offensive traits merely because they're female. If you gave the same depiction you've just listed for a man no one would question it.

Even though we have to allow for individual differences, men are supposed to display traits we consider negative in women. Men that don't are called wimps, sissies, pansies or has-beens. You get the gist. It's not fair but that's what society has imposed upon us. It was even apparent back in Cleopatra's lifetime. That was eons ago. You'd think times would have changed since then."

"Do you have a point to all this?" Amy challenged.

Not in the least offended, Kara laughed. "Of course I do. Women who put the needs of others before themselves unconditionally aren't doing that. When our children are young we might care for them tenderly and with real compassion. As they get older though, most women need more. They crave something else.

It seems to me some women start to put conditions on their love. It might not be a conscious thought. It just builds over time. All the years of sacrifice and denial of personal gain can result in bitterness, unhappiness and cynicism. Guilt becomes part of grandma's repertoire. Rather than being the kind, white haired old person they're expected to be, some women turn into crotchety, spiteful, mean spirited eccentrics.

How often do you see grandpa yelling at the kiddies? Never. It's grandma that dives off the deep end. She's the one who screams like a banshee and looks like a lunatic."

"So what's your answer oh wise and farseeing prophet? I feel as if I should bow down on the ground anxiously awaiting your clever response." Amy wondered if she'd gone too far. Kara responded to some ridicule but there was a fine line. Had she stepped over it?

"Sarcasm, I love it." Kara threw her head back then roared at Amy's outrageous comment.

Amy and Brittany joined in.

Amy was relieved. She'd blurted out the first thing that came into her head. Luckily, Kara took her remarks in the manner they'd been intended.

"Are you waiting with bated breath? Should I perhaps demand a drum roll to herald the occasion?"

Amy and Brittany gamely complied. They drummed their fingers on the edge of the table.

"Thank you."

Kara gave a little bow.

"The answer of course is, wait for it…. balance."

Amy smiled. When it was apparent Kara wasn't going to elaborate she ventured, "That's it?"

"Yes, are you disappointed?"

"Well, I don't know. It's logical. I could have come up with that solution myself."

"Of course you could. Anyone can. That's my point. Harmony and stability are necessary ingredients for happiness and personal fulfillment. When we have balance in our life we feel better about ourselves. Women who give love unconditionally have to allow time for their own needs. By nourishing our souls we replenish what we've given away to others. To remain upbeat, positive, loving and encouraging we need to maintain a healthy balance. It's as simple as that."

"Were you able to do that in your previous lives? Do you feel balanced now, as Kara?" Amy opened her eyes wide, shocked at what she'd just asked. How could she be so thoughtless?

"No, I don't."

Kara hung her head. "I know it's logical and should be an easy thing to do but I never said it was effortless. It often seems the opposite. I wonder what drives us to do that which can destroy us. Rather than settle for something that satisfies us. Why do we always want more? Why must we have it all?"

"I don't know, human nature maybe."

"I guess. Regardless of gender, the human species seems unable at times to derive satisfaction from the simple things in life. We crave excitement, glamour, power, money, prestige, glory and recognition. Then we like to add in harmony, quiet, solitude, a chance to nurture our soul all while striving for balance. Of course everything takes a back seat to our personal drive and blinding ambition. I know that from my own experience."

"How so?"

"Well, I should have been content when Caesarion was born. Instead, I continued to hold grand and illustrious illusions about his future probability of being King of both Egypt and Rome."

"That's not a bad thing for a mother."

"It is when you put aside the happiness and security of your child to further your own aspirations. I went to Rome and flaunted my rank. I was eager to proclaim my status as queen of the most prosperous nation in the world. My ego lapped up the attention accorded to royalty.

A queen is granted many honours when visiting another head of state. I made sure notable Romans paid court to me. It was gratifying to have others bow before me, to acknowledge me as important. I also wanted to get Caesar's attention again. I secretly hoped he'd publicly acknowledge our son."

"Did he?"

"What do you think?" Kara crossed her arms then leaned back.

"I'm guessing, not."

"Bingo."

"You must have been disappointed."

"Devastated was more like it. I rallied forth though and did the best I could with what I was given."

"That's always the lot of women."

"Yes, it is, isn't it? So, Amy, do you think men have a compulsion to treat others shabbily?"

"What do you mean?"

"Well, in many of my lives, my husband or master as they liked to be referred to took great pleasure in having power over my life. Take Caesar for example. When I showed too much independence he behaved in a derogatory manner. I was embarrassed and suitably put in my place when he refused to publicly acknowledge our son. Caesar did not treat me well. He was the one in control though so I bowed to his wishes."

"Oh, now I understand."

"Do you?"

"Yes, I've been treated that way myself. In a bad way I mean, by men, often. As you said I found it unpleasant. I've made an effort not to be around men who behave like that. Do you think it's a male trait?"

Bird of Paradise Drums Beating

"Hmm, well I think it boils down to power and control myself. If another person thinks someone is lesser they rush to demean that individual should the opportunity arise. Derogatory names get thrown about. Their actions show a high level of contempt. They treat people as no more important than the dirt beneath their feet. It's hard to fathom that degree of disrespect yet it happens all the time."

Kara scowled. "I find it interesting people have no regard for what they've done. When confronted with the magnitude of their actions they're aghast. They hasten to point out the person wronged, most likely a woman, has blown the entire situation out of proportion. You see what this person has done when they point the finger of blame at the female, don't you?"

"Made it her fault," Amy guessed.

"Yes, precisely. Then, they often compel the woman to give her word it won't happen again. Rather than apologize, as they should, control freaks crave the last word. They get power when they watch others grovel. Those worms should beg forgiveness. Instead, they turn the tables and make the woman the wrongdoer. This of course demoralizes the woman. It also reduces her self-esteem as she second-guesses her failing memory. This clouds the original matter of dissent."

Kara shook her head. "As I mentioned before, the female now takes great pains not to repeat the subject or initial action for fear of further criticism. Hence the man has won. He retains his power over her. He's like a matador with his foot on the slaughtered bull. He bows then revels in the applause he receives for his bloody deed."

"You make it sound calculated."

"Hmm, do I?"

"Yes, if the situation arises a man might overreact. He might not have the sense to apologize for his boorishness. I don't think it necessarily equates with the level you've described." Amy glanced over at Brittany who was bent over her notebook rapidly taking notes. She seemed content to listen to the conversation rather than engage in it.

"No, not the first time," Kara agreed. "If a man does it once though and gets away with it, don't be surprised when he does it again.

After all, he never got hurt. He managed to switch blame to the woman. I don't think men should be allowed to behave in a thoughtless manner. When should they atone for their actions?"

"I don't know? I've never thought about this."

"What if others witness the man's behaviour towards women? He might conduct himself the same towards his wife, sister, mother or close friend. Do you think they might imitate his manner, particularly if they emulate him? If they're young and male, when they grow up will they treat women the same way?"

Amy shrugged while Kara plowed on.

"You have to keep in mind Amy it's not a man's right to belittle females. No one should make us feel small and insignificant. What lesson is this for others, particularly the young? So the cycle of dominance and abuse continues."

"Don't you think you've exaggerated a bit?"

"Have I? Tell that to a woman who stood up to a man then was beaten or killed for it. Tell them you think it's an exaggeration."

Amy had no answer to that statement. It sounded so final.

"We took the cycle of abuse in one of our classes, mom. I think Kara has some valid points," Brittany chimed in. "It makes me think you've lived through abuse."

"Hmm, perhaps." Kara clammed up.

Since Kara didn't look like she'd be elaborating on the subject Amy asked, "Have you ever dreamt of death? I mean your own."

17

Kara considered Amy's question. "Yes," she admitted. "You wouldn't believe all the times I thought I'd be killed, especially when I had so many enemies."

Kara gritted her teeth.

"Yeah, I remember you alluded to that before. What I mean though, is have you ever dreamt of dying by the hands of a loved one?"

"Why don't you tell us about your dream?"

"I'd like to, I mean if you don't mind," Amy murmured. "It's sort of odd and I don't want to tell Andy. You know, since he's my husband."

Amy glanced at Brittany who stared wide-eyed at her mother. "Brittany, are you all right hearing this?"

Brittany nodded.

Amy took a deep breath. "This discussion about men and negative behavior brought a dream I had a few nights ago to mind. Not that it related directly to this. Yet, it was strange and I'd appreciate your comments."

Amy was torn between relief and embarrassment at what she was about to say. She plunged into her story, before she could talk herself out of it. "I think I might have had an affair. Perhaps I thought about having an affair. I'm not sure."

Amy held her hands out toward Brittany as if in apology. "It was only a dream, but it seemed real. I would never cheat on your dad. I love him too much."

"I've had dreams where I woke up in a cold sweat, ready to scream for help. Our subconscious works in strange ways. Was this a nightmare? Did you feel overcome by e vil?" Kara stretched the word out, to give it further significance.

"I felt frightened and afraid to face the day. I thought," Amy paused. "If I acknowledged the dream it might make it real then part or all of it might happen. I don't want that."

Amy lowered her chin. Ill at ease she pretended to check her nails. Raising her head, Amy shook her hair back from her face. With a distracted air she ran her hands through her locks. She opened her mouth to apologize then closed it again.

"Why don't you just tell us?" Kara urged.

"Yeah mom, you can't leave us hanging like this. That makes it worse," Brittany agreed. "Besides, dreams never mean what you think they do."

Amy reached for her iced tea then took a big gulp. "OK. In the dream my husband was jealous of this other man. My husband didn't look or sound like Andy. I don't know who the men were in my dream. I had a sense of who they were though. I think I was murdered by my husband while my lover led me to destruction."

Amy smiled. "It sounds melodramatic when I say it out loud. Like a murder mystery or movie of the week."

"It seems to me dreams and nightmares are often exaggerated, like books and movies. Don't you agree?" Kara pointed out.

"I guess. I don't remember most of my dreams. Sometimes bits and pieces that don't make sense so it's hard for me to say."

"Hmm," Kara murmured with a slight nod.

"What bothered me about the affair was it seemed premeditated. I went out of my way to see this man. We met everywhere. I saw him at the supermarket, in the park, when I went out for walks, at the dry cleaners. I even saw him at my doctor's office. Isn't that weird?"

Amy jumped up then began to pace in front of Kara and Brittany.

"In real life I never run into the same person every day, just out of the blue. Dreams are too fantastic."

"Are you sure about that?"

"Yes, I mean, I think so. Wait a minute, are we talking about dreams being fantastic or meeting people coincidentally?"

Bird of Paradise Drums Beating

Kara sighed. "Don't you remember our initial meetings? We saw each other daily, at the same spot, for how many days, two, three."

Amy gasped. Her hand flew to her mouth. "I'd forgotten. Goodness, you're right, it has happened before. I can't believe I forgot."

They stared at one another.

"Do you think our meetings were accidental?" Amy pivoted then walked toward the nearby window. She drummed her fingers on her arm.

Suddenly the dream had more significance than before. What if the man, the person Amy thought had been her lover, was a woman in real life? The significance could have been the woman Amy had met by accident. Could Kara be the man in the dream?

"What do you think?" Kara demanded.

"No, you can't play this game," Amy snapped. "I need real answers. Don't you see how important it is to me?"

"I don't know if you're ready for the truth. Our meetings weren't coincidental. The first one was, but not the rest. Have you ever read dream interpretation books?"

Amy shook her head.

"No not in years. As a teen I read about dreams. I don't recall details though. Brittany reads dream interpretation books."

Kara glanced at Brittany. "Want to try or should I explain this one?"

"Be my guest," Brittany offered. "I like to refer to my book and I don't have it here."

Kara nodded. "When we dream about someone murdering us it means denial or we want to control our own nature. With dream interpretation, a part of our life is out of balance when we dream someone wants to kill us. What are you in denial about?"

Amy's eyes opened in alarm. She didn't meet Kara's gaze. Instead she slowly walked back to her chair. "I don't know."

Kara raised her brows then gave Amy a slow smile.

"All right, I guess maybe I sort of know."

"Uh huh." Kara crossed her arms.

Amy glanced toward Brittany. She stared straight at her mother.

Amy knew she wasn't going to get out of this one. She began to fidget. "O.K. This situation with you is, well, odd, I guess would be the word."

Amy started as she glanced at Kara.

Kara had stilled. She looked like a statue as she stared straight ahead.

Wasn't Kara listening?

With a suddenness that caught Amy unaware, Kara covered her face with her hands. Her shoulders began to shake. She appeared to be weeping.

Taken aback, Amy reached out then patted Kara's arm. She shook her head, confused by Kara's reaction. Why would Kara cry?

"What happened?" she whispered to Brittany.

Brittany shrugged. Eyes wide, she was as confused as Amy.

Kara continued to sob while Amy searched for tissues to mop up Kara's tears. There were none in sight. Brittany dug in her purse then handed a wad to Amy.

"Kara," Amy ventured, "We have tissues if you need them."

Kara grabbed blindly for them, then gulped out a teary reply. "Thank you so much. You don't know what this means," she wailed.

Amy gnawed on her fingernails. It was an old habit she'd managed to overcome except for in times of high stress. This seemed to fit the category. What had she done to warrant this level of anxiety? She glanced at Brittany who stared intently at Kara. They waited for a clue about what to say or do next.

Kara appeared to calm herself. She sniffled then turned toward Amy. "Could you order hot tea?"

"Of course." Amy jumped up, grateful to be doing something. She walked over to the intercom then asked for tea. "Perhaps, cookies or biscuits too."

"Do you think they have hot chocolate?" Brittany whispered.

"I'll check." Amy went back then pressed the button again.

Bird of Paradise Drums Beating

"Carl is on his way," Amy reported to Kara. She nodded toward Brittany. "I asked for tea, hot chocolate and a snack."

"I'm a mess. I hate to cry. It makes my eyes all puffy," Kara complained.

Amy studied Kara. Not a hair out of place. "You don't look as if you've been crying," Amy said, startled when she realized it was true.

"Yeah, you're stunning," Brittany agreed. "My nose gets red when I cry."

With shiny eyes, Kara turned toward Brittany. "You think I'm stunning?" Her voice sounded doubtful. "I wish I had a mirror. Thanks for the positive comment."

"I might have one in my purse. Let me check." Amy began to toss items onto the table beside her.

Kara watched with interest as Amy inventoried her supplies.

"Here's one." Amy held up a tiny makeup mirror.

Kara grabbed it. "Thanks."

Pulling lipstick from her pocket Kara began to apply it. She stared intently at her face in the mirror. "Not bad," she admitted, "It'll do."

Kara thrust the mirror in Amy's direction as Carl entered the room with a tray.

Amy shoved items back in her purse any which way so she could clear a spot on the table for Carl. Carl had brought cookies, biscuits and a scrumptious coffee cake. He piled Brittany's dirty plate, glasses and the now empty jug of iced tea on his tray then left the room.

"Would you pour please?" Kara murmured.

"Oh, I'd love to. What would you like in your tea?"

"I'd like cream, no sugar please."

Kara leaned over to peer at the food on the table. "I'd like two biscuits and a tiny sliver of cake." Kara leaned back then rested her head against the chair. She closed her eyes as if weary.

Amy prepared Kara's tea then put the requested items on a plate.

"Here you go," Amy called out in a gay voice. She hoped to generate some enthusiasm into the impromptu tea party.

Kara opened her eyes but didn't move. After a moment she leaned slightly forward to reach for the plate. "Just put the tea there." She pointed at a spot beside her on the table.

Amy did as she was told then turned toward Brittany. "Here's your hot chocolate." She passed the mug to Brittany. "What would you like to eat dear?"

Brittany leaned over Amy. "Yum, I'll have a big piece of that." She pointed at the cake. "And some cookies. Hmm, maybe put one biscuit on my plate too."

Amy loaded up the plate then passed it to Brittany.

"Thanks, yum, this is delish, you've got to try some mom." Brittany stuffed some cake in her mouth. "Kara, take a bite," she urged.

Amy helped herself to a generous piece of coffee cake.

"Mm." Amy sighed. The cake was delicious. It melted in her mouth.

Kara stared at Amy. Then she turned to watch Brittany who appeared as if she were about to inhale the rest of her cake.

"Sorry, didn't mean to murmur aloud," Amy apologized. "Brittany's right, it's tasty. You've got to have a bite. Does Carl bake these goods?"

Kara shrugged. "Yes, I guess so. He seems to be a good cook."

"That's an understatement." Brittany reached across her mom for another piece of cake.

⁌⁍

"Why don't you like me?" Kara demanded.

"What?" Amy blurted, caught off guard by Kara's question. She hastily stuffed the remains of her cake into her mouth. After swallowing she uttered, "I mean, what do you, mean? I never said I didn't like you."

"Do you then?"

"Do I what?"

"Like me? Aren't you paying attention?"

Bird of Paradise Drums Beating

"Yeah, I am, hmm." Faced with the age-old question asked by children as young as three and adults as old as ninety-nine, Amy hated to admit she didn't like Kara. She didn't want to hurt her feelings. It was more than that though. Kara intrigued Amy. She told fascinating stories. Amy didn't want to jeopardize that. Did Amy like Kara though?

"It's not that I don't like you." Amy glanced at Brittany as she stalled for time. Brittany was busy inhaling another piece of cake. "I don't like certain things you do."

Amy sat back in her seat, pleased with her answer.

"I do like your stories and you're an interesting woman. I don't know you well though. After all, we just met."

Amy reached for her tea. She blew on it then took a tentative sip. Ah, it was the perfect temperature. She took another slurp then stretched her hand out to get another piece of cake.

Amy had just taken another bite when Kara blurted, "What don't you like about me?"

Amy swallowed her bite, quick. She took time to place the remainder of her slice on her plate. Then she took another sip of tea. She glanced over at Brittany who had moved on to her cookies and hot chocolate. She was envious for a moment. Why hadn't Kara asked Brittany the dreaded do you like me question?

Amy sighed. "You're so mysterious. When I ask questions you only answer sometimes. You often ignore me as if I'd never spoken. I don't like that."

Amy stole a nervous peek in Kara's direction. She sat on her hands so she wouldn't bite her nails again.

Kara reached for her cup of tea then began to drink it.

"To be honest I don't know whether I believe your stories either. They seem farfetched." Amy was apologetic yet had to say it.

"Is that it?"

"Yes. Wait, no, there's one more thing. The bird, I want you to tell me about the bird and your relationship to it. I mean, if you do have a relationship with it."

Kara continued to drink her tea.

"I have something," Brittany added.

Amy turned toward Brittany then shook her head. She didn't want to tag team Kara. It might unglue her again. She motioned for Brittany not to talk.

Brittany plowed on, oblivious to Amy's sign language.

"I don't understand this age thing. Mom thinks you're old and I think you're younger than me. You talk old though, sometimes like someone elderly. What's up with that?"

Amy stared wide-eyed at Kara. How would she react to Brittany's observations?

Kara glanced at Brittany. Then she turned to Amy. She shrugged, shook her hair back then gave a brief, abrupt laugh.

Amy was at a loss. She pulled her hands out from under her, picked up her plate then polished off her cake. She washed it down with the remainder of her tea. She picked up the teapot then held it out toward Kara. "Would you like more?" Amy asked politely.

Inclining her head Kara held out her cup. "Yes, please."

The gesture reminded Amy of royalty.

"Before we discuss your questions did you tell me everything about your dream?" Kara asked abruptly.

"No. I want to hear what you have to say first."

"Me too," Brittany chimed in.

"Here's the deal. You tell me the rest of your dream and I'll answer three questions for you. How's that sound?"

"Reasonable, I think. You can't answer yes or no though. You have to give a statement. It has to be a longer explanation so I understand what you've said or where you're coming from."

"Agreed."

"What about me? Are you going to tell us about your age?" Brittany persisted.

Kara turned to Brittany. "Not today. You'll learn of this soon though."

"Promise?" Brittany urged.

Bird of Paradise Drums Beating

"Yes."

"OK then. Mom, can you pass me another piece of cake before you tell us about your dream?"

"Sure, here you go dear. Kara, do you want another piece?"

"No, thank you."

"All right, the next part doesn't seem to have anything to do with the beginning. It didn't seem to relate somehow. It started to get quite confusing."

"How so?" Kara wondered.

"I was walking through a farmer's field. It must have been late fall since there were corn stalks and they were high. I tried to walk through them but it was hard to make a path. I couldn't seem to get to the other side. I got turned around often. I was confused and became desperate as I searched for a trail."

Amy stopped.

"Was there more?"

"No not that I remember. What do you think it meant?"

"Let me think."

Amy considered the plate of cookies beside her. Should she have one? Brittany said they were tasty. Reaching over, she lifted one off the dish. She glanced at Kara while she ate her cookie.

Kara's brow was furrowed. She seemed to give great thought to Amy's dream. "Aa ha," Kara announced. "I think I remember."

Amy sat up straight.

"Corn and wheat have to do with fertility and new life."

"What? You mean pregnancy?" Amy screeched.

Kara shook her head then rolled her eyes. "Calm down. Yes, that's what it means. I think it has something to do with new developments in other areas of your life though. That's probably how the dream relates to you."

"For sure Kara, I remember that too," Brittany chimed in. "A friend had that dream and she freaked just like mom. When we read my dream book we realized it meant she should move to Winnipeg.

She had trouble deciding whether to leave home or not. I should phone her. See how it's going."

Amy relaxed. "Oh good, I can handle that. Change is all right. I just don't know about a new addition to the family."

She laughed. "Now that you and the boys are older I can't imagine changing diapers again."

"I hear you," Kara agreed.

"The new development could have something to do with meeting you I guess," Amy suggested.

"Hmm, yes, I suppose so. That would tie it to the beginning of your dream. It might not have been as disjointed as you thought."

"Now that we've covered my dream and figured out self-discovery and awareness it's your turn to share. You were going to answer my questions," Amy prompted.

"Not right now, maybe tomorrow. I have to go."

"What? We made a deal," Amy shrieked.

"Yes, well it will have to be another day. Bye."

Kara waved over her shoulder then bolted from the room before Amy or Brittany could protest further.

Amy sighed as she shook her head.

They'd been dismissed again!

"That woman is infuriating," Amy griped as they left Kara's house. "She led me on, pretended she would answer my questions then bam walked off when the mood struck her. That is so annoying."

Amy stalked off, walking extra fast.

"Wait, mom, slow down," Brittany yelled.

Amy turned around.

"Check it out."

Amy followed the direction of Brittany's extended arm. Her eyes widened at the sight before them.

There were hundreds of birds gathered in front of Kara's house. More than Amy had seen on a previous visit when birds and wildfowl had come together in the area.

Bird of Paradise Drums Beating

"That's odd," Amy began. The rest of her sentence was cut off by what could only be described as an explosion of noise as birds and wildfowl erupted in birdsong.

"This is like last time," Amy shouted to Brittany. "Come on, let's get closer."

Amy grabbed Brittany's hand then pulled her nearer to the impromptu performance. They crept close to the river side of the house then came around the corner. They were rewarded with a front row seat.

Some of the birds had risen into the air while others were perched in nearby trees or in the area around the riverbank. Their beaks were open to emit a pure, blissful, heavenly melody. As notes poured forth Amy and Brittany squeezed their hands together in silent appreciation of the wondrous moment they'd been blessed to witness.

Brittany's eyes darted here and there as she tried to watch as many birds as possible. She understood Amy's description of the sensory overload she'd experienced during the previous performance. The melody was one of pain and suffering.

Brittany felt the intense desire, yearning and anguish as it poured forth. It was almost tangible. Something you could stroke with the very edge of your fingertips, where the sensation of touch was most pronounced.

Brittany sighed. She'd never experienced anything like this. She wanted it to go on forever, a melody frozen in time to consume her senses indefinitely. Brittany smiled, as she knew this level of sensory overload was best achieved in fleeting moments. Her impression of wonder was suspended at an unbelievable, heightened level. How long could her emotions handle this pinnacle of intensity?

Brittany slumped against her mother when the melody broke off with a suddenness that startled her. Caught off guard Brittany was thankful for her mother's comforting presence beside her. She sighed, took a few deep breaths then turned toward Amy.

"Do you think we'll get an encore?"

Penny Ross

    Amy gave her daughter a sad smile as she heard the longing in Brittany's voice. She shook her head. "Watch," she whispered.

    Brittany turned to see the birds rise up as one into the air. With wings silent as their song, they ascended straight towards heaven. The evening seemed eerily still as a hush settled over everything.

    Brittany sighed as she squeezed her mother's hand. They hugged one another then turned to gaze at the quiet. They were silent as they acknowledged the need for calm and peace to reestablish itself. An irreplaceable moment of ecstasy had been shared between mother and daughter, an instant suspended in time.

18

"Now you're being ridiculous!" a woman exclaimed.

"Me, I've never been more serious in my life. Well, in this life anyway." Kara's laugh sounded shrill.

Amy and Brittany hesitated before they entered the room.

Amy saw Kara flick her hair over her shoulder in a distracted manner. Painfully aware of interrupting, Amy coughed announcing their presence.

Two pairs of eyes swiveled in Amy and Brittany's direction.

The eyes belonging to the stranger had raised brows while Kara appeared relieved at their untimely entrance.

Kara couldn't hide her pleasure as she heartily welcomed Amy and Brittany.

"Amy, Brittany, I'm so glad you're here. We've been waiting for you," Kara gushed. "This is the friend I told you about Moira, and her daughter Brittany. Come here Amy, Brittany, meet Moira. Sit here, make yourself comfortable."

Kara fussed around Amy and Brittany. She fluffed a pillow and put it behind Amy's back then patted her shoulder, babbling all the while. She did the same for Brittany.

Amy had never seen Kara flustered. It wasn't something she hoped to witness again. She preferred Kara's calm, haughty persona to this harassed, nervous version.

Kara introduced everyone, her movements jerky as she pointed.

Amy nodded at Moira but stayed quiet. She needed further clues about Moira before initiating conversation. Moira didn't have the same need. She launched into the discussion Amy and Brittany had interrupted.

"Kara, you need to focus more. This isn't about you. It's for the greater good. How could you forget that?" Moira demanded.

"I haven't, I'm just having trouble, that's all. Maybe I need a refresher course. I can't seem to assist Kara and her family with their situation. I feel no ties with this man and these children. I cannot imagine them coming from my womb. I feel helpless. I can't remember an obstacle like this before. It's frustrating." Kara wrapped her hair around her finger like a string.

"Enough with the dramatics, no one likes people who exaggerate. Women who become overwrought at a hint of conflict are the worst. You know that." Moira shook her finger at Kara.

Fascinated by the exchange, Amy felt like a spectator at a lively tennis match. She watched the conversation ball lob back and forth with bated breath.

"I know, I know. I hate being one of those women. I've tried everything. I have no inkling of why I'm here."

Moira glared at Kara. "Why are you babbling?" she shouted. Rising, she paced in front of them as she punctuated the air for emphasis with one finger.

Amy leaned forward, listening with rapt attention to this unlikely friend of Kara's. Moira's combatant attitude showed Kara in a brand new light. Kara seemed more human somehow. Her hesitant manner and fragility exposed her. It portrayed a woman with further depth than Amy had previously imagined.

After glaring at Kara, Moira sat down. She hefted her ample backside into the cushions of the chair then gave a heavy sigh. "All right, let's go over this again. Is it OK to talk in front of them?" Moira gestured wildly in their direction.

Amy thought it was kind of late to inquire about their presence. She tried to appear invisible or at least hardly interested in the conversation as it swirled around her. She was thankful Brittany was quiet. Brittany sat wide-eyed and hadn't taken out her notebook. Perhaps her curiosity was greater than her compulsion to take notes.

"Yes, I've told them stories about my previous lives."

Bird of Paradise Drums Beating

"Of course you have." Moira's voice dripped with reproach. She shook her head like a schoolmarm faced with an unreasonable child.

Chin raised, Kara stared out the window.

Moira continued to shake her head. Exasperation crossed her face, adding further wrinkles to her heavily creased forehead.

"You have to remember why we've been sent here. *She* thinks it's important for women to feel strong. They need to figure out who they are. When a woman is comfortable in her skin, so to speak, she can stand up for herself. Not all women are able to do this. That's why we're here. Remember," Moira stated with arms folded.

"Our purpose is to help women feel more confident, to enable them to speak out and give their point of view. We help women find their inner strength and purpose. We need to understand ourselves before we can have an impact on others. Our strength is from within. Have you forgotten our mandate?" Moira demanded.

"No, Moira, I haven't," Kara whispered. Her voice held a note of desperation.

Amy watched Kara fumble clumsily with her shirt. Part of her wanted to help her new friend yet a bigger part was content to watch the scene unfold before her.

"I'm confused. Perhaps I've lived too many lives. I can't seem to get a grip on the current one." Kara held her hands out, imploring. "Why have I chosen this man? We have nothing in common. He's not a spiritual person. He is one of logic. I can only think it's for the stability. He does have great wealth and I'm comfortable here. Perhaps that's it." Kara trailed off.

Amy felt bad for Kara. Who was the *she* Moira referred to? Amy sat on the edge of her seat fascinated by the conversation. She listened intently, careful to remain as still and quiet as possible.

"You never lived an entire life as any of those women Kara. Let's put this in perspective shall we? You've merely helped women identify who they are. Just because you know their past doesn't mean you were beside them the entire time. You certainly weren't any of them for the duration of their lives. You had to believe you were those women to be plausible but you know you weren't. Don't you?" Moira challenged. "You do know this current life is not your own, don't you?"

Kara hesitated before she answered.

Amy inclined her head toward Kara, willing her to respond. She leaned forward, eager to hear more. Moira was forcing Kara to answer questions Amy had asked. Amy was shocked as Moira's strength diminished Kara.

Amy watched Kara shrink right in front of them. She knew this had to be an illusion. Her eyes widened as Kara shriveled further, drawing inward. They seemed to be losing her.

Startled, Amy put her arm out as if to halt Kara's weakened progression. Amy turned sharply toward Moira. She was about to question what was happening but stopped instead.

Moira shook her head. She gestured silently for Amy and Brittany not to obstruct what was about to happen.

Wide-eyed, Amy turned to Brittany. Should they do something?

Brittany shrugged, eyes wide as well.

As Amy turned back to Kara she watched an amazing metamorphosis take place right in front of them.

Kara continued her downward slide. She began to wither rapidly. Within moments she turned into a small, shrunken shape. Kara's youth disappeared.

The former Kara was replaced by an old, emaciated outline. The person who sat in Kara's chair resembled a dried up apple formed in the silhouette of a little old woman.

Aghast at the rapid change, Amy's hand flew to her mouth as she smothered a gasp. She couldn't take her eyes off the unknown form seated beside her. How could this be the woman she'd spoken to moments earlier? Where had Kara gone?

Guess that answers the age question, Brittany uttered. Her eyes darted to Amy then Moira. No one gave her a second glance. Great, she hadn't said the words aloud, just in her head.

Bird of Paradise Drums Beating

Brittany turned to her mom then mouthed, "Wow," followed by an open mouth and wide eyes.

Amy mimicked what Brittany had done.

Oh, My, God, Brittany thought, this is awesome. She swiveled her head to stare at Kara, eager to see more.

After what seemed an eternity, the person who had been Kara spoke. It was halting at first, as if she were unsure of her voice. Barely recognizable, the tiny woman answered Moira's earlier question.

"Yes, I know I wasn't any of them," Kara croaked. "I had to believe I'd been reincarnated as every woman I helped. It was the only way I could accept my destiny as truth. Otherwise, I couldn't continue to do it.

I'm not like you Moira. I need to immerse myself. I have to pretend to be the woman I'm helping. I crave total submersion. I need to take on each woman's identity entirely. I had to believe I was her, and she was me. Can you understand that? Do you think *She* will let me continue or will I have to go back?"

Kara gulped then covered her mouth with her hand.

Amy watched the former Kara gaze at Moira with tear-strewn eyes.

"That's not for me to decide. You know that Kara. Only *She* has that power. We're merely *her* vassals," Moira stated firmly. Then she seemed to soften for a moment. "Perhaps if *She* thinks this has something to do with your own personal journey, you may receive some leeway."

With bowed head Kara gave a slow nod.

"Do you think that's why she's here?" Moira pointed at Amy.

"Perhaps." Kara sounded vague and withdrawn. "At first I thought Amy was here to befriend me. I've been lonely and out of sorts. Amy felt my pain. I've begun to think either she's here to help me find strength to continue or replace me. I'm not sure which. Then again, maybe she's here for a reason I haven't identified yet. It could even have to do with Amy's own personal journey. I have no idea."

While they stared at her, Amy found her voice. "What do you mean Kara? I don't understand how I could replace you. What journey? This conversation has me confused. When you refer to *we,* do you mean each other, and who is *she?*"

Moira peered at Amy, her gaze intent, penetrating. After careful consideration, Moira seemed to come to some decision.

"I don't think it hurts to answer your questions." Moira's tone was pleasant. "First though, why did you bring your daughter here Amy? If you came to visit as Kara's friend, why bring your daughter along? Were you afraid to come alone?"

Before Amy could answer, Kara whispered, "I invited Brittany."

"Oh, I didn't realize."

Brittany didn't say a word. She merely nodded.

Amy wondered if it was because she didn't want to be caught up in Moira's anger or if Brittany just wanted the conversation to keep on track. She smiled. Yes, Brittany always was smart about things like this. She knew agreement would soothe Moira's ruffled feathers and speed things along. What a clever girl.

"Well, since Kara requested your company that's good then. It's fine to include both of you in this conversation," Moira conceded with a slight incline of her head. "After all, Kara already spilled her guts about previous lives."

Amy and Brittany began to smile as they nodded agreement at Moira's comments. Their smiles froze at her glaring criticism of Kara.

"Lighten up," Moira admonished. "That was my attempt to be carefree." She flashed a broad grin.

Amy and Brittany returned her wide smile with a halfhearted attempt.

Moira shrugged. "No matter, now back to your questions Amy. When I mentioned the word *we,* I referred to Kara and I. We have the same purpose. We exist on earth to further the cause of women. We've helped females throughout the centuries while they identify who they are. Women gather strength from one another as they strive for equality. We give them silent encouragement, like a private cheering squad." Moira chuckled at her last statement.

"The stronger they become, the less they need us. When they're comfortable and able to speak for themselves, we are no longer needed. Kara and I are vassals of strength, like slaves who carry out the wishes of our master. When women have found their inner power and are able to address issues of importance our work is done. Women must travel their own personal journey of discovery to realize their potential. Does that make sense?"

"Yes, it does," Amy admitted. "How long do you stay with these women?'

"That depends on the situation and the woman. It could be anywhere from a few years to twenty. There's no formula for the length."

"So, you and Kara are timeless?" Amy ventured.

Moira laughed. "I guess that's one way to put it. I like that term." She turned to Kara, "Do you feel timeless?"

Fortunately, Kara saw the irony in the comment and rose to the occasion. "Oh, definitely, when I gaze at myself in the mirror years evaporate before my eyes."

Kara gave a short laugh. It sounded more like a bark.

Amy averted her eyes. She found it difficult to converse with Kara in her present form. She knew it was shallow but couldn't control her reaction.

Instead, Amy focused her full attention on Moira. Amy wanted to gather as much information as she could. It would make her feel better prepared to deal with Kara.

"What about *she*?" Amy prompted.

"Ah, now you've come to the crux of the matter. Do you believe in God?" Moira's manner was thoughtful.

"Yes, I do."

Moira smiled, a sweet saintly expression on her face. "Have you ever thought about the image of God?"

Amy was slow to speak, thoughtful. "I guess I've equated God's appearance with the pictures I've seen. You know angels on high, the pearly gates, illustrations in books."

"How about you?" Moira demanded as she turned to Brittany.

"I'm going to take *'Intro to World Religion'* next term. I imagine we'll read and discuss the image of God then. So my answer could differ after I've done research. For now though, I'd say long hair, flowing white robe, clouds and angels. He's gentle, kind and benevolent."

Moira's grin broadened. "Well, I have news for you." She leaned forward in her chair eager to share a secret.

"God is a *She,* not a *He*," Moira whispered.

Sitting back in her chair Moira smirked. She reminded Amy of the Cheshire cat, from *'Alice in Wonderland.'*

"How do you know?" Amy blurted. Quick to cover her mouth, Amy was shocked at her audacity. She felt blasphemous as she dared question Moira's claim. On the other hand, Moira was a stranger who'd made an outrageous statement. Perhaps Amy's question wasn't far off the mark.

Moira laughed, not in the least put out by Amy's boldness. "Why I've seen *Her* of course. So has Kara." Moira waved breezily at her old crony.

Kara nodded. She appeared anxious, yet silently confirmed the announcement as true.

"What do you see *Her* as?" Amy leaned forward, toward Moira, almost tipping over her chair.

"I can't tell you that." Moira's voice held reproach. She shook her head as she admonished Amy by waving her index finger in the air. *"Her* image is indescribable. Everyone sees *Her* in the likeness they're most comfortable with. Isn't that right Kara?"

Kara grinned. She had no teeth. "Yes, our comparisons were wildly different from what I recall."

"Uh huh." Moira leaned forward toward Amy, eager to share. "We see what we need when we gaze at *Her*. It's personal and can't be shared with others. At least it shouldn't be."

Bird of Paradise Drums Beating

"Oh." Disappointment made Amy's answer more abrupt than she'd intended.

Moira laughed, not at all put out. "Disappointed are you?"

"Well, yes. I expected more."

"Don't we all? Look at Kara. She requires more than the average person, don't you Kara?"

"Yes." Kara sounded reluctant as she added, "I've always been a bit demanding." She shrugged. "So what, people can take me for who I am or leave me be. I don't care most of the time."

Moira chuckled. "Ah, come on Kara, fess up. Regard your present image. You've dropped the mask you wear and your natural persona has emerged. It's clear to Amy, Brittany and I. We see you for who you are. You seriously don't care what we think of you? What about Kara's family? What if they walked in right now?"

Kara regarded them with half-closed eyes. "Since you're my friends I was able to show my true self. What's wrong with that?" Her tone was defiant. "I would like you to leave Kara's family out of this."

Moira burst out laughing. "Liar, liar pants on fire. You didn't willingly drop your mask for us Kara. It happened because you were weak and despondent. You let my strength diminish you. It wasn't something you did on purpose. Come on, admit it," Moira badgered. She stood with hands on hips as she towered over Kara.

Kara put a hand out as if warding off an enemy. Moira maintained her pose. Amy thought Moira could intimidate Kara indefinitely.

Amy had had enough of Moira's bullying. She jumped up from her chair then moved beside Moira. "That's enough," she bellowed. "There's no need to pick on Kara, Moira. Why don't you leave her alone?"

Moira glared down her long nose at Amy. She appeared to measure Amy's worth. With a huff she turned abruptly, strode across the conservatory then stared out the window.

Kara touched Amy's arm then smiled. "Thank you," Kara whispered.

"No problem." Amy felt pleased with herself. She returned to her seat. They sat in companionable silence watching Moira at the window.

Amy glanced at Kara. She noted Kara sat straighter than she had before. What type of control did Moira have over her? How did Moira's strength physically diminish Kara's appearance?

Moira wandered back to her seat. She fussed with her skirt then sat down. Without preamble she demanded, "So, where were we?"

Kara gave a brief glance in Amy's direction then answered. "We'd been discussing masks and personas."

"Ah." Moira folded her arms. She turned to Amy then commanded, "What do you have to say on the subject Amy?"

Amy was flustered. She took her time to respond, unsure of her approach. Should she address the way Moira personally attacked Kara about her assumed role? Was it better to discuss the topic in more general terms?

Amy chose the safer path. To forge ahead single-handedly and tackle Moira about her behaviour seemed foolhardy. Moira was a formidable woman and Kara didn't seem up to verbal sparring.

"I think we all have masks." Amy's tone was thoughtful. Gripping the arms of her chair she leaned forward. "We often don the mask most beneficial to us. If it's natural, we maintain our persona for a given time. If it's foreign to our character, we have trouble sustaining it. As one would expect, our true self emerges. Then the mask is exposed for what it is, a farce. Some people slip effortlessly from one mask to another while others have a harder time."

Amy nodded as she warmed to the subject. "I think when we're emotional it's tricky to hide our feelings with a mask. When we grieve, are in pain, or angry, our true identity surfaces. Of course, we can try to cover it with another mask but that can be confusing. What is reality and what's a façade?"

Amy leaned back. She folded her arms then nodded pleasantly at Moira.

Bird of Paradise Drums Beating

"Hmm, interesting points you've presented." Moira sounded indifferent, bored even.

Amy felt oddly disappointed. She glanced at Kara, eager to hear her opinion.

Kara stared at the fruit trees. She gazed ahead, far away, distracted and unfocused.

Amy turned to meet Brittany's eyes. Brittany shrugged.

Amy continued where she'd left off. The topic had captured her interest and she wanted to discuss it further, even if no one else cared. "I've noticed people respond differently to an individual based on their gender."

Amy paused, fascinated to note Moira and Kara now appeared to be listening. They'd turned toward her, so Amy rushed on. "I'm sure we've all seen women act a part. They may be coy, helpless or flirt outrageously around men. One woman might give another a tight, polite smile then walk away. Or, she could beam fully at a woman engaging her in silent conversation."

Amy glanced in Brittany's direction. Brittany flashed Amy a bright smile followed by a nod of encouragement.

"Women often communicate silently without a man's knowledge. You know what I mean, don't you?" Amy leaned forward, eager to get her point across.

Moira shrugged. "I guess." Unmoved, she added, "So what?"

"Well, for women I think it can be another level of social skills or the ability to converse with others. I'd describe it as the presentation of masks. We might want to present our self in the best possible light. The more effective one is with a mask, the better others respond."

Amy held her hands out to underscore her point. "Think of the nerd or socially inept individual who bumbles along through conversations. Their emotions are clearly shown on their face, open to everyone's interpretation. It's an effort for these people to put on or remove a mask. We have to accept them for who they are. They might pretend to be something they're not, but we see through them. I think they're more pure and real than others who naturally don masks."

Amy nodded. "I think they're better off than people who have a multitude of masks. When you're proficient at exchanging one mask for another, how do you relax and be yourself? Being true to oneself might involve more effort but it pays off in the end."

Pleased to share her thoughts Amy added, "It's important to know who you are and be comfortable with yourself."

"Do you know who you are?" Moira demanded.

"Yes, I mean, I think I do. I make an effort to be true to myself. I think it's important to my self-worth."

"Hmph," Moira snorted.

There was an uncomfortable silence.

"What do you mean? Do we admit our weaknesses out loud or only privately to ourselves?" Kara wondered. She sounded uneasy. "How much do we want others to see? More important, when is it their business?"

"I don't know," Amy admitted. "I guess we should reveal ourselves to others in a manner we're comfortable with. When we admit we're vulnerable or hurt emotionally, it shouldn't put us at a disadvantage.

I feel better when someone shares their personal feelings with me. I don't judge it as weakness on their part. It makes them more human. I find them easier to approach and relate to them. That's not something to scoff at. Frailty is a trait we all have in common," Amy pointed out. "Of course one has to have a vested interest in a relationship. I don't feel the same depth of feeling for strangers or a casual acquaintance."

"You're right." Kara was pleased. "I should have realized it earlier. I don't have to be perfect, nor is it wrong to show my true self. I should be proud of who I am. I can hold my head high no matter what my faults are. I don't know why I deceive myself or have to prove I'm better than other people."

Kara sighed. "I guess that's one of my weaknesses. I have to say the right thing. I act according to the role I see myself in.

It's exhausting to say the least. I'm often tired and want to just let myself go. I want time to myself, just to be."

Giggling, Kara confessed. "There are advantages when you come across as a hag. People don't peer too close at your face. I bet I could eliminate personal hygiene and no one would be surprised. This mask could work for me," she quipped.

While Kara talked she tossed her hair over her shoulder. She sat up straight then held her head erect. Before Amy's eyes, Kara transformed to the young, beautiful woman she'd been earlier. Like a butterfly shedding its cocoon her slight frame increased.

Kara was restored to her former size. Her skin smoothed out then became almost wrinkle free. Her hair was long and lustrous like before, her teeth white and even. Her chin no longer sagged unbecomingly. Her eyes had widened while her lips were fuller.

Amy smiled at Kara, relieved at the physical change.

Kara beamed at her friends. "I never realized I'd be uplifted by admitting my flaws," she joked. "I feel better now that I've confessed to human frailty."

Amy laughed then admitted she preferred this appearance to the haggard one.

Moira turned to Amy. "I admire you. You were able to talk Kara out of her funk then help restore her confidence. That takes a special ability. Perhaps you were right Kara. There's more to Amy than meets the eye."

Amy's smile died on her lips. What did Moira mean? When Kara and Moira talked like this it made her nervous.

"Yes, that's why I wanted you to meet her. I think Amy has potential."

Kara grinned at Amy as if she'd personally discovered her. Amy wanted to protest but remained silent.

"Hmm, perhaps. I want you to do me a little favour." Stroking her chin, Moira gave Amy her full attention.

"What?" Amy's voice was heavy with distrust.

"Oh, don't worry," Moira was quick to add. "It's nothing out of the ordinary."

"Hmm," Amy hedged.

"Why don't I tell you what it is? Then you can decide if you want to do it? No strings attached."

"Well, all right." Amy was reluctant to grant Moira's request yet curious what it would be.

"I want you to tell us about a woman you admire."

Amy waited for more.

"That's it?"

Moira laughed, "Yes, that's it. Are you disappointed?" She raised her eyebrows at Amy as if daring her to challenge this request.

"No. I expected something more difficult, that's all. This seems too easy."

"Ah, a doubting Thomas."

"No, it's not that. It's just when you and Kara refer to my gift, or potential, it makes me nervous. You're both out of the ordinary so I'm not sure how to respond to you. I feel like I'm being tested. It makes me apprehensive." Amy admitted this with reluctance while she crossed her arms in front of her like a shield.

"I'm your friend though," Kara protested.

"I know, but I only met you this week." Amy tried to adopt a reasonable tone. "It sounds like you've known one another for ages."

Moira glanced at Kara with a broad smile. "That's an understatement." Moira began to laugh as she shook her head.

"What's so funny?" Amy demanded.

Moira flashed Amy an impish grin. "Nothing important," she hedged. "You're right though. Kara and I have been acquainted with one another throughout the centuries. Sometimes it's taken us awhile to identify one another. We've been around together for an awful long time though. Haven't we Kara?"

"Yes." Kara chuckled. "We certainly have. I don't think Amy can relate to our unique situation though Moira. Why don't we get this conversation back on track? We can talk about this later."

Amy frowned. Why did their exchanges seem layered with hidden meaning? She was exhausted as she tried to keep up with their discussion. She sighed then glanced over at Brittany who had been quiet for ages now. Brittany smiled at her mother. As Amy returned her smile she thought how fortunate she was to have an uncomplicated relationship with Brittany. She might never figure out Kara and Moira but she was infinitely blessed to have Brittany for her daughter.

Moira brought her back to the present as she repeated her earlier request. "Will you please tell us about a woman you admire Amy?"

"Yes. Of course I will. I'd love to."

19

Amy hesitated. She'd never thought of herself as a storyteller. She wrote stories, yet rarely gave them to anyone to read. It was time to share. "This is a woman I've admired since I was a little girl. Her name is Josephine and she was my paternal grandmother. She died years ago. She's part of me though. I feel her life story will live on forever through family and friends."

Amy smiled. "My grandma was a great storyteller. She rivaled Kara with her tales."

"Oh, I find that hard to believe," Kara quipped.

"Grandma wasn't nearly as boastful as you Kara. Quiet dignity became her."

Kara dropped her eyes, embarrassed.

"Oh," Amy exclaimed. "I didn't mean to put you down Kara. I only meant, well, you know…" She trailed off. What had she meant?

"No big deal." Kara shrugged then tossed her hair back. "I won't take it personally."

"Great, so Moira should I tell a story or two about my grandma?"

"Sure, tell us whatever pops into your head."

"Well, my grandparents were in their sixties when I was born. I guess they were kind of old but I never realized how elderly until I got older. Children aren't aware of a person's age. It's only as we mature that some people fixate on certain milestones like thirty, forty, fifty and sixty."

"In particular women," Kara agreed.

"Yes, must have to do with how we perceive ourselves or something. Anyhow, I never knew their age nor did it seem to slow them down. My grandpa died when he was eighty-one. The only thing that

Bird of Paradise Drums Beating

bothered him was a limp. It got worse as he got older, probably from arthritis. I guess grandpa broke his leg when he was around ten. They took the cast off too early so the leg didn't set properly."

"That's unfortunate."

"Yeah, well he was young and active. I guess he complained about it being itchy all the time and in the way so his parents took the cast off. You know how kids are."

Amy laughed. "My grandpa was so much fun. He played jokes on us all the time. He used to chase us around with water balloons, played hide and seek with all the grandkids, he was a vibrant, happy go lucky guy. I never noticed his age.

My grandma seemed the same in her eighties as she was in her sixties. She was ageless. She always took time to talk to us. She paid particular attention to me since I was the only girl in our family. We were very close."

Amy was eager to portray her grandmother in an accurate manner.

"I remember one summer I got to stay at my grandparents. I would have been around ten or so. I should give you background to put this in perspective. There are eleven kids in my dad's family and thirty-some grandchildren. You can imagine all the great grandchildren.

I'm not sure if this was a rule or something that just happened. None of the grandchildren ever stayed overnight at my grandparents' house without their parents. Nowadays, an overnight visit at grandma and grandpa's is quite common. It wasn't though at my grandparents' house.

They also didn't give us presents at Christmas or on birthdays since there were so many grandchildren. It wasn't a big deal, that's just the way it was. If we questioned our parents they said our grandparents didn't have much money and that was the end of it. It's true, they didn't."

Amy grinned. "Guess I was a favourite of grandma's though since she continually gave me treasured objects. I still have them."

Amy was thoughtful as she continued. "They've always meant more to me than usual presents. They're precious. I often take them out to look at and recall special moments with my grandma."

"What sort of objects?" Kara wondered.

"She gave me earrings, brooches, handkerchiefs, a few teacups and saucers, plates, pictures of my dad when he was young. Some of them are tarnished and pieces of jewelry have fallen out but that doesn't matter.

My grandparents favoured money starters as a gift. You put a few quarters or dimes in and save them until you have ten or twenty dollars. They'd start us out with a few coins and we'd continue saving. We often got those for Christmas or on birthdays."

"I thought the grandchildren didn't get presents," Moira remarked.

"Well, it wasn't on a regular basis, not every Christmas or birthday. Now that you mention it though, it did seem quite often. I think my brothers and I got more than some of my other cousins."

Amy nodded. "My cousins in Fort Qu'Appelle and our family were closest geographically. I think my cousins in Fort Qu'Appelle got presents too but I'm not sure. Since it was never expected it was more special somehow. None of my cousins ever compared what we got. Maybe we hoarded it away and pretended we never received anything. Who knows, maybe we all got presents and never knew the others did?"

Amy laughed. "It doesn't matter. We saw my grandparents on a regular basis. They'd come visit us in Regina at least once a week and we went out to the farm every Sunday."

"They lived out of town?" Kara inquired.

"Yes, by Indian Head, right off Highway #1, on a farm. That's in Saskatchewan, by the way. Speaking of which, I was going to tell you about the time I stayed with them for a week."

"Ah, yes, the big visit." Moira's fake smile looked twisted.

"It was, yes." Amy was suddenly shy. She glanced at Brittany who gave her thumbs up. Amy felt better as she launched back into her story. "One thing my grandparents never skimped on was time. They gave it freely. They were interested in what we liked to do. When we were together I always felt special around them."

"You use that word a lot when you talk about them," Kara remarked.

"What word?" Amy's tone was eager.

"Special."

"Well, I guess that's how I felt, so it's an appropriate term." Amy smiled. "My grandparents had a warm, accepting attitude toward life. When you talked, they listened. When they spoke, we acknowledged what they said was the truth. At least I did. They were wise, knowledgeable and interesting. They lapped up information, were fascinated by everything going on around them, particularly in the lives of their children and grandchildren, and were eager to learn. Their loving relationship helped me see what a marriage should be. When I was with them I felt safe, special and loved."

Amy stopped. "I guess I've gotten off topic again. I didn't mean to ramble. My storytelling ability certainly lacks style." Amy grinned at her audience.

"No, it's captivating." Kara leaned forward eager to hear more. "Please continue," she encouraged in an enthusiastic voice.

Moira said nothing, but nodded.

"All right. I'm going to tell you about a walk my grandma and I went on when I stayed there on the famous overnight trip." Amy smiled at the recollection.

"We talked about everything around us. Nature, trees, herbs and flowers were a favourite topic with my grandma. She had a green thumb and her garden was a riot of colours. There were a wide variety of flowers, herbs and spices. They had an immense garden. One part was dedicated to vegetables then there was grandma's flower and herb area while trees and shrubs bordered the entire space.

Inside the house, grandma had flowers and plants on every available space in the living room and near every window. They had windows on two walls in that area. I loved to walk by her side and listen to her talk while she fussed with her plants and flowers."

Amy paused. "Grandma had plants in her house close to the day she died. My aunties replaced some of the real ones with silk flowers. Her doctor said it would be easier for her to breath with fake ones. Relatives planted more flowers outside for her though every spring. She loved her plants.

We'd walk down the gravel road," Amy whispered, as if alone with her thoughts. "She'd show me all the varieties of wildflowers that lined the road. She knew every name and what medicinal purpose they had. Now that I know more about First Nations people I realize grandma was passing down what she knew about plants and shrubs to me. It was part of her oral history and tradition. My plants grow well but I don't know much about them," Amy confessed. "I never remember their names and healing abilities are way beyond me. I should have written down what she told me. Of course you never think of those things when you're young."

Amy lowered her head, self-conscious as she added. "I do remember grandma's stories though. I've written some of them down. That must count for something. She was smart too, you know," Amy was quick to add.

"My grandmother was well educated. She went to residential school until she was eighteen where she learned to read and write. She was born in 1900 so that was quite an accomplishment for a woman in those days."

"It certainly was," Moira agreed. "What did your grandmother tell you about residential school? Was it as abusive as they say?"

"I don't know. Grandma never said much about it. I remember stories she told about being instructed to forget her native ways. The nuns were her teachers and they were very strict. She used to show me this picture of her in the school with dozens of other children. Her sweet little face stared out of the picture straight into your eyes. She was so tiny. They came to get her when she was barely five years old. Her hair was short. They'd cut it off when she got to the school. I never saw her with long hair.

Can you imagine?" Amy's voice rose. "Someone comes to your house, an official government person. They take your children away from you. Wrench them out of your arms. You have no recourse but to let them go. It would have been heartbreaking. I shudder when I think about it. In fact, I'd rather not think about it."

Amy closed her eyes, took a deep breath. When she spoke there was a catch in her voice. "If someone had taken my boys or Brittany when they were so little, a part of me would have died. Even now, when they're older, I couldn't stand it. As a mother, my mind refuses to think about that possibility. I don't know how parents did it. I wouldn't be able to handle the pain, the hurt, the longing." Tears ran down her face.

Amy rubbed her cheeks, hard. She swiped away the tears then opened her eyes, shiny with unshed tears. "My grandma was born on a small reserve called Little Black Bear. It's part of the File Hills Qu'Appelle Tribal Council in Saskatchewan. She lived with her mother and two half brothers. She didn't get to visit her mother or brothers often after they took her away. It sounded like they only let her come home for a short visit every few years. She said it was hard to adjust and get to know your family when you barely had time to be with them."

Amy rubbed her forehead. "I know grandma was grateful for the education. She didn't dwell on the unpleasant aspect of it. She wasn't like that. Maybe she didn't want to tell us that part because it was too painful. I don't know. I only hope she was treated well." Amy whispered the last part, the subject made her sad.

She took a deep breath. It was time to move the story along. "My grandmother knew Cree and French so when she had to learn English she said it wasn't that difficult. Children weren't allowed to speak their native dialect at the school. Since they rarely left most of them forgot how to speak their language. My grandma remembered a few phrases and words but that's all. She called me *'Mon chi'* a lot before she died. I think it means *'my little one'*.

Grandma would sometimes say a word or phrase in Cree but I don't remember them now. Just *'Mon chi.'* Grandma also called me *'my girl'* all the time. That's a common term with First Nations people. The older ones call the young ones that. I like it."

Amy smiled. "Grandma liked to write letters to her children and grandchildren. She wrote down facts and recipes. I don't know if she ever wrote stories though. If she did they were either misplaced, lost or someone's taken them and not told the rest of the family. I wish she would have kept a journal." Amy gazed off, wistful.

"That's why I write stories about her so she won't be forgotten. Not that she would. She was the family matriarch and everyone wanted to be by her side when she was in the room. My grandparents were popular people, positive and interested in others. They liked to tell stories and listen to peoples' narratives. I think that's a favourable ability to possess."

"I think so too," Kara agreed.

"Grandma was always keen to hear about my university days. I think she would have liked to attend university or college. When you have eleven children to raise and no money, school is a distant dream. They never would have been able to afford it. I don't even know if they let women attend post-secondary education in those days, especially First Nations women."

"Money often hinders people from pursuing their aspirations," Moira agreed. "Your grandmother sounds like she would have been a good women's advocate given a chance. What sort of things did she teach you about the household or a woman's role in society? Do you remember?"

Amy laughed. "Well, to hear it from my dad and aunties' viewpoint, grandpa treated grandma like a princess."

"As it should be," Moira pointed out.

"I remember I'd sit for hours and listen to her stories. She'd pat the cushion beside her on the sofa then we'd talk, often an entire afternoon. They always listened to my brother and I practice when they came for weekly Regina visits. He played the guitar and I played the accordion. They patiently sat and applauded our efforts.

When my mom visits she always encourages my children to play the piano. I notice they play longer and more enthusiastically when they have an audience. It's a great way to get children to practice their music lessons. Brittany and Eric still play the piano while Sam has moved on to the guitar."

"Hmm, I'll have to remember that," Kara commented.

"I've always enjoyed when grandma listens to us play," Brittany noted. "You're right mom, it does encourage me. Grandma claps for every song and has her favourites. I know those songs really well," she added with a grin.

"Perhaps your grandma told stories since she didn't like to cook or clean," Moira commented.

"Oh, I don't know if it was that. After all, we'd come for a visit or they'd called at our house. So it was the polite thing to do. My mom has always liked to cook and clean so she'd putter around while my grandparents visited with us. I think mom cooked most of the time when we went to my grandparents' house now that I think about it. It probably gave my grandma a break since she was elderly already."

"That's true. I guess I should wait till I'm seventy or eighty to see how much energy I have to cook and clean. What am I saying?" Moira slapped her forehead. "I'm way over eighty. Being timeless has its disadvantages when you appear young." She shook her head. "I can't even say what my real age would be right now. Can you Kara?"

"Umm, no, I can't. I don't like to think about it. Now that you mention it though maybe that's why I like to have Carl in the house. He cooks, cleans, does errands and keeps us all organized. Maybe my age has caught up with me." Kara's voice was grim.

"Hah, somehow I doubt that. Don't get morbid or theatrical on us Kara," Moira warned.

Amy stepped in before Moira browbeat Kara again. "Age is strange, my grandparents were in their sixties when I was born yet

Penny Ross

I never thought of them as old. They had a young attitude while my mom has always seemed old. She says she was born ancient. We generally agree with her. Maybe we're all born with the propensity to remain forever young or long to be old."

"Perhaps," Moira murmured. "Did you have any more, meandering stories you want to tell Amy?"

"No." Amy pursed her lips. How rude. Moira was more of a pain than Kara. It made Amy appreciate Kara more. Amy hoped Moira would leave soon.

Moira stared at Amy. "I find it interesting you picked an Elder to tell your story about. Your grandmother sounds like the type of woman I would have enjoyed meeting. Perhaps we'll see her on the other side."

"You can do that?" Amy demanded.

"Sometimes, but I wouldn't dwell on it if I were you. It rarely works out." Moira's voice held a hint of mystery.

Damn the woman. Why mention it then. Amy glared at Moira.

Moira gave Amy a tight smile. "You're right Kara. She does show potential. I like her spunk. With time and patience she could be trained. The choice of your grandmother shows infinite wisdom Amy. If you play your cards right we might ask you to join our merry band of women."

Amy shrugged. "Is that a threat or promise?"

Moira laughed heartily as if Amy had told a hilarious joke.

Kara gave an uneasy smile while Brittany remained silent.

"We'll see," was all Moira said.

There was an uncomfortable silence.

"Should I call Carl for refreshments?" Kara's tone was anxious.

Staring right at Amy, Moira replied, "None for me thanks, I should go."

Amy smiled at Brittany as Moira stood up. Once Moira's back was turned Amy gave Brittany thumbs up. They exchanged a quiet high five then grinned at one another, happy Moira was about to depart.

Kara joined Moira. They walked toward the door of the conservatory. She spoke in a low tone then in her regular voice commented, "It was good of you to drop by. Come again when you have a chance."

"Oh, I will. Kara, you know who you should have over," Moira said in a casual voice.

"No, who?"

"Invite Nellie for a visit. She might have an opinion about your friend here. It would also show Amy and Brittany another dimension regarding who you are. It's just a thought. Bye now. Bye Amy, Brittany."

"Bye." Amy remained in her chair. She didn't add, *'nice meeting you,'* since it hadn't been.

Brittany chorused good-bye with her mother then pulled out her notebook. She began to write at a frantic pace obviously keen to record the days' events.

Kara stopped by the intercom to order tea from Carl. "Would you prefer sandwiches or cookies?"

"Either one is fine," Amy replied.

"Cookies," Brittany almost shouted as she looked up. "Do you think Carl has any more of that cake?" With a distracted air she bent over her notebook again.

Kara mumbled something then returned to her chair.

"I found your stories fascinating." Kara sounded thoughtful. "I think people born at the turn of the century must have seen a great deal of change throughout their lifetime."

Carl appeared with refreshments. They were quiet while he served. He'd brought tiny cucumber sandwiches, cookies and another attractive coffee cake.

Brittany jumped up, said, "Sorry, I'm gonna grab some of this then get everything down while it's still fresh in my mind. Don't say anything too interesting. I have to tune you guys out for a while." She filled her plate then sat down to resume her writing.

Amy took a little bit of everything, suddenly hungry. The tea was Earl Grey, one of her favourites. Amy took a sip then resumed their earlier discussion. "My grandma told me stories about the first train she saw as it streamed across the prairie. My dad and his sisters never tire of farm tales about thrashers, combines and the horses they had. I've always found stories of their life on the farm fascinating."

Amy took a bite of cake. "Yum, tell Carl this is excellent. They sure had to work hard back then. Chores never seemed to end. They baked bread, hauled water, cut wood, fed farm animals and tended the garden. Cleanliness was even an effort. When they had a bath in the *'good old days,'* it sounded like quite the undertaking. We're certainly spoiled with all our modern conveniences. I hate using an outhouse." Amy shuddered at the thought.

"Eew, don't remind me. That's one of the worst things about being a pioneer woman."

"Mom, you're not supposed to talk about interesting stuff. How am I gonna remember that too?" Brittany griped.

"Don't worry honey," Amy soothed. "I can fill you in later. Hey," Amy asked her tone eager. "Were you ever a pioneer or native woman?"

"Yes, of course I was."

20

Amy licked crumbs off her fingers, eyeing the coffee cake again. She reached for another piece hoping it wouldn't offend the weight conscious Kara.

"Would you like to hear about a pioneer woman?"

Amy nodded. She was quiet since her mouth was full.

"Hey," Brittany uttered. "You still have to tell us a story about vampires and werewolves."

Kara sighed. "Yes, how can I forget? That will have to wait for another day Brittany."

"No problem, I'll remind you again." Brittany grinned as she reached across her mom for more food.

"Women have always had to assert themselves, no matter what century they live in. It's rare for us to be accepted in our own right without having to fight for recognition."

"What do you mean by that?" Amy furrowed her brow then wiped crumbs off her skirt. She greedily eyed the cake. No, she shouldn't eat another piece, maybe later. She glanced at Brittany who had no qualms about her calorie intake. Ah, to be young again with a fast metabolism.

Amy turned back to Kara. The woman Kara had chosen to talk about must have advocated the rights of women. Kara enjoyed throwing out inflammatory remarks about women she professed to have been. Amy imagined Kara would have risen to the status of rabble-rouser should the occasion arise.

"Think about it Amy. Rise to your potential," Kara taunted.

"What? I don't understand."

"It's time for you to begin the process of discovery."

"Wha…what? I mean, now, but, why," Amy stammered.

Penny Ross

"Amy, you need to open your eyes and embrace the gift you've been given." Kara leaned forward, her tone patient. "You can be so much more. You need to begin your journey. The path has broadened. It's time to discover and nurture your hidden potential. Unlock the door and gaze deep within. Learn what your special gifts are and how to balance your life. The time to begin is now."

"I don't understand what gift you refer to Kara. What journey of self-discovery? Why choose me to help with whatever it is you've hidden from my view? This is confusing," Amy wailed. Her eyes darted about.

Brittany glanced up, frowned, shook her head then bent over her notebook again.

"Don't worry. It will become clearer to you. The mist will rise and you'll observe what you need to see," Kara prophesied.

"There you go again. When you talk in that convoluted manner it drives me crazy," Amy complained. She rounded on Kara with displeasure.

"Ah, your self-pity has turned to anger. That's good."

"I find you maddening when you use all this mumbo jumbo. Why can't you talk in plain language?"

"You're right," Kara admitted. "As a teacher I have a lot to learn." Kara spoke in a slow, clear, measured manner. "Listen to what I'm about to say Amy. It will change your entire life."

Amy gulped. Kara made this sound serious.

Brittany glanced up, interested in what was about to happen. She put her pen down.

"When we set out on a journey of self-discovery we need teachers and protectors to guide us. We often begin on one path then realize we're better off on another. People may stumble about confused at the direction their life has taken. Once we knowingly decide to embark on a journey of awareness we're never the same. Your eyes will be opened.

Our potential is infinite Amy. As you travel on your path you will discover this. Once you've fully developed your gift, then and only then, will you be able to serve others."

"Why are you telling me this?"

"Why do you think I am?"

"You think I've begun my journey of self-discovery," Amy ventured.

"What do you think?"

Amy sighed. Her eyes filled with tears of frustration. "I don't know," she moaned. "How could I not know?"

Kara gave Amy a moment to compose herself.

Wiping a tear away Amy wondered, "Do you think I've stumbled about on this journey awhile now? Maybe I just haven't been conscious of it." Almost to herself she murmured, "If I have, how long has it been since the process began?"

Kara shrugged.

"So, now that I'm aware of this journey what will happen now?"

"You'll be open to knowledge, wisdom and truth. Some of what we've spoken of will make sense as you travel towards your potential."

"Oh."

"There's someone I think you should meet. She might help clear up a few matters. You might also understand more about who I am."

"Sure," Amy agreed as she reached over for another piece of cake.

"Here she is now."

Amy jerked her hand back fast. "What?" She forgot about the cake.

⸺

Amy and Brittany glanced at one another. Amy hoped this woman would be more sociable and agreeable than Moira had been. She felt ill prepared for another strange visitor.

Amy rose to her feet unsteadily. She felt lightheaded. As she stood she searched the doorway where Kara had gone to welcome someone. Brittany jumped up then reached out to grab her mother's hand. Amy squeezed her fingers gratefully. Would this woman, who'd appeared out of the blue, help clear things up or provide further confusion?

Penny Ross

Amy watched the two women approach, intrigued by the woman's clothing. It didn't resemble anything women in this century wore. The newcomer's hat was right out of a vintage fashion magazine.

Amy gazed with interest at the woman. Who could she be?

Fortunately, Kara wasn't in the mood to torture them.

"Nellie, this is a friend of mine. We've only met this week but it seems as if we've known one another forever. Her name is Amy. At my request her daughter Brittany has accompanied Amy here on her visits."

Amy and Brittany smiled at the newcomer.

"Amy, Brittany, this is a woman legends are made of."

"Oh," the woman whispered in a gentle, soothing voice. "There's no need to exaggerate Kara." Her smile was pleasant.

"Her name is ... .." Kara paused. It sounded dramatic since she didn't finish her sentence.

Amy squeezed Brittany's hand then moved forward to shake the woman's outstretched hand. She almost fell over when Kara filled in the blanks. She realized her mouth had opened like a fish flung out of water, gasping for breath. Amy closed it, quick before anyone noticed.

"Pardon me, what did you say your name was? I couldn't have heard. The air conditioner must have kicked in." Amy leaned toward the woman, expectant and eager to hear her name again.

"My name's Nellie," the woman announced with a smile, "Nellie McClung."

"That's impossible," Amy stammered. She fanned her face, suddenly faint. How could someone born in the late 1800s stand there? She seemed real, with flesh and blood and everything attached. With a tentative motion Amy reached out to touch Nellie's shoulder.

Yes, the woman definitely was real.

Amy's eyes darted toward her daughter. Brittany's eyes were wide as she stared at the newcomer. Amy grabbed Brittany's hand again for reassurance.

Perhaps this wasn't the famous Nellie McClung. It could be another woman with the same name. Yes, that must be it. Then again, why was the woman wearing outmoded clothing?

Kara and the person who professed to be Nellie McClung just stood there. Kara seemed smug while the woman was apologetic.

"I have to sit down," Amy mumbled. She groped behind her for a chair then collapsed heavily into it. Brittany moved to her side.

"Perhaps she needs water or something," the newcomer suggested.

"Hmm, well, if you insist," Kara grumbled. "Would you like more tea Amy or shall I call Carl for water?" Kara shouted.

"I'm not deaf," Amy hissed. She brought her fingers up to her temples then gently massaged the area. "I'm merely disoriented, that's all. I thought you said your new friend was a woman who would have to be over one hundred years right now." Amy pointed. "She doesn't appear to be a day over forty."

Kara glanced at the woman beside her.

"Hmm, appearances can be deceiving can't they? Think of the old hag you saw less than an hour ago. Nellie, grab a seat. This could take awhile."

The woman sat down on the edge of a chair. She placed her hands in her lap, her back ramrod straight.

Amy fixed her gaze on the stranger. Could it be possible she was from another century yet sat beside them gazing around with interest? It would explain the clothes and hat, yet the likelihood was improbable. Amy sighed. She should keep an open mind and let the woman speak her piece. She was obviously here for a reason.

Kara broke into Amy's thoughts. "Nellie and I have a lot in common."

Nellie nodded.

"Aren't you going to ask me why?"

"Oh, yes, sorry, umm, why do you and Nellie have so much in common?" Amy felt like a parrot forced to reiterate a phrase for her master. The thought brought a small smile to her lips.

Kara grinned back, mistaking Amy's smile for positive reinforcement. "Well," Kara paused, for effect maybe. She leaned toward Amy.

Instinctively, Amy sat further back in her chair. She felt news Kara was about to share might be hard to take. The way Kara eyed Amy made her nervous.

Brittany sensed her mother's uneasiness. She moved a chair to Amy's side then sat with her arm around her mother's shoulders.

Amy leaned toward Brittany. Her presence comforted Amy. She smiled her gratitude then turned to Kara. Brittany's familiar touch made her infinitely stronger.

"Women have talked about having the same freedom and rights as men as long as I can remember. It's not a new topic by any means."

"Mm hmm," Amy agreed.

"What are your views on the subject?"

"Women and rights," Amy clarified.

"Yes."

"Without certain women we wouldn't be where we are today. I like being able to raise a family and have a career. I feel as comfortable in the kitchen as the boardroom. I applaud women that helped make this possible. I feel their contributions were important to our present society." Amy glanced towards the stranger who had been introduced as Nellie. "Women like Nellie McClung make me proud to be a Manitoba woman. Without you and your friends Canadian women might not have gotten the vote until much later. Thank you."

"Besides the right to vote I think Nellie helped women win political equality. There was a group of five women weren't there, mom? I'm pretty sure Nellie was known as one of the famous five," Brittany clarified as she watched her mother frown at Nellie. "I remember one name, it was Emily Murphy. Was that your friend?" Brittany turned toward Nellie.

Nellie just sat there, a polite smile on her face. She ignored Brittany's question and Amy's previous comments.

Bird of Paradise Drums Beating

Amy had her mouth open to engage Nellie in conversation. She leaned closer to Nellie.

Kara jumped in and continued where she'd left off before Amy could address Nellie. "Some of the women I've embodied accomplished more than most people could in a dozen lifetimes. I don't think they ever got sick or too tired to continue with their project or crusade. Their diligence was exhausting. If sheer determination could result in a positive outcome they demonstrated anything is possible when you put your mind to it."

Amy nodded. "Those are the women legends are made of, like Nellie McClung. Why is she ignoring us?" Amy waved her hand in Nellie's direction.

"Yes, I agree with you." Kara ignored Amy's question about Nellie. "Without many of these women we wouldn't hold our place in history books. Men dominate the archives of libraries and museums. Women have always been overshadowed. We make small backstage appearances now and then. Women need more presence in the past, present and future to assert our rightful place as worthy citizens of this society."

Amy nodded. Kara hadn't stated anything new. If Kara had been involved with other women who had led the crusade for freedom and social reform, Amy was eager to applaud her efforts.

Amy turned toward the woman who claimed to be Nellie McClung. The conversation should have been near and dear to Nellie's heart. Yet Nellie seemed preoccupied and had ignored Brittany's direct question about her friend. Nellie gazed around the room with interest yet didn't appear to be listening to their conversation. When would she speak up? Perhaps she wasn't feeling well.

Amy had a thought. Had Kara ever mentioned any of the women she'd embodied being sick or even tired? How could Kara keep up her tireless pace? She must have had some breaks. Did she rest up between causes?

Kara seemed relaxed and claimed she had no friends to speak of. Yet, Amy had just met two of her friends. She also said she never went anywhere. Had she exaggerated her loneliness? Amy hadn't noticed Kara involved in any current projects, she wasn't writing or publicizing the plight of women. She didn't seem to be doing anything significant right now.

So, what was Kara's purpose? Was she a homemaker? By her own admission Kara didn't cook, clean or spend much time with her children.

"This is it," Kara stated, as if she'd read Amy's mind.

"What is?"

"My purpose," Kara repeated.

"Is what?"

Amy felt like she'd stepped off an elevator with no floor beneath her, confused by the lack of concrete foundation. The direction the conversation had taken tilted from the known to the unknown. Had Kara read her mind? Was that part of her shtick? Amy glanced at Brittany. Brittany shrugged, apparently as confused by the conversation as Amy was.

Kara spoke in a slow, calm, measured manner, like one would to a small, frightened child who was lost or disoriented.

"The reason I am here," Kara enunciated in a clear voice. "It must be to tell you and Brittany these stories. I haven't done anything noteworthy as Kara. My time here has been relaxing though. I've enjoyed the luxurious splendor. No one expects anything of me. I spend my days in a leisurely manner. This has been a pleasant interlude."

She smiled. "I'd hoped the spouse and children I had this time would interact with me more than they do. We don't understand one another. It doesn't matter." Kara shrugged. "Had it been important to the cause it would have happened. Everything in the universe happens for a reason," she concluded.

"So yes, to answer your question, sometimes I do get to rest up. My purpose changes to a certain degree now and then."

Amy stared, transfixed by Kara's matter-of-fact tone. Kara made everything sound reasonable, plausible even. It was almost as if some supreme being mapped out a plan for Kara to follow faithfully. Kara believed in God. She had confirmed this in their previous conversation with Moira. Did that explain it? Amy furrowed her brow. She was still confused.

"How do you do that?" Amy asked.

Instead of asking *'what'*, Kara answered the question. "I don't know. It just happens. I guess it's natural. Perhaps I'm psychic."

Kara grinned. The thought obviously delighted her.

"Hmm." Amy knew she'd get nothing concrete out of Kara in this mood.

"Do you remember your childhood in each of your lives?" Where had that question come from? It popped out for no reason. Amy saw no connection to their discussion. Mere curiosity had prompted it.

"No, I don't, now that you mention it. I remember being a young or mature adult. I was a teenager occasionally. In centuries past, thirteen and fourteen were old enough for a woman to be married though. So, no, I don't ever recall being young. How odd, now that you mention it."

Kara's brow furrowed. She stared before her, caught up in only something she could see.

Amy gazed at Kara's profile. Why had Kara chosen them for her stories? What had they done to deserve this? Was it an honour to be chosen as the recipient of these legends or a chore they were duty-bound to uphold? Amy wondered if there were more to this than storytelling.

"Is it all right for me to take notes again?" Brittany whispered.

Amy nodded.

If Kara's purpose was to tell them stories Brittany's notes were invaluable. Perhaps Kara's narrative would answer why Kara never experienced childhood during her reincarnations. That was a topic worth exploring.

"Do you think you projected yourself into women's bodies when they were of a certain age to have them further the cause? Were you there to help them complete an assignment they didn't know they'd been given?"

Kara glared at Amy.

"OK, so that sounds a bit far-fetched."

"Where do you think these women went, when I, what was the word you used, projected myself into their bodies? Is that a body transference trick? Strange, I don't remember learning that one."

Kara snorted, not bothering to hide her contempt for the notion.

"You admitted you don't remember everything. Why does my suggestion sound so outlandish? It's no more preposterous than you being reincarnated from one body to the next, repeatedly, throughout the centuries. Maybe you were only physically in their bodies for short periods."

"Moira said there was no formula for the length of time," Brittany pointed out. "I remember she said you stayed with the women anywhere from a few years all the way to twenty years."

Brittany glanced at Kara. Whatever she saw on Kara's face caused her to quickly turn back to her notes.

Kara frowned then opened her mouth to respond.

Amy shook her head. Brittany hated conflict and sensed Kara didn't appreciate her comments. Returning to her note taking helped Brittany avoid confrontation. It was a smart move. Amy jumped in before Kara voiced her possible displeasure.

"Yes, I recall Moira's comments Brittany. To take this further, the women could have gone someplace. I don't know where, a holding site perhaps, while you borrowed their body. It would have been for a certain time, whatever was necessary."

Kara seemed ready to burst, eager to interrupt Amy.

Like a traffic cop, Amy held her hand up to halt Kara's words. "It would enable you to accomplish what you were there to do. We can assume your purpose is to further women's causes such as freedom, social reform, justice and self-actualization. I'm sure the list will become clearer when we record your stories."

Kara didn't speak. She shook her head, rolled her eyes then scoffed.

"Could you agree to keep an open mind to the possibility? See what happens when we explore the idea further. Then we'll discuss it. The accounts you remember now could be significant. Maybe that's why you're here. Perhaps we're supposed to help you find the key to the puzzle you've been unraveling."

Kara seemed less skeptical now.

"Good, that's all I ask. We'll figure this out together. If I'm way off, hey what's the big deal? After all, friends talk things through, don't they?"

"Yeah, I guess you're right. Friends would do that," Kara admitted. She still sounded annoyed.

Amy smiled. She was relieved when Kara returned it with one of her own. Kara was a beautiful woman when she smiled. Had she been pretty in every one of her lives?

Amy shrugged. What did it matter what Kara looked like? It was the memories they needed to retrieve. They had to delve into the recesses of Kara's mind. Kara's purpose was important not her physical attributes.

"Are we ready then?" Kara asked.

"Ready? For what?" Amy blurted.

Kara rolled her eyes.

"Sorry, I need to pay better attention. My mind wandered. I was distracted. I imagine this has to do with her." Amy nodded toward Nellie.

"Yes, it does."

They turned toward the woman seated between them. With hands clasped comfortably in her lap, the woman in question was still oblivious to their presence.

Amy peeked at Brittany. Had she noticed how disengaged Nellie appeared to be? Of course she had, Nellie had ignored Brittany's earlier question about whether or not her friend was Emily Murphy.

Brittany glanced up from her notes. She met her mother's gaze then shrugged as if to say, *'I have no idea about her either.'*

Kara frowned then cleared her throat.

"All right, I'll begin. As you know, this story is about a Canadian woman born in the late 1800s. You already know who it is."

Amy nodded.

"Yes, well, I did a great deal to further a number of worthy causes. I'm sure you and other Canadian women have me to thank for your right to vote."

"Let me be the first to thank you then, or I mean, I should thank Nellie. I did thank her earlier but she didn't appear to be listening. She still doesn't seem to be." Amy included Nellie in her statement but received no response.

Kara ignored Amy's musings. "I was born in Ontario then moved to Manitoba when I was seven."

"Do you remember moving to Manitoba or being seven years old?"

Kara paused to consider the question.

Amy wondered why Kara insisted on speaking for Nellie. It reminded Amy of a marionette spoof except Nellie was real. Kara didn't even pretend to be her puppet master. Amy was about to point this discrepancy out when Kara answered her earlier question.

"No, now that you mention it, I don't recall moving to Manitoba or being seven years old. I remember facts. They're etched into my memory, part of my database. I retrieve the information to relay my stories. Recollections about my own family, parents, siblings, those aren't available. When I search for Nellie's life, I see five children and a husband who moved us often."

"Can you describe it in greater detail for us?" Amy hoped to get further clues about Kara and Nellie's strange relationship.

"Sure, I have this sensation where I appear to gaze into a looking glass. Or I see these images and they're in a body of water. As I watch people go about their daily business I become conscious I know one of the individuals. It turns out I'm the woman who's always the central character in the scene. That's when I begin to remember everything else."

Bird of Paradise Drums Beating

"Reminds me of a kaleidoscope," Brittany noted. "You know, where you have changing images and you turn them until you recognize something familiar."

"Yes, it does sort of begin like that. Once I identify the pattern, or sequence I see myself there."

"It sounds like the sensation you have when you gaze at the imaginary looking glass or body of water is the prompter of your memories," Amy guessed.

"I expect it could be something like that. I clear my mind of all thought then immerse myself in the images before me. Then everything comes back to me, as if it happened yesterday, not years or centuries ago."

"I want you to try something Kara," Amy urged. "Go into Nellie's life at the point you began your story. While you're there, see if you can recall earlier years."

"I'll see what I can do."

After a brief moment, Kara began to talk. Amy watched her closely. Was she in a trance when she had these recollections or was Kara actually reciting a story from her past?

"I see myself sitting at a table. I'm writing something. Now what is it? Oh, yes, I remember now, it's one of my books."

Kara chuckled, she sounded embarrassed.

"I'm an author among other things."

"Yes, of course, you're a famous Canadian author. Well, to be more appropriate, I should say, she's a famous Canadian author." Amy nodded toward the woman who claimed to be Nellie McClung.

Nellie nodded at Amy in a distracted manner, content to be silent.

Amy frowned at Nellie then turned back to Kara. "What year is it now, or more specific, when you wrote your first book?"

"It was published in 1908. I'm not sure when I wrote it though. Odd, I don't remember writing the first book," Kara confessed. She turned to Nellie with a puzzled air, seemed about to say something then changed her mind and remained quiet.

"That's all right." Amy was quick to reassure Kara. "This is close enough. Let's be clear on our facts so far. You were born in Ontario, you live in Manitoba now with your husband and you'll have five children. You write books and you campaigned for women's rights. Manitoba was the first province in Canada where women were allowed to vote. It was sometime in 1916 if I'm not mistaken."

Amy nodded toward Kara for confirmation.

"Yes, it was January 29, 1916."

Kara spoke as if it had been yesterday. It was clear she wasn't in a trance. To Amy it appeared this was her own personal story.

"I was instrumental as an advocate of suffrage for women. Even though our family had moved to Edmonton when the vote was passed in Manitoba, I like to take some credit for the campaigning that was done."

"You did move around a lot. You lived in Ontario, Manitoba and Alberta. Did you move anywhere else?"

"We moved to British Columbia when I was around fifty years old according to the history books. I don't remember that part. I do know I kept on writing. I also worked with other noteworthy women to further the role of women in politics. I was a member of the legislature as well. Not the first female member though, that was Louise McKinney. She was elected in 1917. In 1921 I was elected as a Liberal member of the legislature in Alberta. It was quite an honour I must say."

"You sound like you led a fascinating life. What was your family like?"

"They were involved in a number of activities just like me, or her." Kara nodded in Nellie's direction.

"One of my sons, I mean, one of Nellie's sons, was a Rhodes scholar. Another one became a deputy minister. Of course I was equally proud of all their efforts. It didn't matter that any were more prestigious than the others. A mother doesn't think that way about her children.

Bird of Paradise Drums Beating

I found joy in all their accomplishments, from their first tentative steps toward me, to good grades, to continued education. A mother's life involves pleasant memories of her offspring, or so I'm told...." Kara trailed off.

Kara's face bunched up with confusion. It seemed as if something had just dawned on her.

Amy didn't want to lose the moment. She jumped in with another comment to keep the story rolling. "So you were fulfilled by your family life in addition to your career. What an inspiration, to hear about Canadian women leaders who were able to balance home, career and personal aspirations."

"Yes, fortunately we've had many women with notable stories. I'm glad I wrote mine down to share with others. *Sowing Seeds in Danny* was my first book. I'll never forget how surprised people were to learn a woman wrote a popular tale. Of course I didn't personally write that one, Nellie did." Kara nodded toward Nellie who remained silent. She seemed oblivious to their conversation.

"How many books did you pen in total?" Amy was quick to ask.

"Ah, fifteen, or was it sixteen?" Kara appeared distracted for a moment. Then she added as an afterthought, "As well as numerous magazine articles. I guess I was quite the prolific writer."

Kara shrugged.

"Imagine that. I've written articles, newsletters and promotional material for years. I'm on my sixth novel. Maybe there's a chance for me to be published one day like Nellie McClung," Amy fantasized.

"I love to sit down and put pen to paper. The challenge of portraying what I imagine in my head in a logical yet captivating manner brings me immense pleasure. It's quite the balance, to create interest, tempo and appeal to a wide variety of readers. I've practiced my craft for years. Your story is fascinating Kara. I'd love to record it for you."

"Yes, I love the intrigue of a great story. As with all things, the more one writes and rewrites, the better one gets. It's like storytelling. I think I've improved." Kara chuckled.

"Writing is a craft you perfect with practice. It's understandable some people are better at it than others. That's like anything. Some individuals are skilled and reach a high level of ability while others are not as proficient in the same area. When one puts their mind to something of interest one can accomplish anything. As a writer Amy, your next step should be to get your works published."

Amy raised her eyebrows then rolled her eyes.

Kara laughed at her expression.

"If only it were that easy," Amy deadpanned.

"All right, maybe that's a bit simplistic. What I meant to say is many people write. Some are even successful. Like any career or hobby there are different levels of skill, that's all."

"When you put it that way, I agree."

"Good, I like when you're agreeable."

They laughed.

"Do you remember writing in any other lives?" Amy prompted.

"I'd have to think about that. Since it's something I like it could be possible. Then again, having a fondness for something doesn't seem to have bearing on the lives I was reincarnated into, now does it?"

"I don't know about that. Didn't you say you've always been an advocate of women's rights? That you spoke out against injustice to further women's causes?"

"Yes," Kara agreed.

"Then perhaps that's the common thread of all your lives."

Brittany jumped in. "I wouldn't say you spoke out against injustice in every one of your lives Kara."

Kara raised her eyebrows at Brittany.

"Well, I don't see how getting sacrificed as a Mayan girl furthered the cause of women or what about when you were that anorexic singer?" Brittany persisted.

"Hmm, yes, you do have a point," Amy agreed. "I guess we'd be safe saying you were an advocate of women's rights for many of your lives Kara."

Kara nodded.

Bird of Paradise Drums Beating

Amy glanced over at Nellie.

"Why haven't you contributed to the conversation?" Amy demanded. She couldn't stop herself.

"If you claim to be Nellie McClung, shouldn't you know about your life? Why did Kara describe it and you just sat there? You don't appear to listen to our conversation yet it's about you."

Amy couldn't help it. She didn't mean to be confrontational. How could Nellie tune them out while they spoke highly of her?

Nellie turned toward her. "I'm sorry dear. I don't know the story as well as Kara since I wasn't there. I can tell you about my children if you'd like. I remember the precise details of every one of their births. They were lovely babies."

Nellie nodded. "I remember writing my books, well, most of them anyway. Now that you mention it, a few novels seem to have been written without my knowledge. The style is decidedly different. I do recall my first one though, '*Sowing Seeds in Danny.*' You never forget your initial attempt at writing. It's a memorable occasion."

Nellie smiled, after a moment her grin turned to a frown. "You know though, for the life of me I can't recall the finer points of the years Kara knows so well."

"Why is that?"

"Why, I assume it was because I wasn't there. It seems Kara was there in my place. When I returned, I finished the work Kara had begun. That's why I'm here today. To show you a living example of a woman Kara knows intimately."

Amy was aghast. How could Nellie and Kara be so cavalier about this subject? Amy found it mindboggling.

21

"So you claim Kara was you, I mean, was Nellie McClung, from when, 19, what?" Amy ventured.

"I'd say it was about 1915 or so. Thereabouts, wouldn't you agree Nellie?"

"Yes, that sounds about right."

"When did you come back Nellie?"

"Well, I'd guess it was sometime in the twenties, wouldn't you say Kara."

"Yes, I left after the move to Edmonton. That was an exciting time. Rabble-rouser was the term they used to describe me. I found that exhilarating. Woman suffragettes, they're the best."

"Yes, they certainly are," Nellie agreed.

Amy frowned. "So where did you go when Kara was you?"

Kara, Amy and Brittany all leaned toward Nellie, eager to hear her answer.

Nellie pursed her lips, furrowed her brow then brought one hand up to delicately tap her chin.

After a few moments, Nellie met Amy's gaze. "I don't know where I went," she confessed. "It was never an issue before. I mean, I've never thought about it. Perhaps I went somewhere to rest up or something."

"The holding site," Amy, Kara and Brittany chorused.

"Good theory," Kara acknowledged. "It could have merit. You know Amy, until we had this conversation I never thought about where the women went whom I replaced. I always assumed I was reincarnated. You've raised a number of pertinent questions."

"Yes. Where did the women go while you took their place and how long were you there?"

Bird of Paradise Drums Beating

"I didn't seem to be gone for long," Nellie piped in.

"No, you're right. It was only about what, seven years?" Kara agreed.

"Maybe that doesn't seem long to you two. For those of us with only one life, that seems significant though," Amy pointed out.

"Yeah, that's almost half my lifetime," Brittany added as she glanced up from her notes.

They chuckled.

"Yeah, maybe," Kara conceded.

"I still don't understand something," Amy began.

"Only one thing Amy, my goodness you are quick. Nellie, pay attention," Kara crowed as she turned to Nellie, "She's perceptive."

Amy frowned. "No, there are numerous things I don't understand Kara."

Kara made a face at Amy then stuck out her tongue.

Amy shook her head at Kara like a mother chastising her child. "This is specific and applies to our discussion."

Amy turned to Nellie. "If you went back to your life in 1922 or so, then you can't possibly be in your forties or fifties. You should be dead. I'm sorry," Amy rushed to add, "But it's true. If you're dead, how can you sit here now, in the flesh? You're dressed like someone who walked out of a magazine from the twenties. I think you've got some *'splainin'* to do lady," Amy quipped.

Kara laughed.

Brittany glanced at her mother then frowned. "I don't get it," she confessed.

Amy and Kara laughed harder.

Amy turned to Brittany. "It's from an old sitcom, *'I Love Lucy.'* Her husband, Ricky Ricardo used to always say that to Lucy. It was hilarious. The show was way before your time though dear."

"I must say, I've never heard of it either but I like the sounds of this sitcom you refer to." Nellie flashed a mischievous wink. "I've definitely got some *'splainin'* to do." She turned to Kara. "Should I tell them?"

203

Kara shrugged. "Sure, why not. They think we're from the loony bin already. Why not tip over the edge? Besides, maybe it will help with Amy's prognosis of our exceptional situation." The last part was said with a wide smile.

"Well, Amy, Brittany, I'm like Kara and I travel through time."

Amy nodded. This didn't sound new. Now they'd met Kara, Moira and Nellie. They were quite the merry band of ladies who claimed to be reincarnated in women's bodies on a regular basis. Perhaps they merely replaced women for short periods of time. The notion was certainly open to one's interpretation.

"Since we're similar to time travellers to some extent it is important for you to understand how we travel around. First, we get an assignment." Nellie turned back to Kara. "Did you and Moira explain that part?"

"Yeah, sort of." Kara waved her hand as if to dismiss the question.

"All right. Then we go to the woman who's in need of our help. She can be in any century. Right now I'm in 1926. I took a little break to come here for a visit. I'll go straight back there since it will be teatime soon. I'm expected you know."

"Of course you are," Amy quipped. "Are you trying to say time isn't linear?"

"Yes, exactly, you've got it." Nellie clapped her hands enthusiastically.

"No, I don't have it, but maybe it'll become clearer later on," Amy confessed.

Nellie motioned toward Kara. "I agree Kara, Amy is a rather perceptive young lady. Of course your youthful curiosity might have to be curbed to some degree. You have so many questions."

Nellie tapped her cheek, thoughtful while she gazed at Amy. "Hmm, I don't quite know what to make of this. I like how you stated you're willing to wait for issues to become clearer. That shows potential. Patience is important. So is blind faith." Nellie nodded at Amy then turned back to Kara.

Bird of Paradise Drums Beating

"Yes, I'm glad Moira suggested I come here personally. Amy shows promise yet there is a great deal of work to do. Hard to say, hard to say," Nellie murmured. "We'll see."

"It's become more obvious to *Her* though," Kara commented.

"Yes, well," Nellie trailed off. "I assume you'll give your personal endorsement?"

"Mm hmm," Kara concurred.

"I do have a special favour to ask *Her* first though. If *She* agrees then I'll discuss it with Amy tomorrow. Do you think I should bring up what we've discussed?" Kara wondered

Nellie started. "What do you think Kara?" she countered.

Amy was enthralled by the conversation. Nellie had just used Kara's favourite tactic of answering a question with another question.

"Hmm, you're right," Kara replied as if Nellie had answered her.

"Well." Nellie's tone was brisk. "That's that then. Tell *Her* I concur with your recommendation as well."

Nellie turned toward Amy then beamed. "Amy, it has been a real pleasure meeting you. I hope to see you in the future." Her smile widened. "I'm sure we'll get to know one another better. There's always room for another friend. I expect you might be one of us soon. You've done a fine job spotting her Kara," Nellie praised.

"Well, now that we've cleared everything up here I do need to run. It's almost teatime. Ta, ta for now ladies."

Nellie stood then waved at Kara and Amy. She called out, "Good bye young one, take care of your mother," to Brittany then left the room.

Amy expected Nellie to disappear in a cloud of smoke. She was speechless as Nellie departed. What had Nellie and Kara alluded to now?

Kara continued the conversation as if Nellie had never been there.

"I wonder how being sacrificed fits with your premise I've been in lives where I like to be involved in something I care about such as writing? The common thread theory you mentioned. Sacrifices don't make sense."

Amy tried to focus on Kara. It was annoying how Kara resumed their last conversation as if nothing of note had just happened.

"Well, no, you're right, it doesn't."

They were silent for a moment, lost in thought.

Amy noticed it had gotten windy outside. She glanced at her watch. With surprise, she noted it was later than she'd realized. Andy would be anxious for them to go grab a bite somewhere. She glanced at Brittany who was busy with her notes.

"Brittany, we have to leave soon. Don't you have a night class tonight?"

Brittany started. "Oh man, what time is it?" She dug through her purse for her cell phone. She opened it, glanced at the clock then said, "Can I borrow your car tonight mom? Then I can stay a few more minutes and we can walk back together."

"Sure Brittany, your dad and I will probably go somewhere nearby for supper. We can use his car or walk."

Kara interrupted their conversation. "What if I was sacrificed that first time to lead subsequent lives I've led? I'm convinced I've had a special purpose all along. I mean, even more cause than Moira, Nellie and the rest. A force beyond simple comprehension has led us all. My lives have differed than theirs though." She nodded toward Amy. "I had a thought. It happened when you mentioned I might only be in women's bodies for a relatively short time. Something twigged just now."

"What?"

"It was the length."

"Sorry, you've lost me."

"I think I was about fourteen when I was sacrificed."

"Mm hmm, and," Amy coaxed.

"What if I was in each woman's body for that length? You suggested I wasn't born, nor died in each body. It was something I assumed but it's not true. Nellie just proved that." Kara cocked her head

Bird of Paradise Drums Beating

to one side. "I don't remember being a child. Each life seems to be stored in that databank I mentioned earlier. So, perhaps I was selected to be a host of those bodies for a specified length. After which, the original woman was restored."

"It does fit with my theory," Amy agreed. "You were only in Nellie's body for seven years though."

"Hmm, you're right."

"It's the number seven," Brittany exclaimed. "You were Nellie for seven years and sacrificed when you were fourteen. It sounded like you were Cleopatra for a considerable time, at least fourteen or even twenty-one years."

"Brittany, you're onto something," Amy praised.

"You could be extra special," Brittany acknowledged. "I mean, really, you were Nellie McClung, Cleopatra and how many other women who are famous historical figures? Nellie is one of the women whose purpose was to further women's causes. Were you ever Moira or any of the other women who are now part of your group?"

Kara stared at Brittany, a shocked expression on her face.

"Yes, I was," she blurted. "I'm like a, a recruiter or something."

Brittany laughed. "Yeah, well, that's one way to put it Kara. Maybe that's why you've got your eye on my mom."

Kara still looked upset.

"Let's keep an open mind and explore all the possibilities we identify," Amy urged. "We can go over your stories then try to figure out the time span for one. Brittany has taken notes. We can tackle the other issues we've raised later."

"Ah, sure, sounds great." Kara's voice was hesitant.

Amy smiled at her new friend. "I'm glad you expressed an interest in what I've said. It makes me feel as if my opinion counts for something."

"Well, that's what friends are for, or so I'm told." Kara laughed then squeezed Amy's arm in an affectionate manner.

"Hey. What about me?" Brittany interrupted. "I've come up with some kickass comments too, ya know."

"Group hug," Amy announced as they congratulated one another on their cleverness.

Amy and Brittany took their leave, after they agreed on a time to meet the next day.

∽∽

"This is an exciting project," Brittany remarked as they briskly set out for home.

With head down Amy agreed. "I'm glad you've taken notes Brittany. We'll have to go over them when you have time. Or, you could leave them with me and I'll read them over. I realize you're busy with classes, studying and visiting Kara."

"Yeah, that's for sure. I'll give you the notes when we get home and you can check them out. Feel free to add anything to them or change stuff. I could have gotten a few facts wrong. Everyone talks so fast. Man is it ever windy out," Brittany griped. "You're right about me being busy. I haven't had time to get together with Brad as much as I'd like either."

"Brad? Have you mentioned him?" Amy swiped hair out of her face. She wished she had something to tie her hair up. It was going to be a mass of knots when they got home. Brittany's hair was in a ponytail so she wouldn't have that problem. "Is this some new guy?"

"I haven't told you about Brad yet? What? Jeesh, talk about busy. This Kara stuff takes up a lot of time, that's for sure." Brittany shook her head then lowered it again as she realized it was easier to walk that way. "So, he's this cute guy I have in my Biology class and lab. We've had coffee a few times now. He mentioned going to a movie one of these days. Hey, maybe we'll go to a late movie tonight since I have the car."

"Sounds serious," Amy joked.

"Mom, come on, I just met him. What do you expect? A marriage proposal." Brittany snorted.

"No, I'm happy with the pace," Amy reassured her daughter as she backpedalled. "Tell me more about him."

Bird of Paradise Drums Beating

Brittany gave Amy a full-blown description of Brad from his looks, to the number of siblings he had, his second year status, his love of sports, how he was a rural kid from Beausejour, the whole bit.

Amy was happy for Brittany. Her daughter liked to jump headlong into a relationship. It was all or nothing for Brittany. She enjoyed meeting new friends and liked to surround herself with people.

"Caitlin's great too."

"Is she another new friend?"

"Yeah we met in Bio lab. She's got a boyfriend already so I don't have to worry about her trying to hook up with Brad. Caitlin made sure we exchanged cell numbers and she suggested Brad and I go out for coffee the first time." Brittany hurried up the sidewalk then rushed to open the door. "Man that wind is annoying. Thanks for lending me your car mom. Now I won't have to wait at the bus stop in this wind. Is it OK if we go to a late movie if Brad has time?"

Amy nodded.

"Thanks mom, you're the best. I gotta go get ready."

Amy watched Brittany bound up the stairs. "Should I make you something to eat?"

"Sure, that would be great mom, thanks."

"Remember to leave me your notebook," Amy called up the stairs.

⁂

"What did you think of the show Brittany?" Brad pushed the door open for Brittany as they left the theatre.

"It was great. I loved that scene with Paula, Laura and Sam on the bed. It was hilarious."

"Yeah, when Laura slugged Sam that was priceless." Brad laughed while Brittany giggled.

"I like how they had it from Paula's viewpoint," Brittany added. "When the three of them sat on the bed in the hotel room and watched everyone else party I wasn't sure where the scene was going to go."

They crossed the road headed for Brittany's car.

"It was so funny how Paula heard Sam say '*Blah, blah, blah, look at me I'm a man, wanna go make out*,' then Laura yelled '*Jerk*' and wham Laura slugged Sam." Brittany laughed. "The expression on Sam's face was priceless."

"Yeah, when they panned in on his face just before he keeled over on the bed, that was a great shot," Brad agreed joining in Brittany's laughter.

"Wanna drive?" Brittany handed the keys over to Brad.

"You sure your mom won't mind if you let someone she doesn't know drive?"

"She'll be fine. As long as you don't go nuts."

Brad grinned. "I'll control my road rage, how's that sound?"

"Perfect. Do you think that happens in real life?" Brittany fastened her seatbelt as Brad adjusted his seat then started the car.

"What, road rage?"

"Oh right, I need to be more specific." Brittany chuckled. "It's not as if you can read my mind, duh."

"Not yet anyway. We probably have to be going out for at least a month or so." Brad started to back out of the parking space.

Cool, we're going out, Brittany thought. She grinned at Brad. Aloud, she said, "I was referring to the rest of that scene in the movie. After Sam got slugged by Laura. It was interesting to see everyone's reaction at the party. I expected the guys to be all, '*Yeah Sam, go get her.*' But it was the opposite."

Brad pulled into traffic. "Guys don't want to see women used or taken advantage of anymore than girls do Brittany. Especially since Sam was drunk. Laura and Paula hadn't even been drinking before they got to the party. When Laura called Sam a jerk then slugged him everyone thought he deserved it. I've seen that happen in real life. It wasn't pretty to see Sam called down by everyone but he deserved it."

"Yeah, it wasn't nice how most of his friends belittled him. It was definitely a gang mentality. Even though he was a jerk I kind of felt bad for him."

Bird of Paradise Drums Beating

"That's good. I'm sure the director and producer would be pleased by our reaction. Imagine producing a movie that people line up for then talk about later. We'll probably tell our friends about that scene and that promotes the movie more. So they'll get more people to the show just by word of mouth. How awesome is that?"

Brittany nodded. "You're right. I never thought of the promotion angle. It was a powerful scene and made me feel like I was part of the experience. We related to what happened in the movie. That's why it's a success. Hmm, I'm going to have to tell my mom about this."

"Do you think she'll want to go to the movie? Is it the kind of show she likes?"

"Oh, no, I don't think so. I want to tell her about that scene and how powerful it was. She writes books and she likes to hear stuff like this. You know, like how I personally felt I was part of the experience. She tries to get in the mind of her readers. I think making movies is kind of similar."

"Wow, your mom sounds cool. I'd love to meet her and your dad one of these days. Does she have any books published?"

"Not yet. We met this new woman, her name is Kara and my mom might write her next book about her. I've been taking notes so mom says maybe we'll write it together. This could be the one she publishes."

"You're going to write a book with your mom. Wow, I'm going out with a writer. Wait till my mom hears about this. She's going to love you." Brad grinned.

"Don't get your mom too excited just yet Brad. I think we're kind of far away from having the book written. Plus we'll have to convince Kara it's OK to write her stories. She hasn't agreed yet."

Brad turned to her while they waited at a red light. "I'm sure she'll agree Brittany. You just wait and see. By this time next year you'll be a published author."

Brittany grinned. "I hope you're right Brad. That would be so cool."

22

When Amy and Brittany arrived Kara greeted them with a welcoming smile. It was a pleasant start to the afternoon.

"I've been thinking," Amy began.

"So have I," Kara interrupted. "I've decided to answer some of your questions today."

"You have," Amy cried. "When, now?"

"No, not right away," Kara hedged, "later on today. First, I want to tell you a few more stories. You'll like these ones," she added mysteriously.

"Are you going to tell us about the vampires and werewolves?" Brittany sat down then bent over to remove her notebook from her purse.

"Hmm," was Kara's reply as she frowned at Brittany.

Brittany shook her head. "Jeesh, you said I should remind you."

Amy sat down. "I'd like to discuss something before you start."

Kara nodded.

"When Nellie mentioned time wasn't linear yesterday I wondered if you've ever gone forward in time. I assume as time travellers you travel through some sort of portals or something. Can you go forward and backward?"

"No, never forward, only backward. We can't foretell the future. We're there to ensure women have a significant place in the past."

"That doesn't make sense though," Amy argued. "The past has already happened. We know who played an important part in history. Why go back now?"

"You still don't get it, do you Amy?" Kara shook her head.

"When you read a history book they hardly mention women. We barely exist. We're there as vassals to the men, bearers of their

Bird of Paradise Drums Beating

children, slaves to their passion, whims to their fancy and backbenchers to their gallery. Our primary purpose is to ensure men have all their creature comforts addressed."

Amy shrugged. "Well, Kara, it's not that black and white. You make our fate sound worse than it is."

"Yeah, sure," Kara mumbled, "whatever you say Amy. Now back to my point. That's why we go to the past. We want to help rewrite the stories. To ensure women are included as part of history. There are always people to research and write about legendary men. We need to ensure there's enough information provided to highlight legendary women. Without it, we're nothing. The notes Brittany has taken, they're invaluable."

Brittany grinned as she uncapped her pen then bent over her notebook.

"When we, the group of women, who have been sent back in time, come back to this century, we find women who record the facts as we know them, while it's fresh in our memories. We ensure proper research is done. Then the real woman who was the hero, leader, prophet or advocate who we've left behind is acknowledged in print."

Kara smiled. "It furthers our cause. It ensures women are given their rightful place in history alongside men. There's no need for women to always be in the background. Their role should be obvious to future generations."

"OK, yeah, that makes it clearer. When you answer these questions today we'll be so knowledgeable you'll probably want us to start writing your stories lickety-split," Amy added with a quick laugh. "After all, Brittany has already taken expansive notes."

Amy turned to Brittany. "By the way dear, I read over your notes last night. You're very thorough. Together we could formulate an enjoyable novel should Kara agree."

"Perhaps," Kara commented.

Amy was surprised. Hmm, imagine if Kara cooperated? They'd have a bestseller for sure! She smiled at Brittany. They could co-author this.

"Oh, while I think of it, I need to leave early today. My parents are bringing the boys here for the weekend."

Amy laughed. "Andy has been teasing me since I've spent more time with you than at the conference this week. He's threatened to lay me off if I don't quit goofing. I'm going to have to work harder at the next conference."

Kara frowned.

"I'm joking of course." Amy didn't want Kara to think Andy was serious. He'd be in Kara's bad books for sure.

"Oh, right. Perhaps you'd be willing to bring the boys by for a visit. Andy too of course," Kara added.

"What about me?"

"I thought you were a given Brittany, since you're part of our group already. You're welcome here anytime. I haven't met the men in your family though."

"Great, thanks Kara. Not tonight though, I've got a date." Brittany smiled then sat forward with an expectant look on her face, her pen ready for action.

"Sounds good, I'm sure we can all drop by sometime this weekend when everyone's around. How about that story," Amy urged.

"Of course, this one fits directly with the teaser I threw out when you and Brittany arrived. It's about women, history and being well-known because of a man."

"Ah, sounds fascinating. Should we guess who she is, or will you tell us?"

"You try to guess." Kara flashed a mysterious smile. "I can give you numerous examples of famous women who should have been admired for their own traits. Many were well known though because of their relationship with a man. How well do you know your Canadian history ladies?"

"I guess as well as the next person. Depends who you're referring to of course," Amy admitted. She'd always been bad with names. Twenty questions wasn't one of her strengths.

Bird of Paradise Drums Beating

Kara arched her brows at Brittany who was bent over her notebook. "Brittany," she prompted.

"Oh, I'm pretty good. We took Canadian history in grade 11. It wasn't that long ago."

"Perfect, here's one for you then. Name a famous Métis person."

"Oh good, an easy one, Louis Riel," Amy shouted as if she were in a game show.

"Yes, it was a good one to start with. I'm sure the fact he was a male solidified his recognition factor," Kara pointed out.

"Well, I don't know," Amy mumbled. Now she wasn't sure whether she'd guessed the right person or not. She glanced at Brittany who was no help as she was immersed in her notes.

"Hmm, no matter, you were right Amy. I was related to Louis Riel you know."

"What? How astounding. That's fascinating." Again, Kara had surprised her. "So you've been many races throughout your lives?"

"Of course I have. I couldn't be a white Anglo-Saxon every time now, could I? Otherwise, how would I have represented women throughout the ages? Take Harriet Tubman for instance, she was born a slave, escaped to freedom, then led more than 300 slaves to the north and Canada where they obtained freedom. Progressive women have stood up for women's rights and been from a variety of ethnic groups. In this instance I was white though."

Had Kara just alluded she'd been Harriet Tubman? Amy wasn't sure if she should mention it or not. She chose not to as she wanted to hear more about Kara's ties to Louis Riel. "You're right. Louis Riel was Métis so one of his ancestors must have been European. Were you his mother?"

"No, I was his grandmother. His mother was my seventh baby, Julie. She was a cute little thing, so docile and easy going."

Kara's expression was dreamy.

It surprised Amy.

Kara didn't strike Amy as maternal. It was unclear whether she had birthed any children herself. Kara barely mentioned the two sons she had now. Although, now that Amy thought about it, Kara had talked a great deal about Caesar's son, Caesarion. Perhaps Amy had misjudged her.

"You must have had scads of children if you added all of them together throughout your lives."

"Yes, I imagine I have. I only remember some offspring though. My lives are hazy around the edges. We established that yesterday, remember?"

Amy nodded.

"You always recall children who are particularly easy going or rambunctious though. Those in the middle seem to fade from memory or meld together somehow. It's sad, but true."

Kara seemed lost in thought.

Watching her, Amy thought of Kara's earlier comment.

"You spoke of women who asserted themselves then mentioned it was rare for them to be recognized in their own right."

"Yes, men generally rule the world and hold the place of power and honour in most households, kingdoms and domains. I don't think it's right but it's been accepted and familiar. It seems women who try to rule the roost or reign as a monarch are thought of in rather derogatory terms."

Amy frowned. "Women are supposed to be feminine, have good manners, look decorative and be healthy and strong enough to bear children. Words like assertive, powerful, tough, courageous and honourable are equated more with men than women." Amy shook her head. "When we exhibit these characteristics we make men uncomfortable. It's always been that way. Change takes a long time to come about. Of course, as you've shown, there are many women who are famous in their own right."

"Yes. That's what happened to Marie-Anne. I was considered foolhardy for the risks I took. Risk-taking is something men are revered for while women are frowned upon as thrill-seekers. I was determined to go with my husband though. The men had no other choice but to allow me on their trip."

Bird of Paradise Drums Beating

"Where were you headed?"

"Oh, I guess I should start at the beginning," Kara offered.

"My husband was a voyageur. In those days, this was back in the early 1800s, men were farmers and women were wives and mothers. Not my Jean-Baptiste. He wanted to paddle in a canoe and explore the Northwest.

We got married when I was twenty-five. He thought I'd stay at home and have a family. I had other thoughts. I told him if he was going west, I was too. So we paddled down the St. Lawrence and came here."

Kara laughed. "I mean to what is now known as the Province of Manitoba. Not right here, literally, to my house."

"You mean you never landed nearby. After all, your house is on the river."

"Yes, it is. Jean-Baptiste and the rest of us landed at the spot where the Pembina joins the Red River."

Amy nodded.

"We traveled around the West. Then we came back to Pembina Valley when I was expecting my first baby. It was a girl as I recall. I had her in a little log shack. A Cree woman helped me with the delivery. That reminds me, do you know why I'm famous in the history books?"

Kara smiled, raised her eyebrows then gave Amy an encouraging nod. "Come on, take a guess. Brittany, you too."

Amy furrowed her brow.

"Well, you mentioned being Louis Riel's grandmother. What was your name?"

"Marie-Anne Lagimodiere. You're right about the Louis Riel part. I already told you that though. Come on, there's more. I'll give you a hint. It had to do with the babies."

Kara grinned.

"The babies," Amy mused, thinking Kara seemed pleased with herself.

"I don't know I give up." Amy threw her arms out in a gesture of defeat.

Kara smirked, barely able to contain herself. "Brittany," she prompted.

"Can't help you." Brittany shrugged. "This is way more detail than we took in our history class."

Kara's grin widened. "I was the first white woman to become a permanent resident of the West. I had the first legitimate white baby born in what is now known as Manitoba, Saskatchewan and Alberta."

Kara glowed with pride.

"I had Reine, my little girl, in early January of 1808. Another girl had her baby at the end of December in 1807. She wasn't married though so mine was the first legitimate baby. If Jean-Baptiste had thought of it at the time we could have paddled to British Columbia and had one of our children there. That would have solidified my notoriety I'm sure. Then you might have heard of me."

Kara laughed. "Can you imagine? My claim to fame was to have children in different provinces while we paddled from one place to another. How many women can boast of that?

I remember we paddled back to Manitoba with three young children. It wasn't something I'd care to repeat now I'll tell you. I can't believe we did it then either."

"Yeah, sounds like an unlikely scenario," Amy agreed. "Driving in a car a great distance with three children is memorable. I can't imagine paddling in a canoe. When you think about it though I'm sure Marie-Anne was also known for bravery, strength of character and her will to survive in those harsh times. Imagine the determination it took to convince her husband she could accompany him on his journey. Let alone traveling with three young children on these rivers."

"Yes, you're certainly right about that. None of the voyageurs had ever had a woman along with them before. It took awhile, but I became a member of the group and they accepted me. I recall as we paddled through Saskatchewan some of the Aboriginal people hosted

Bird of Paradise Drums Beating

a summer celebration. We joined them and I became something of a celebrity with my baby girl Reine."

Kara chuckled at the memory.

"I recall the Chief came and told me about how they'd heard about the white man's queen who lived across the ocean. They'd never had a queen so they asked me to do the honour. Of course as you know I'd been a queen in earlier lives. This was a special tribute though since I hadn't been born to the position. To be acknowledged as a queen in my own right gave me a mark of distinction. For a while there, Jean-Baptiste and the other men treated me with a high level of respect. It was a heady experience I'll tell you."

Kara tossed her thick hair over her shoulder. "They wanted me to stay at Cumberland House to serve and honour me. I listened intently while an interpreter repeated the Chief's words. I'll admit I was tempted by the privilege. I had to turn them down though since we were continuing westward."

Kara gave a long, dramatic sigh. "Ah, the life of a common woman as she flirts with thoughts of royalty, it makes me giddy when I think about it." She flashed a warm grin.

"So you were famous for that too."

"Well, now that you mention it, I guess I was. I also arrived in Manitoba five years before the Selkirk Settlers. I witnessed the birth of the Province of Manitoba. I had many tales to tell my children and grandchildren. I hope you're getting this all down Brittany. It's important for Marie-Anne and other women like her to be represented as part of Canadian history."

Brittany glanced up, "Yup, got it." She bent back over her notebook.

"Marie-Anne was a true pioneer woman in every sense," Amy noted.

"Yes, she certainly was."

"Is that why you mentioned you'd been a queen more than once? Did you consider Marie-Anne a queen?"

"You know Amy, I never thought about it before. I don't think a pioneer woman like Marie-Anne could be considered royalty even though the Chief wanted me to be. I never had servants, although the Chiefs' people would have served me. There were no riches to speak of.

When it came to power, I certainly had no authority over Jean-Baptiste and the men. When we paddled I obeyed them since they knew what they were doing. I certainly never tried to control any of them. Marie-Anne would have been a good ruler though, she was fair and had good judgment."

Amy smiled. "Marie-Anne and Cleopatra sound quite different."

"Yes, they were in many ways," Kara agreed. "They lived in uncommon circumstances though. They rose above what they had been given in life to make a name for themselves. As courageous, independent females they stood up for their rights and forced men to look upon women in a different manner. They certainly didn't represent your stereotypical female by any means."

Kara nodded toward Amy. "When we discuss women as equals we could take a few lessons from the Aboriginal people."

"How so?"

"You mentioned the research you've done about Aboriginal people Amy. Here's a fact you might have missed. In 1450 within the Iroquois confederacy women had an equal vote, the same as a man. In many ways, women have gone backwards in our so-called *'modern'* age."

"What was that date again?" Brittany asked.

"1450. Now, I think I'll tell you two stories. One is slightly unbelievable. At times, I think the second one never happened and was just a dream. Then I remember everything I learned and believe it had to have taken place."

Kara nodded as if she had decided something. "I'll start with the first memory since its more current and from this century. The earlier recollection is from the late 1800s. It illustrates how we need awareness to gain knowledge of our surroundings."

"What? I'm confused," Amy admitted.

"Fair enough, point taken. The first story is about my immersion in a sweat lodge as a white woman. In the second instance, I take on the spirit of a medicine woman and experience everything through her eyes. The second occurrence is sketchier than the first. It's more of a shadowy image. I feel as if I've grasped wisdom. I speak from afar but it's not my story. It's hard to explain but I think you'll like it."

"How is the second one possible?"

"I'm not sure." Kara shrugged. "The recollections recently surfaced. They could be the result of stories about your native grandmother and personal journey. One point of interest for you to note, especially you Brittany, since you're recording this, is you'll notice a difference in my understanding and level of involvement."

Amy frowned. She opened her mouth, about to ask a question.

"I'll explain further." Kara held up a hand to halt any questions. "You'll notice initially, I seem to be on the periphery even though I experienced the sweat lodge firsthand. In the second memory I feel more as my insight reaches a high level of intensity. As I mentioned though, I don't know if the second one is my voice. I don't think I'm a specific medicine woman, more a compilation of them. Listen to the stories. See if you notice a difference between them."

"Of course. I'm interested already since they involve the First Nations culture. Perhaps I'll learn more about my ancestors."

"Hmm, perhaps." Kara closed her eyes. She clasped her hands across her lap as she began her story. She seemed to sink into a trance-like state.

"Drums beat in the background. It was dusk. Nature decreed thunder would rumble along as background to the chants that radiated from the sweat lodge. The intense heat of the sweat differed from anything I'd ever experienced. Sweat poured down my forehead and through the crevices of my breasts as my heart palpitated like a hummingbird."

Eyes closed, Kara gave a slight nod. "It wasn't like a sauna or steam room. That's the only comparison I've had with hot rocks and steam. It's hard to describe, not something one is used to. When we're faced with an unfamiliar situation I find it's easier not to dwell on what might happen." Kara opened her eyes. "Don't you agree Amy?"

"I guess, although I can't control what I feel. Sometimes, while I wait for something to happen or look forward to an event my stress level builds. I tend to worry as well. Not a good trait. I often have a hard time controlling my reaction." Amy flashed Kara an apologetic smile.

"Oh well, no matter. To each his own I guess. I did have a few preconceptions," Kara continued. "I thought the sweat lodge would be quieter. I never expected it to be dark either. I imagined candles or thought the firelight would provide illumination. It kind of threw me when we were plunged into darkness. It was so intense. The noise level overpowered me at times."

Kara gazed off. She appeared to replay the scene in her mind.

"Why was it so loud?"

"Hmm, well, as I mentioned there were drums, thunder, as well as women who chanted outside the sweat lodge. Then there was all the commotion inside."

"What commotion?"

"I'm not sure if the noise is typical. I admit I was disconcerted at first. I must have blocked some of it out later on though. I don't recall a loud volume as the sweat progressed." Kara rubbed her chin. "Hmm, interesting, I haven't thought about this in a long time. It's what happened though. I'm sure of it. Perhaps I went to another plane or some further level of consciousness for a short time. Whatever happened, I managed to tune everything out. Well, not everything." Kara chuckled as she wound a piece of hair around her finger.

"Inside the lodge, Mary Jane led the group. I'd describe her as the medicine woman or healer. If this had been a workshop she would be called a facilitator. It was a woman's gathering."

"Why did they call it that?"

"There were only women allowed, silly. Kind of obvious, don't you think?" Kara laughed in a good-natured way.

Amy chuckled. "Well, when you put it that way, yes."

"Yeah mom, duh," Brittany added as she joined in.

"Now where was I?" Kara peered around as if she'd lost a script she'd been reading from.

"Mary Jane and the commotion inside the lodge," Brittany read.

"Right thanks."

"There were far too many of us in the lodge to begin with. Since we were known as '*first timers*' I guess they piled more than usual into the lodge. I know they did, since Mary Jane apologized for it a number of times. There were at least twenty-two of us. I think an acceptable number was more like, fourteen, or sixteen. The less the better since you need to spread out."

"Ah, that makes sense."

"She said that a lot."

"Who did?"

"Mary Jane, the medicine woman, haven't you been listening?"

"Yes, of course I have," Amy was quick to agree.

"Mm, well all right then. Mary Jane mentioned Elders comment '*ah*' when they listen to people speak. She said it often throughout the day, while she did her teachings."

"Ah." Amy could have bitten her tongue off as Kara frowned in her direction. "Sorry, I don't know what came over me. I didn't do it on purpose."

"Perhaps your native blood has surfaced without your knowledge." Kara flashed Amy a sly, sidelong smile.

"Ah," Amy said, on purpose this time.

They laughed.

"Now I've forgotten where I was in my narrative again. Have I gone off on a tangent or lost my mind? Why can't I remember where I am in this story?"

Kara frowned as she tried to figure out where she'd left off.

As she glanced around it reminded Amy of a child who had lost their marbles. The thought made her smile. Should she share the comment about Kara losing her marbles? What an interesting play on words. Before Amy could decide Brittany piped in. The moment passed.

"You mentioned more than twenty-two people were in the lodge," Brittany read from her notes.

"That's it, yes, now I remember. Thanks." Kara bestowed a benevolent smile upon Brittany.

It brought an image to Amy's mind of the Pope holding his ring out for someone to kiss. Kara might like that. Paying homage would be up her alley.

"I was scrunched up. My legs were crossed and I held them close to my chest. I do not find that a comfortable position. A woman was in front of me and the people on either side touched me with their sweaty bodies. Eew." Kara made a face. "Mary Jane said we should have our own space. It was better if we didn't get too close to anyone since we'd have our own personal experience. We were packed in like sardines so this wasn't possible at first."

Kara shuddered. "The heat, it was so intense in there. Even before the grandmothers arrived."

"The grandmothers?" Amy wondered.

"Yes, there were sixteen of them in all. Four for the first round then four more were added for each subsequent round. There were four rounds in total."

"Where did they sit if you didn't have any room?"

Kara gave a big belly laugh.

Amy smiled although she wasn't sure what the joke was.

"I'm glad to hear you phrase it that way. I thought the same thing myself. When I heard we'd have sixteen grandmothers in the lodge I couldn't comprehend it. Where would they sit I wondered? I was just like you."

Kara smiled at the memory. "I looked around the circle of women throughout the day then counted how many women looked like grandmothers. I only came up with four or five. I wondered if more people would join us later that evening. There were over fifty women around. The majority of them were younger than grandmothers though. Some were even teenagers."

Kara laughed again. "Imagine my surprise in the lodge. We were packed in there waiting for the grandmothers. When the first one arrived I almost doubled over from shock. Well, it was either that, or the intense heat." She smiled at Amy and Brittany. "I was glad it was dark so no one could see the initial confusion on my face."

23

Kara turned toward Amy and Brittany. "It was a rock."

"What?"

"Yes, you heard me correctly. The grandmothers are the rocks. They arrive on this wooden slab placed in the open doorway. We welcomed each one as they appeared. They were pushed one by one into an earthen pit in the middle of the lodge."

"So there were never real grandmothers?" Brittany wondered.

"No, the spirits of the grandmothers were called in to help us in the lodge. As you know, the original Indigenous society here in North America valued women. Many tribes and bands were matriarchal. That meant women ruled the family and the grandmother was respected, as all Elders should be.

You need to understand, the sweat lodge is there for women to bond with Mother Earth. While a woman experiences the wonder of the sweat we all exist on this earth because of our mother and grandmother."

Kara nodded. "Women give birth. Therefore, they are linked with the Creator. None of us would exist without a mother or grandmother. That's why the earth is referred to as Mother Earth and the rocks for the sweat lodge are called grandmothers."

"Wow, fascinating, tell us more," Amy urged.

"The grandmothers had been heated for hours before they came into the lodge. They glowed from the intense heat. We received four of them first. Another surprise was the bulk of the grandmothers. They were mammoth, the size I would imagine dinosaur eggs to be. I had expected them to be the size of coals you use in a briquette fireplace."

"Yes, I would have thought the same," Amy agreed.

Bird of Paradise Drums Beating

"I drew my breath in, amazed when the first two arrived. They were so large and burned steadily. Flames shot out blue, white, a little red. They'd put the rocks in a fire then piled huge amounts of wood on it hours before."

"Why did you receive four rocks? I thought you said you were told sixteen grandmothers would join you?" Brittany wondered.

"Yes, we had four initially though. Since we sweated four times, the rocks were added four at a time until we had sixteen in total. Did you know the number four is significant? For many First Nations cultures, I'm told."

"Ah."

"There you go again," Kara quipped. "Mary Jane explained the meaning of the number four. She spoke of the four great winds and our need for body, mind, spirit and emotion to embrace our surroundings. Gifts given to the earth are often in fours. If you think of it, the number four is all around us."

"You're right, like the four directions," Amy added eagerly.

"Exactly. Mary Jane explained the teachings in a manner that captivated my interest. I knew what she meant yet hadn't thought of it before in those terms."

"What do you mean?"

"Well, take the elements for instance. There's fire, water, earth and air. I know that, but never paid attention to how there are four of them. Mary Jane spoke of the need for fire. Imagine what our life would have been like without it? It represents heat and was given to us so we could survive. Fire can mean the difference between life and death."

"The elements are explained a lot in pop culture," Brittany remarked as she glanced up from her notes.

"How do you mean?" Amy wondered.

"Well, they're in comics, graphic novels, board games, video games, on TV shows and pretty much in anything that involves fantasy."

"Hmm," Kara murmured. "That's interesting. Now back to the topic, I must say, I was fascinated by my immersion in the First Nations culture. I always meant to do more research on the specific bands. I was touched by my sweat lodge experience and I'd like to be involved in further teachings. I'd forgotten until now though how enthralled I was by the opportunity."

Eager to learn more Amy cleared her throat. "Kara, you mentioned the four elements. Were you going to expand on them? I realize from Brittany's comments she's probably pretty familiar with them. I'd like to hear more though."

"Of course, it's logical when you think it through. The teachings I mean. Water represents life itself. Everything needs water to survive, plants, animals, insects, people. So we need to treat water like the precious resource it is.

The earth is important as well. We need the land to have somewhere to live. The earth, or land, represents our security. It gives us a sense of place. Of course the wind, or air, is absolutely necessary to our survival. We need to be able to breath or we die."

"It sounds like all the elements are of equal importance," Amy noted.

"Yes, without any one of them nothing can survive. It's not just us. We're but one of the creatures who depends on the elements. That's another thing the teachings show us."

"What do you mean?"

"Everything that lives on this earth is of equal importance. Humans are known as two-legged. There are animals, they're known as four-legged. There are also winged ones. Those are the birds. Then there are the aquatics. That includes fish and other aquatic animals that like to live in the water like beaver and muskrat.

So, to take it a step further the two-legged and four-legged are responsible for taking care of the land. The winged ones watch the sky while the aquatics take care of the water."

"That covers all the bases."

Bird of Paradise Drums Beating

"Yes, it does, doesn't it?" Kara grinned. "It's simple, yet we forget these basic truths. It seems children learn this easier than adults. We tend to get bogged down in details while the little ones just open their ears and listen. I bet if I asked a six year old to come up with ways to use the number four in nature, they'd have this big list. It would include the parts of a plant, seasons and directions. Who knows what else they'd come up with?"

Kara laughed.

"The number four and elements were used in the *'Harry Potter'* books and movies," Brittany noted.

"Yes, remind us how Brittany," Amy urged.

"Well at *'Hogwarts'*, that was the *'School of Witchcraft and Wizardry'*," Brittany explained as she turned to include Kara, "There were four houses."

"Ah yes, I vaguely remember this," Kara admitted. "You may tell us more Brittany."

"Well, let me see if I can recall the names and elements. I might mix them up but hopefully not." Brittany scrunched up her face, deep in thought. "There's Gryffinder and the element associated with that house is fire. I know that one since Harry Potter was in that house. For sure Slytherin was water. That's an easy one since the troublemakers were always in Slytherin. They always competed with Gryffinder." Brittany gave an emphatic nod. "I think Hufflepuff was earth and Ravenclaw must have been air. Yup, that's it for sure."

Brittany grinned. "Like I said, movies, books, fantasy, they almost always include the elements."

"Yes, that's interesting how youth know these things more than people my age," Amy noted. "I guess we need to embrace our innocence more. If we concentrate on the basics, like the elements then we can figure out the bigger issues from there."

"Yes, that's why the grandmothers were at the sweat," Kara agreed. "They were there to teach us of the need for respect, truth and honesty. It's important to respect oneself, others, the land, animals, birds, fish, insects and plants, everything that surrounds us. It was a gratifying moment when I was allowed a glimpse into the First Nations culture."

Amy was touched by Kara's explanation. "What happened next in the sweat lodge?"

"When each grandmother arrived we welcomed it. One of the young girls threw a small amount of tobacco on each one as an offering. We'd also thrown tobacco on the fire before we went in the sweat lodge. Oh, and we were purified before we entered. One of the women smudged us first."

"What's that?" Brittany wondered. "The word you used, smudging."

"I know this," Amy interrupted. "Can I explain it Kara?"

"Sure, go for it."

"When you have a ceremony you always smudge first. The ceremony can be part of a group or private in nature. It's to purify and cleanse. When we're involved in healing in any way a person must be cleansed of bad feelings, thoughts, spirits or negative energy, both in a spiritual and emotional sense. Then positive, pure and good influences can enter the area. People usually use three herbs to smudge, sage, cedar and sweet grass."

Kara nodded. "Yes, it's just as your mother said Brittany. This woman had the herbs burning in a small bowl. She had a feather and as each of us lined up to enter the sweat she lightly passed the smoke over each one of us. Some people used their hands to cleanse more areas of their body."

"Have you smudged before mom?"

"Yes, I have. When I've attended ceremonies and some workshops I've gone to have smudging as an option. It's never forced upon people."

"Yes," Kara noted. "From what I understand, nothing is done unless an individual is open to it. Honour and respect are of the utmost importance. In the sweat for instance they didn't put much tobacco on each grandmother. So it only produced a faint smoky smell. The smoke didn't overpower you or anything. I found it pleasant."

Bird of Paradise Drums Beating

"Yes," Amy added. "The herbs and tobacco have never bothered me. People who have allergies or asthma might be affected though. When smudging is done outdoors there's no problem as there's natural ventilation."

Kara laughed. "Yeah, well there wasn't much ventilation in the sweat I was in. It was hot already since there were too many women in the lodge. The heat increased as each rock was pushed into the pit, you could feel the temperature rise."

"Did you feel dizzy?" Brittany wondered.

"No, I was fine. I concentrated on breathing. That seemed to be the key. It helped me out anyway. Did I mention I made it through all four rounds?"

"No, you didn't," Amy noted with a smile.

"Yes, there were less than a dozen of us at the end of the four rounds. Everyone seemed proud of us first timers that made it through the entire ceremony. Before the first round started, a few women left. I imagine they were more cramped than I was. They might have felt dizzy or claustrophobic. I don't know."

"How did they leave? I mean was it a big deal or anything?" Brittany asked.

"No. We were told before we entered we should leave if we felt uncomfortable, too hot, dizzy or nauseous. I thought the women were very supportive and nurturing."

"That's good."

"Yes. It made me more at ease about the experience. Perhaps that's why I was able to go until the end since I knew I could leave any time. There was no shame when someone left the lodge."

"No shame, what an odd way to put it."

"What do you mean by that Amy?"

"Oh, nothing. I was surprised by the word shame, that's all. I assume you meant no one was embarrassed when they left the lodge before the ceremony ended. Is that right?"

Kara gave a slow nod. "Yes. It's hard to explain though. As I mentioned, everyone was proud when we completed the four rounds.

Penny Ross

They were supportive so no one felt bad when they left. That's what I assumed. I never asked any early leave-takers what happened when they exited from the lodge though. I think they felt fine with it. Now that you've brought it up I'm not so sure though."

Kara tapped her cheek. "It's interesting how you look at something from your own perspective. Then one makes assumptions based on their experience. What each of us took from the day was personal. I can only speak for myself yet I've made blanket statements about how others felt. I shouldn't have mentioned shame and embarrassment since I didn't come across it. Yet, I spoke as if I knew about it. Interesting how our mind works."

Amy liked to hear Kara's positive comments about her First Nations experience. She flashed a wide smile.

"When the grandmothers arrived, after the tobacco offering, they were splashed with water, almost as if they were given a drink. I felt the heat rise up. It went right through me. It was so intense. I felt warmed throughout, to my very core. The sensation made me feel almost as if the grandmothers had given me a hug." Kara hugged her arms as if reliving the moment.

"I felt loved and secure in their patience. It was a tender feeling. The entire lodge seemed filled with affection. Almost as if we were protected, safe, like we were in our mother's womb."

Kara turned away, slightly embarrassed.

Amy reached out to touch Kara's arm for reassurance.

Kara cleared her throat then continued, "Mary Jane talked a lot about how we shouldn't judge others or interfere in the lives of people we know. Some of the women mentioned having a hard time accepting the path their adult children had taken.

Mary Jane was adamant about letting others choose their own journey, to not meddle in their affairs. She said Creator accepts everyone even if they do drugs, are alcoholics or prostitutes. It doesn't matter since we are all children of Creator and regarded as equals. Mary Jane felt we should remember this and not judge others for their actions. We should accept and tolerate differences."

Kara smiled. "I was fascinated by Mary Jane's teachings. I especially enjoyed the discussion about recognition. Of particular meaning to me was when she spoke of how each person is at a distinct stage in life. Mary Jane spoke of how we need to recognize and acknowledge this reality.

I've mentioned your journey of self-discovery a few times Amy. It's important for you to know you're not alone. We're all on a journey and we're at different stages. Many people have barely begun to discover themselves. Others have advanced to a higher level on the path of understanding. It has to do with spirituality and what one believes in."

Amy was surprised when Kara reached out to briefly brush her fingers across Amy's arm. It was the first time Kara had voluntarily touched her.

"I can't tell you what your journey will be like nor can you relate to mine. That's because we're all individuals. We connect to experiences in distinctive ways. Embrace your gifts and be open to knowledge. Remember that balance is the key."

Kara flashed Amy a warm smile.

"I think much of what Mary Jane said relates to self confidence, acceptance and the level of consciousness each person has of themselves. Some people are happy to be who they are. They appreciate the stage they've entered in life. Then there are others that have never been content. Serenity is a state many people search for yet can never achieve. Don't underestimate it."

Amy nodded.

"People who are lost search endlessly for something. Yet they don't even know what it is they're looking for. It's easy to lose your way when you don't know where you're going. We all have choices and can go down a variety of paths on our journey. It seems the best way to achieve satisfaction is by recognizing there will be bumps and detours along the way. We need to allow ourselves some latitude on our journey.

If we learn to be less hard on ourselves, perhaps it becomes easier to let others choose their way. Tolerance, patience, compassion, empathy and love are traits we should try to nurture."

Kara laughed. She ran her fingers through her hair then tossed it back off her shoulders. "Listen to me, I sound like I should be up on a soapbox preaching to my followers. I didn't mean to give you a lecture yet I just passed out free advice. I guess it's easy to fall into the trap of giving one's opinion under the guise of information sharing. I haven't let either of you get a word in edgewise."

"That's OK, it was fascinating. I didn't find your story preachy at all. I must say I'm star struck by your words of wisdom. I'd like to attend a women's gathering and a sweat lodge. I love to hear about the teachings."

"Yeah," Brittany added. "It sounds like you had a memorable experience. I was mesmerized like my mom for most of your story. In fact I forgot to take notes for part of it. I think I'll remember what you said but we might have to review this area. That's OK though since I'm pretty sure mom and I will want to hear about this again."

Amy agreed. "Thank you for sharing your personal observations with us. We'd love to hear more."

"You're welcome." Kara gave Brittany a warm smile then reached her hand out to briefly clasp Amy's hand.

Amy was touched by the gesture. Their relationship had moved to another stage.

24

"You know, it's easy to get caught up in other people's lives as Mary Jane mentioned," Amy noted. "Humans have a natural tendency to give advice. Discussions about others often center on what we'd do if we were in their shoes. We think it's easy to live another person's life and we could do better. I wonder why we have that inclination."

Amy nodded toward Kara, interested in her opinion.

"Perhaps we don't want to look within ourselves and deal with our own issues Amy. It's easier to forestall our journey when we pretend to deal with the inadequacies of others. It shifts the attention away from us."

"You're right Kara. Another thing about human nature is we want to look better than others. If we think other people are inadequate, our defects aren't so predominant. Unfortunately, we can become shallow, self-centered and arrogant as a result. Those aren't desirable traits." Amy made a face.

Kara laughed at Amy's expression. "No, being human isn't all it's cracked up to be is it? That's why I especially liked Mary Jane's final message. She focused on tolerance, patience, compassion, empathy, love and honesty as traits we should try to nurture. Those are positive characteristics. If we work towards them on our personal journey we can accomplish a great deal."

"Sort of liking reaching a Zen-like state."

"Yes, Buddha is another form of teaching and enlightenment. Remember? We spoke of it the other day."

"As yes, the four virtues, what were they?"

"They are loving-kindness, compassion, sympathetic joy and equanimity. Admirable qualities, don't you think?"

Penny Ross

"Just a sec," Brittany interrupted. "Can you repeat those virtues again? I think I missed one last time."

"Sure." Kara listed the qualities for Brittany's notes. "I think the teachings are similar. It doesn't matter what religion one is or what form of spirituality one follows. Accuracy in terms isn't the essential point. It's important to remember positive traits are desirable. We need to overcome hatred, greed and ignorance. Then we follow the light as compared to fumbling aimlessly in the dark. Of course, light is good and dark is bad. Conversely, some people label it good and evil. It's all about the description."

Kara chuckled.

"Yeah, I got that part," Amy said as her and Brittany joined in Kara's laughter.

Kara turned to Amy. "I need to talk to my husband Morey for a few minutes. Do you want to come to the other part of the house or stay here?"

"I'll stay here. I can rest my eyes for a while."

"Are you tired?"

Amy grinned. "Well, it's always pleasant to have a little nap. Makes me feel decadent."

"How about you Brittany?"

"I'm fine here. It will give me a chance to catch up on my notes."

"I'll get Carl to bring us a snack when I get back."

"Sounds great, see you soon."

Amy must have dozed off for she awoke to hear Kara's voice.

"I'm back. Did you miss me?"

Amy shook her head. She hadn't realized how deeply Kara's story about the sweat lodge had touched her. She'd dreamt just now, a vivid, realistic vision that stayed with her upon waking.

Amy turned to Kara, her expression eager. "I have to share this dream I just had. It was so real."

"Carl is bringing our snack. Would you like a cup of coffee?" Kara pointed at the coffee urn beside her.

Bird of Paradise Drums Beating

"I'd love one." Amy watched Kara sink into the chair beside her.

"I'll pass," Brittany said.

"I told Carl to bring you iced tea since I know you like it."

Brittany smiled her thanks then bent over her notebook.

"I see you're brimming with news. Why don't you share your dream before you burst?"

"It's more like a vision. It was so lifelike. I felt as if I took part in a sweat like you described."

"Hmm, interesting, go on."

"While I gazed into the fire and the smoke filtered lazily upward, the lodge was heated to an unbearable degree. That's when I saw my grandma's face before me. I closed my eyes to further appreciate the image of my loving, wise grandmother stirred from ancient memories. Well, not ancient, less than a century. In reality it was less than thirty years ago. I'm practicing my storytelling. How am I doing?"

Amy laughed, slightly embarrassed.

Kara gave her an indulgent smile. "Continue."

"I saw myself when I was eighteen. I was away at university but happened to be home for the holidays. I was at the kitchen table and it was suppertime."

"Wait." Kara put up her hand like a policeman about to stop traffic. "I'm confused. Were you in a sweat lodge or at home in your kitchen? Where was your grandmother? Your story has no logic Amy. You'll have to work on that."

"Yeah mom, embellishment is fine but the story has to be told in sequence or it loses all credibility."

"I know. It sounds strange," Amy apologized. "First, I was in the sweat lodge. I experienced what you described to us earlier."

"Uh huh," Kara deadpanned.

"Then I saw my grandmother's face. She was about eighty years old so I would have been around eighteen."

"OK, I understand."

"That's better mom. I can write this down in order. Now it makes sense."

"Right, so next I watched a scene unfold when I was eighteen between my grandma and I. My body was still in the sweat lodge though."

"Ah, now I see. Like a flashback," Kara suggested.

"I guess. I've never experienced anything like it before. Perhaps that's a flashback. It's strange, the message grandma passed to me is clear. Yet I don't remember it from when I was eighteen."

"Perhaps it held no significance for you then." Reaching for the coffee urn Kara refilled their mugs.

"Could be." Amy paused to take a sip of coffee.

Carl arrived with their snack. They took a moment to fill up their plates.

"What happened next?" Kara asked.

"We ate supper. My mother brought dessert to the table. It was raisin pie."

Amy stared off in the distance as if watching the scene in her mind.

"That's it? This is a boring story, mom."

Amy stirred. "Oh, no, sorry, I was thinking, that's all."

"Do you want to continue?" Kara gave her a slight frown.

"Yes, sure, of course. It seemed so real. I see grandma in my mind's eye and she's so clear. Like I can reach out and touch her."

Amy leaned forward with her hand outstretched. "It's like she's here now listening to my description. Isn't that odd?"

Amy gave a short, nervous chuckle.

"No. If you believe your grandmother is here with you, she could be. Depends how strong your faith is."

Kara raised her eyebrows at Amy's expression.

"So you wouldn't think it odd if I have this feeling often?"

"No, I wouldn't. You can tell me anything Amy. After what I've lived through, nothing shocks me. Spirits and ghosts are a comfort to those of us that believe in them. Of course, I'm only reassured when they're friendly, kind and supportive.

Bird of Paradise Drums Beating

When ghosts are in pain, grieving, confused or lost they can be disconcerting. Then I'd rather not be aware of their presence. That's just me though. I'm sure people have their own level of comfort. Fortunately, I haven't dealt with ghosts who are in pain or disgruntled. Not yet anyway," Kara quipped.

Amy smiled then took a deep breath. "I feel better sharing this," she confessed. "It's not a subject I've felt comfortable broaching with just anyone."

"Mom, what about me, I could have handled it," Brittany interrupted.

"Thanks honey, I'll know that now."

"It's good you feel at ease. Do you want to continue with your dream or talk about your grandmother's spirit?"

"I'll finish the dream first. Her message might pose more questions and I'm eager to get your opinion."

"Sounds good," Kara agreed.

"I mentioned the raisin pie we had for dessert. It seemed to be the catalyst that set grandma off. It was like an omen, heralding bad news. It opened the dams of her unhappiness as her tears poured forth. There was so much grief, and all because of the damn raisin pie."

"You've lost me again," Kara interrupted. "I hate to be critical but what's with all the melodrama when you mention your grandmother. Must you utter words like omen, dams of unhappiness, tears pouring forth? Isn't that a bit much?"

Amy laughed. "I guess my stories leave something to be desired. My creative juices overflow."

"Like your grandmother's tears perhaps," Kara noted dryly.

"Yeah, maybe," Amy admitted, not in the least put out by Kara's sarcasm. "I have a reason for being overdramatic though."

"Uh huh, we're listening."

"My grandpa had just died in December. This was grandma's first visit to our house following his death. Raisin pie was grandpa's favourite dessert. Mom didn't think of that when she served it, so grandma was emotional about the pie."

Kara nodded.

"Grandma got up clumsily from the table, hurriedly wiping her eyes. She dried them with the apron tied at her waist. Grandma always wore an apron, with flowers on them. I think she liked to sew them herself. It seems to me grandmas love to sew, knit, crochet, mend clothes and bake cookies. I can bake cookies with the best of them but am sadly lacking in the other categories. Wonder what kind of grandma I'll make?"

Kara raised her brows at Amy then frowned.

Amy was quick to continue before Kara or Brittany could comment. "Sorry, I've digressed again. Grandma walked upstairs to her room, there was no sound, as if her feet barely tread on the carpet. Absolute stillness greeted her retreat."

"You're doing it again," Kara warned.

"Oh, sorry, didn't mean to embellish. Where was I?"

Kara drummed her fingers on the arm of her chair.

"Your grandmother went upstairs to her bedroom," Brittany read aloud.

"Hmm yes." Amy's voice was dreamy. She sounded far away as if in a trance. "My parents sent me upstairs. Always the peacemaker, that's me. As I climbed the stairs I got an image in my head that refused to budge. It was a picture of grandma sitting on the bed nurturing her sorrow. She slowly rocked with arms crossed in front of her while tears rolled down her cheeks. I stood outside her door for a long time, reluctant to intrude. I sensed she needed me though. With a hesitant knock, I inched the door open then slipped inside.

Grandma looked the same as the image in my mind. I stopped on the threshold, loath to enter her domain of sorrow. When grandma focused her teary eyes on me, I hurried to her side. I felt her grief. It coursed over me while I lovingly embraced her. We rocked together, silent, while tears flowed from our eyes. My poor grandma."

Amy broke down. Tears ran down her face while she gazed sightlessly past Kara and Brittany at something only she could see.

Kara got up then brought back a box of tissues.

Bird of Paradise Drums Beating

"Thanks." Amy whimpered as she reached for a tissue.

After wiping her face then blowing her nose, Amy appeared better. Kara waited patiently for Amy to get herself under control.

Brittany put her notebook down, stood then gathered her mother in for a hug. "Better," she whispered a few minutes later.

"Yes," Amy whispered back. "Thanks honey."

"I assume there's more," Kara noted.

"Mm, hmm. The bed we sat on and the sweat lodge melded together after that. I saw grandma's face in the dying embers of rocks in the lodge. Her face was clear. I stared into the darkness, rocking, chanting and shaking my rattle. I heard drums beat in the background. With wide eyes I gazed about, anxious. I felt empathy and fellowship with my grandma. It was true emotion, then and now, past and present, joined as one."

Amy smiled. "I heard her voice, her sweet voice as she spoke to me. She felt my compassion, at eighteen and now, in this time and place. Grandma told me I had bonded with Earth Mother. I was connected through time to grandma and all my relations."

Amy brushed her hair from her face. "Grandma was there beside me. She helped recall memories I didn't know I had. She reminded me of the words she'd confided that day long ago when I was eighteen and we rocked together in her room.

Grandma had faith in me. She knew I'd know what to do. Her words were branded into my soul. They've ached to fly out, here, forever, over a lifetime. I just had to remember them," Amy whispered. "Now, I have."

Amy stared ahead, sightless. She was in another time and place, with her grandma, where memories linger.

"It was the pain," Amy whispered softly.

Kara and Brittany leaned forward to hear Amy's words.

"The pain is unbearable," grandma murmured. *"My grief overwhelms me. I am so alone. The pain is here."* Grandma pointed to her bosom. *"Here,"* her heart, *"and here,"* her forehead. *"It surrounds me like a shroud to be worn. It never goes away. It will stay with me forever."*

"Those were the words of my grandmother." Amy shook her head. "I'll never forget them." Amy moaned, as if coming out of a trance.

"I remember my grandmother's sigh, aching and lonely. I couldn't sooth her that evening, words empty and hollow to my ears. I hugged grandma and we were quiet. I was content to share her sadness as it drifted then lingered in the room. I hoped to ease her pain with my loving presence. I embraced her throughout the long night. When she spoke, I listened. It was all I could do."

Amy bowed her head as she sat, motionless.

Kara rose then left Amy alone to her thoughts.

Brittany was quiet, careful not to make a sound as she caught up on her notes.

Sometime later, Kara returned.

The room was silent. Amy gazed out the window while Brittany wrote.

Kara sat down. "Do you want to talk about it?"

Amy silently eyed her new friend. "Yes. I wish my grandma was here, right now," Amy blurted. "She could have told me about the pain. I have many questions, yet no answers. Memories I have linger like sticky cobwebs, fragile and adrift on the breeze. They confuse me. I turn, in one direction then another. It's as if her pain has been resurrected. I know we need to address it before moving on."

Amy shrugged. "I can't figure out whether my grandmother's pain is tied to yours. When I met you on the path I felt your pain, the physical intensity. Now I feel the pain of my grandmother."

Amy bit her lip. "Is there significance between your pain and my grandmother's? Kara, if you know anything please tell me." Amy held her hand out to Kara.

Kara sighed then glanced down at Amy's hand. Reaching forward, she grasped it within her own. "Yes, it's time to answer your questions. I don't know if you'll feel better about this, but certain items may become clear."

25

Kara gazed deep into Amy's eyes.

"What I'm going to tell you reaches beyond centuries. It grasps women roughly while they blindly walk among the masses, hoping to avoid that which is unavoidable. We've all felt it, and by we, I mean women. Pain is part of life. It includes the physical, mental, spiritual and emotional. What you felt the other day was a magnification of pain women have experienced throughout the centuries."

"Is that why it was so intense?"

"Yes."

"I heard *'what about the pain,'* Brittany piped in. When you passed me on the path the first time, as the bird," she added. She returned back to her notes.

"Of course you did. That's why I asked your mother to invite you to our sessions."

Brittany nodded.

It seemed the matter had been settled to Brittany's satisfaction. Amy wished she could be as relaxed. "I had a nightmare after I met you," Amy whispered. "Women tore at my clothing. They implored me to heal their pain. I felt their anguish."

"Tell me Amy. Have you ever experienced pain on a daily basis?" Kara released Amy's hand from within her grasp.

Amy placed her hands in her lap. She sensed her reply should be well thought out. Now was not the time to be flippant about the fleeting pain of a temporary headache.

"I broke my leg skiing. When I had my wisdom teeth out, all four at once, I thought my head would burst from throbbing. I had many painkillers both times though, so that deadened the pain. I've experienced the pain of childbirth.

You know, I've never lived with pain on a constant basis though. Everything has been short-term. I've never been abused nor had anything violent happen to me. No chronic diseases or life altering, heart-wrenching decisions touch wood." Amy knocked on the table beside her.

Kara raised her eyebrows at the action.

"I've been blessed."

"Indeed, you have. You know women have a higher threshold of pain tolerance than men. We can endure a great deal." Kara smiled as she added, "Perhaps that's why God decided women were more suited for childbirth."

Amy laughed. "Yeah, think of the jokes men make about childbirth. They have no idea."

"That's true. Pain can be described in a manner of ways. People relate to the word pain. We've all had a headache, earache, sore tooth, sprained ankle or infection at one time or another. When it comes down to it though, pain is personal. At the end of the day, you're alone with your pain. It may be intense or slight. The pain I refer to eclipses these minor nuisances."

Amy leaned forward, intent on Kara's words.

"When people live with daily pain be it physical, mental or emotional their outlook on life changes. They may become more optimistic if their spirit hasn't been broken. That is, if they have the strength to go that extra mile. Or, they may sink into depression and despair, pessimistic and beyond the reach of a kind word or gesture. Have you met people who can be described by those polar opposites?"

"Yes," Amy whispered.

"Of course, most people don't gravitate toward one extreme or the other. They often lean towards a single inclination, yet have their good and bad days."

Amy nodded. A childhood friend had come to mind out of the blue. Amy hadn't thought of her in ages. Her friend, Trisha, had chronic pain. Amy was ashamed to admit she didn't know what disease Trisha had, something to do with her muscles or joints.

Bird of Paradise Drums Beating

Amy recalled Trisha's strength. Determined to live each day to the fullest it seemed Trisha knew her days were numbered. Perhaps she wanted to fill every one to the brim until they overflowed with positive outcomes and happy moments.

Trisha's energy level had been erratic. Trisha would bounce around, oblivious to the constant ache of her limbs. She played games with Amy and the other neighbourhood children at a frantic pace. Some days though, Trisha would be unable to leave her bed.

Amy and the other kids had been puzzled by Trisha's behaviour. To this day, Amy wondered how Trisha maintained a vigorous pace when her illness should have minimized her activity. Amy made a mental note to call Trisha. A visit was in order.

Aloud, Amy said, "I had a friend who lived with chronic pain. It was part of her daily reality. She never seemed down though. I don't remember Trisha ever complained or bemoaned the fact her health was bad."

"Did she make allowances that you noticed?"

"Like what?"

"Well, conserve her energy for one. Take breaks from activity so she didn't get fatigued as easily."

"No, she was the opposite. Her energy was boundless. She crashed and burned some days though. She often couldn't get out of bed to play with the neighbourhood kids. Her pace seemed frantic at times. It was as if she were afraid to stop or take a break. Almost as if she thought it was the last time she'd play that game or eat the disgusting candy we bought."

Amy smiled. "I'm going to phone and see how things are going."

"Yes, you do that," Kara urged.

"You know people who experience pain as a daily reality react differently to everyday occurrences."

"Uh, huh," Amy murmured, still thinking of Trisha.

"The physical adjustments and emotional loss people experience in their present state, affect their ability to deal with current relationships and life overall."

"What do you mean?"

"Well, think about it. What's worse than pain that never ends? A person must admit their agony and suffering is never going to let up for more than brief, fleeting moments. Can they bear to think of another forty, fifty or sixty years of grief? That's why people who experience pain at a level beyond comprehension have a high tolerance level."

Kara leaned toward Amy. "People with a positive outlook find it easier to accept the inevitable. Their reality is different from the average person's. They're more open-minded, flexible and charitable. Why worry about little problems? Don't sweat the small stuff is a healthy attitude when you think about it."

"You're right. I've never thought about it that way before." Amy paused. "So, do you think people who experience constant pain live in their own world or are they grounded in reality?"

"Hmm." Kara stroked her chin. "Maybe a little bit of both. I guess it would depend on your situation. For instance, if you lose a child, you would be beyond grief. The pain would be intolerable if you let it penetrate your consciousness. Therefore, you live in the past and let pleasant memories carry you over your initial sorrow.

Who knows how long a person would avoid the reality of the situation? I'd guess as long as they had to. Just to maintain some level of sanity. Otherwise their sadness might push them over the edge into that chasm of madness. I think many people teeter on the brink of insanity. It would follow that a major occurrence like the death of one's child could shove you into that abyss."

Kara raised her finger in the air as if to emphasize her next point. "What about the woman who lives in mortal fear of their spouse? Abuse plays havoc with one's mind. Not to mention the damage it does to your physical, emotional and spiritual being. Then there are people who have a life threatening disease. What if you were told

Bird of Paradise Drums Beating

you had anywhere from one week to a year to live? How would you spend your time?"

Kara paused. "Do you think you'd be grounded in reality? Would it be better to fantasize and pretend you were healthy? To blissfully go about your day, professing everything was all right. It's the way humans deal with things Amy. People, in particular women, have carried the weight of the world on their shoulders for centuries now. We handle difficult situations in our own way.

How we manage pain depends on our personality and attitude towards life. Do we see the glass as half empty or half full? Are people gloom and doom or pleased to greet each day? That's what it comes down to in the end."

"What kind of pain do you experience?" Amy held her breath, on the edge of something, unsure of what.

Kara gave a quick glance toward Amy before her eyes darted away. She paused for an inordinate amount of time, a long, pregnant pause.

While the silence lengthened a great weight descended upon the room. Stifled by the closed air, Amy felt claustrophobic. She gripped her hands, afraid of the silence.

The only sound in the room was the scratching of Brittany's pen. Amy stared, transfixed by the pen. As she watched Brittany write, she marveled at her daughter's ability to maintain an air of calm. Could Brittany sense what was about to happen?

When Kara opened her mouth, words would pour forth. Amy knew they would change her perception, possibly her entire existence. Was she ready for this? Should she warn Brittany?

Torn between the need to protect her child and a curiosity to hear Kara's words, Amy's eyes darted between Brittany and Kara. What to do, what to do?

When Kara broke the stillness Amy released the breath she hadn't realized she'd held in for so long. The room cleared. Amy gulped fresh air, greedily replacing pent up breath with healthy, wholesome refreshment.

Penny Ross

Amy sunk further into her chair, eyes closed tight she shook her head, a silent entreaty to stop the flow of words. Torn between her desire for knowledge and need for self-preservation, Amy held her hand toward Kara, a mute appeal for Kara to stop. Her eyes flashed open as Kara's harsh voice penetrated her mind. It was too late to stop the forward motion.

"Some might call me mad, others delusional. When you refer to people who live in their own world, I'd fall into that category. My world is vast and limitless. I am you, and you are I. I am *She* and *She* is me. I am all women and none. I exist, yet I'm not here."

Kara closed her eyes then flung them open again. "I live in constant pain. I see and feel more than you can ever imagine. My heart aches, for loss I've experienced yet never had the benefit of living. I've suffered for so long it's a part of me. I don't know how to live without the constant ache."

Kara reached over to grab Amy's hand. "When you speak of the pain of your grandmother you refer to the sorrow of women. I feel a kinship with your grandmother. Her loss is my loss. Tears she shed, line my face like raindrops as they fall unseeing down a windowpane.

That's what you felt when you passed me on the pathway Amy." Kara brought Amy's hand up to cover her heart. "The pain never ends. It follows me like a shroud and dogs my footsteps. It cloaks my shadow. My soul has become heavy and cumbersome, anchored down by weight."

Kara released Amy's hand as she closed her eyes then began to massage her temple in a slow, steady manner. "I realize my past and present meld as one. I am no more grounded in this reality than I was in the last. Yet, I continue to exist. I live for the moment, for that's all I have. For me, there is no future and the past is not mine."

Kara flung her eyes open then fixed her steady gaze on Amy.

Brittany scribbled madly in her notebook as if intent to get Kara's words down in their entirety.

"Does that help?" Kara's voice was shaky. "I'm not sure how to be more clear. My situation is not real and therefore indefinable. The vagueness of my answers has become the norm of my days. I don't understand my condition fully. It's hard to describe what I experience. My feelings and emotions are alien to women like you, who are real.

You've seen some of my friends, heard their stories and mine. Our reality is not one people relate to. We are ultimately alone with our pain, thoughts and purpose. When it comes down to it though, that defines the human condition.

So how bad is it?" Kara turned to Amy. "As we've mentioned, it all comes down to perspective and one's ability to live a life of balance. Discovery through awareness while we nurture our hidden potential is of the utmost importance. Of course, it helps if along the way we meet a teacher or mentor who exemplifies positive qualities. In the end though, it's a personal journey. How we choose to live our life and the paths we select are ours and ours alone."

Kara flung her arm out to include Brittany. "That's how it is for normal people," Kara blurted. "You don't know how fortunate you've been. How can you relate to someone like me? How can I make you understand the pain, longing, constant ache and yearning for all that is ordinary? My life is not my own, nor has it ever been. Are you ready to cross the threshold, listen to my tales, delve further? The moment is near Amy, decision time races forward."

Amy gulped, unsure how to respond. Kara was spent. She leaned back heavily in her chair as if the effort of verbalizing her thoughts had taken her last ounce of strength. Drained and haggard Kara closed her eyes as she wearily laid her head against the chair.

Amy looked to Brittany for assistance. Should they do something? Brittany was bent over her notebook writing at a furious rate. Amy was unable to catch her eye, as Brittany never glanced up from her efforts. Amy sighed, at a loss. She hoped Kara wouldn't change into the old woman again.

With bated breath, Amy waited for Kara to transform. When nothing happened she boldly sneered. "I suppose there's supposed to be a moral in all these flowery words you pour forth Kara."

Brittany's head flew up. With wide eyes she made a face at Amy waving her arms for attention. Amy shook her head then mouthed *'Don't worry.'* Annoyed, Brittany scowled then quickly returned to her notes as if loath to get involved.

Amy's taunts penetrated the fog that surrounded Kara.

Kara came alive again. She sat ramrod straight then snarled, "Why yes Amy, how astute of you. Care to elaborate? Shall I explain it further or do you care to take a spin?"

Kara voice dripped pure venom.

Amy nodded as she gave a slight smile, used to Kara's mannerisms. The angry façade didn't bother Amy anymore. Kara's barbs were armour she used to protect herself, a form of deflection. Amy knew Kara didn't like others to get too close, to penetrate her defenses.

"Yes, I think," Amy began, "I think we, all of humankind, are here to live each day to the fullest."

Kara gave a grudging nod.

"The wisest choice we make while we're alive is to live in the present and not dwell on the past. We should challenge ourselves to experience all that is possible. Options vary from one person to the next. It's important to be aware of the simple pleasures in life. After we satisfy our basic needs we can welcome unlimited enjoyment from intense pleasure."

Kara raised her eyebrows as if wondering where Amy's thoughts were headed.

Amy laughed. "Get your mind out of the gutter Kara."

Kara shrugged as she gave Amy a slow, grudging smile.

Brittany glanced up, smiled at her mother then continued to make notes.

"We should rejoice in our ability to engage in relationships where pure, complete happiness is laced with love and kindness," Amy continued. "The rest, sorrow, pain, grief, loneliness, in essence the negative side, is something that comes with the positive. We can't have one without the other. It would be impossible to attain the high points in life without occasionally experiencing moments of despair.

They're a point of comparison. That's what I think your moral was," Amy concluded.

"You've done well, Amy," Kara acknowledged. "Now, I'll tell you how this relates to me. You've touched on it. I am the flip side of happiness, love and ecstasy."

Kara's expression was bold. "That is who I am. I am sorrow, grief, tears and pain. You can't recognize me for I am in disguise. I'm in every woman I've ever wanted to be and more than you can imagine. I've experienced all there is to life, more than I'll ever remember."

Kara looked away. "I am the past, present and future. I'll continue in this respect indefinitely. The flip side of life, you referred to it as negative, needs somewhere to rest." With an aggressive gesture Kara elaborated. "I am but one receptacle. I regret not one moment of my fleeting days through the endless years. I sing forth the joys of what I am as time allows. Originally, I longed to be normal. I admit I dwell on the possibility now and then."

Kara sighed. "Yet, I rise above these human frailties to realize my potential and rejoice in my stature."

Kara's voice rose slightly, as if to emphasize her words. "For I am pain and I'll never cease to exist. That's why I'm different from Moira and Nellie. I'm able to recruit others for our overall purpose. Yet, I've never led my own life like they have. I am similar to the others as we help *Her* to further the cause of women. We must find people to tell our stories to. I alone am pain."

Kara sat back in her seat, spent again.

"Were you always pain?"

Kara surprised Amy with a quick answer.

"What an astute question Amy. I'm pleased to note you've followed my stories. You've digested the information and gleaned it worthwhile." Kara bowed her head toward Amy in a queenly manner.

"In fact, I was what we refer to as the flip side of pain for countless years. It was centuries, if truth be told."

Kara nodded, like a wise old matriarch.

Penny Ross

"Women are their own worst enemy. We proclaim that love, happiness, kindness and joy are what we desire in life. In reality, we surround ourselves with those who spout pessimistic statements. We long to hear stories about the downtrodden toadies."

Kara chuckled. "It's true. Many women are at the height of ecstasy as they bemoan their grief stricken life to dismal cohorts. Who doesn't like to chortle gleefully at the problems of close friends, relatives or neighbours? There are types who derive pleasure by living vicariously through others less well off than they are. Why do women become cynical, bitter and jaded by what they proclaim to have worked toward or dreamt about in their youthful innocence?"

Kara didn't wait for an answer. "I frequently affirmed the belief that enjoyment and delight in a simple surrounding results in happiness. A childlike curiosity pervaded many of my lives."

She shrugged. "Others described me as a person of humour. It's pleasant to be thought of as fun loving, lighthearted and a joy to be around. Pain and sorrow seem far away when you've never been touched by grief or loss." Kara sighed. "Then one day, I couldn't do it anymore. I can't remember the life I led at the time, it was so long ago. I just gave up. The effort was too great."

Kara hunched over then began to cry. "Tears of grief were easier to shed than energy required being optimistic."

Amy watched the tears run down Kara's face. Brittany glanced up, her eyes widened as she watched Kara weep. "When I attempted to be a powerful force as a ruler, or stated women should have the same rights and freedom as men, I was shouted down by those superior to myself." With a furious swipe, Kara brushed her tears away. Anger replaced her sorrow.

"Of course, they were men. Many women who should have supported my efforts were as callous as the men though." Kara narrowed her eyes. "It's hard to maintain high self-esteem when others batter at your emotional door to destroy your sense of worth. After centuries of happiness and joy, when it was suggested I become pain, I embraced the idea wholeheartedly."

Bird of Paradise Drums Beating

Kara laughed. A brittle harsh sound filled the room.

"Who knows? Perhaps I'll be given power or evil for my next portfolio? The possibilities are endless. Of course, I'll have to join the dark side."

Kara grinned. As it turned into a wicked smirk she managed to convey her openness to the idea.

Amy shuddered. Was Kara serious?

"You do realize I'm desperately needed though," Kara whispered in a soft voice. "The women I replace can't handle pain indefinitely. I give them a break while they go to the holding site."

With relief, Amy smiled at Kara's use of the term. Kara must have been kidding around with her dark reference.

"While they're away, *She* helps them come to grips with their pain. They learn how to handle difficult situations. They're able to enhance their life when they return to their body. A positive, serene outlook is needed to ensure longevity.

It's important, as you've no doubt gathered, for these women to return to their rightful place in history. We need them. They must ensure other women have the necessary support and guidance to further women's causes. Women need to champion one another. Brittany, are you getting all of this?" Kara demanded.

Brittany gave a brief nod totally immersed in her notes.

"Perfect. Women need to lessen one another's pain, not increase it. When one takes the weight of the world, figuratively, on one's shoulders, it can only be done for a short time period."

"Kara, you've just reminded me of something," Amy interrupted. "I read about a North American Indian man who was a political activist. One of the things the author said was Indian people take the hurt from other people they care about, into their own body. When they take pain from someone, they help that person heal. That's similar to what you've just described."

"Was this author female?"

"Yes, she was. How did you know?"

"She has wisdom. What she wrote had an impact on you. You've remembered it and are able to pass it on to others. That's a special ability don't you think?"

"Definitely."

"I'm glad something I've done reminds you of people you admire. It makes some of the pain I've experienced worthwhile."

Amy reached out to give Kara a quick hug.

"Thank you," Kara gulped. "Now I've answered your question about pain. What about your other queries, are you still interested?"

Amy nodded.

"I found the drumming you've heard to be an interesting phenomenon. It ties in closely to your life."

"My life, why do you say that?"

"Don't you see it?"

Amy shook her head. She had no idea what Kara meant.

"You need to open your eyes and heart. Let what is there, the necessary part of your soul encompass you fully as you search within. Empty your mind of earthly distractions. Welcome the silence. This is an important part of you. Any other questions?"

"Yes, you've mentioned I might join your merry band of women. You said my moment is near and I'll need to make a decision. I have. I don't want to leave my family." Amy strained forward in her chair, eager to make her point.

"Mom, no, I didn't realize," Brittany began. Her eyes darted to Kara, a panic stricken expression on her face.

Kara was quick to reassure Amy and Brittany. "Your journey will not begin until your natural life has ended. There is no need to worry. It won't be your time for many, many years."

Amy leaned back in her chair.

Brittany jumped up, grabbed her mom then pulled her into a frantic hug. Amy squeezed back.

"I think it's time for me to tell my last story of the day," Kara announced. "It might help clear the clouds from your mind and dispel the fog that surrounds you. Yes, it's time."

Bird of Paradise Drums Beating

Kara stood, went over to the intercom then spoke quietly into it.

Brittany gave her mother a reassuring smile. "Are you OK?" she whispered.

"Yes, just uncertain of where this is going," Amy admitted. "How about you?"

"I'm good. It hasn't been dull has it? We never would have envisioned any of this a few days ago." Brittany made a sweeping motion with her arm to include the entire room.

"Hey, Kara, I know this isn't going to happen for like a gadzillion years, you know with my mom hooking up with your merry band of women."

"Yes," Kara agreed.

"I've got the perfect woman my mom could help out with, you know, for her first assignment."

"Well, that's not exactly how it works Brittany. We don't have our loved ones choose the women we assist."

Brittany huffed. "Kara," she began.

Kara held up her hand. "All right, why don't you give me her name and tell us something about this woman. When the time comes I promise to put in a good word for your mom. How's that sound?"

Brittany flashed a triumphant smile in Kara's direction. "That's fantastic, thanks Kara." She turned to her mother. "I think it would be cool if you could be Laura Secord."

"The chocolate woman?" Kara's voice held a note of disbelief. "That's your suggestion?" She sniffed as if Brittany's choice wasn't worthy of further comment.

Brittany ignored Kara. "Laura Secord was a hero. She saved the British and Canadian forces during the War of 1812. She's a big deal for Canadians. When I heard her story in grade 11 history I thought she was so cool."

"Why don't you tell us about Laura Secord honey?"

"Sure, her name was Laura Ingersoll Secord. She was born in the United States, moved to Upper Canada with her family then married a settler. I think they lived near Niagara, in Ontario. Laura and her husband were loyal to the British Crown.

One night these American officers forced their way into their house and ordered Laura to make them supper. I guess they drank a lot of wine and got all rowdy. They started to talk about their game plan while Laura was nearby. She heard how they wanted to crush the last of the British resistance in the area."

Brittany leaned forward in her chair, elbows bent on knees while she recounted an important part of Canadian history. "Laura washed dishes and listened to these guys boast about a Lieutenant named Fitz...Fitz..." Brittany rubbed her forehead with one hand. "Just a sec, I'll remember his name, it was on the test and I aced it. Hah, FitzGibbon, that's it."

"Great job Brittany," Amy praised.

Brittany nodded. "Thanks. So Laura told her husband she had to go warn this FitzGibbon guy."

"Let me guess, the husband encouraged her to go warn an officer about some attack." Kara shook her head then raised an eyebrow at Brittany.

"Yeah, he did. Her husband was wounded from some battle so he couldn't come with her. Laura took off early the next morning and walked for a real long time, I think it was something like 32 kilometers. It was dangerous too. If the Americans caught her they would have killed her for being a spy. Death by firing squad." Brittany shuddered.

"Laura eventually got close to where this FitzGibbon guy was. She ran into a band of Iroquois. I don't know how she did it, she would have been a mess by then." Brittany shrugged. "Laura managed to get across to the chief it was urgent she get a message to FitzGibbon. One of the Iroquois took her to the British headquarters where she warned FitzGibbon of the attack."

Brittany grinned. "Laura was a hero. The British, along with the Iroquois, captured 500 American soldiers. It was because of Laura

Secord's bravery that the British and Canadian forces were saved during the War of 1812."

"That was a lovely story Brittany. I've heard of Laura Secord but never knew those details. I would love to help women like her one day far in the future when I join Kara and her merry band of women."

"Yes, your tale had merit," Kara acknowledged.

Carl arrived with a blanket, clay bowl and other small containers. He placed them next to Kara, then left.

Brittany forgot about Laura Secord as she leaned forward to view the items. "What's this?"

26

Kara spread out the blanket then sat cross-legged on it. "Come." She motioned for Amy and Brittany to join her.

Amy stood, held her hand out to Brittany then walked over to Kara. She mimicked Kara and crossed her legs on the blanket. Curiosity got the better of her. She leaned toward Kara, eager to see what the containers held.

Brittany followed suit.

"Remember, I mentioned in the late 1800s, I felt or dreamt I was the spirit of a medicine woman. Well, to be specific, I think I represented more of a gathering of medicine women."

Amy and Brittany nodded.

"I want to tell you about the experience I had. More than that though." Kara gazed deep within Amy's eyes. "I want you to join me in the experience."

Amy gasped. "Is that possible?"

"I think so. I've never done it before. I believe we can do it. It simply requires faith. Are you game?"

"Yes," Amy replied eagerly.

"How about you Brittany, do you want to come along for the ride?"

"Sure, I'm up for it."

"Good, let's begin. First we'll smudge. It will purify us."

Brittany nodded as she realized the containers were used for smudging.

"I use this clay bowl." Kara showed Brittany the bowl. "If we were outdoors with a fire we could use a piece of wood as our smudging stick. This is sage." She took some sage from one of the containers.

Bird of Paradise Drums Beating

"I like to sprinkle a little bit of cedar on it. You don't need to add cedar, but I prefer the smell of the two when they blend."

Kara took a piece of cedar and added it to the dried sage.

"Now we light this with a match. When the smoke curls up we use it to smudge."

"You mentioned we smudge to purify ourselves," Brittany observed.

"Yes, we smooth it over our head, eyes and mouth with our hands open." Kara demonstrated the motion as she spoke. "Then over our shoulders, heart and body."

Kara held the smouldering smoke toward Amy then Brittany, who copied Kara's motions.

"We purify our mind, body, spirit and emotion. When we smudge it brings out the positive and makes us more centered. Then we concentrate on our breathing and pray to Creator. Thank Creator for everything you're grateful for. Like your family, home, health." Kara closed her eyes then began to move her lips. She appeared to be praying.

Amy closed her eyes then followed suit. She felt more centered by the experience. Smoke continued to curl around them while they prayed. It was soothing and inspiring at the same time.

Amy thanked Creator then thought of all she was appreciative of. She concentrated on her breathing. She could almost hear the faintness of her heartbeat.

After a few minutes, Kara brought them back to the present.

"All right. Keep your eyes closed. I'll tell you what I experience. Be open and aware of your senses. Let the messages flow through you, unfettered by your mind. Your heart and soul will guide you as we take this journey together.

My insight may reach a high level of intensity. Drift with it and don't be afraid. Be calm, open to the possibility of reaching a high level of understanding. Allow yourselves to be healed, purified, by this experience."

Amy and Brittany nodded.

"Oh, I forgot to mention. You may feel something different from me or be carried along by my thoughts the entire time. I'm not certain how that part will work. If you drift away and gather your own knowledge don't be frightened by it. Be open, and all will be well. Remember, balance is the key. A calm, tolerant, patient attitude will hold you in good stead. Whatever happens, I'll be there. We'll come back together."

Kara smiled while Amy and Brittany gave an eager nod. Then Kara reached for Amy's hand on one side, Brittany's on the other. "Join hands and we will form a circle," she said as they began their journey.

"We're high up near a field of flowers. A stream gurgles nearby and the sun has risen on the horizon. We've smudged and will continue to pray. Hmm, stretch your neck and lean toward the sun. It feels warm, doesn't it?"

"Mm, hmm," Amy and Brittany murmured.

Kara began to chant softly.

Amy prayed to Creator while the soft sounds of nature enveloped her in their embrace.

"Visualize yourself becoming lighter and lighter," Kara directed. "In a moment, you're going to have the sensation of floating out of your body."

Amy immediately felt lighter, as if a load was lifted from her back.

"See the women in the background. They gather herbs and flowers to dry. They've just begun now that the day is new. We'll wander over there in a few minutes."

Amy gave a complacent nod. Her limbs felt loose while her mind was clear of everyday thoughts.

"Think of your ancestors while we're here," Kara urged. "They will help guide and give you strength."

Amy thought of her grandmother and grandfather. She had seen a picture of her great-grandmother once and her image was clear. In her mind's eye she imagined her Cree relations who walked in areas similar to these throughout the centuries. Her Cree people, Amy

Bird of Paradise Drums Beating

realized, were here long ago. Years before the white man came, before ships arrived with people, eager to explore this new world.

One of those ships had carried Amy's Scottish great-great-great grandfather. The Hudson's Bay Company recruited men from the Orkney Islands and Scottish Highlanders since they were hardy survivors of a difficult climate. They were brought to what was then called Rupertsland. They settled in what is now known as the Red River Settlement of Manitoba.

Hugh Ross married a Métis woman named Sarah Short and their children walked this land. Amy's relations had merged, with European and First Nations culture as their center. Amy was proud of her people. The more she learned of her culture and ancestors, the more she wanted to know.

"I wonder what it was like back in the 1800s when Europeans began to spread out in Canada and the States?" Amy mused. "Were Europeans friendly with First Nations? Since First Nations people have an oral tradition there isn't much written from the Aboriginal perspective. It's hard to know what took place.

When I read about the treaties, relations seemed strained much of the time. Of course, it wasn't fair since First Nations people lost their land, livelihood and way of life. I think the original intent was to share everything but something went wrong along the way."

Amy shook her head.

"I hope while we're here you get some idea," Kara commented.

Amy started. "We're not here though, are we? I thought we'd see what was happening, yet it was, I don't know, an illusion or mirage."

"We're sort of here. I'm not sure of the details. Let's concentrate on the moment," Kara suggested.

"All right, sounds good."

"Is there anything specific I should search for? Are we dressed all right?"

Amy glanced down at her clothes then did a double take.

261

"Where did these clothes come from? I wasn't dressed like this before, neither was Brittany, or you."

Kara sighed. "When you arrive in another century you have to adopt the style of clothing and hair so you blend in. Do you think we'd be like everyone else if we came in high top sneakers and shorts? I don't think so. Now quit wailing. You sound like a drama queen. If Moira were here she wouldn't be impressed and neither am I."

Kara stood with hands on hips then glared at Amy.

Amy backed down immediately. Whew, Kara was testy sometimes. The last thing Amy needed on this little jaunt was to antagonize Kara. After all, Kara was their ticket home. Amy wasn't prepared to get lost somewhere in the countryside, back in the late 1800s. She was sure Brittany wouldn't appreciate getting dumped here either.

"Sorry, I was just rattled, that's all," Amy apologized. "Didn't mean to be obnoxious, or what did you call me, a drama queen?"

"Yeah," Kara said laughing.

"Takes one to know one," Amy countered.

"Ooh, that's nasty."

They chuckled at that one.

"Who are those women?" Amy pointed at the group gathering herbs and flowers.

"Some of the local people I imagine. Do you want to go over and meet them?"

"Could we?"

"Let's see."

They strolled toward the group.

The women continued what they were doing, oblivious to the newcomers.

"Should we say something?"

Kara shrugged.

"What beautiful flowers." Amy bent to inspect them closer. "Do you know what kind they are?"

"I haven't got a clue." Kara sounded bored.

"Check out the butterflies," Brittany noted. "It's nice to know we still have the same insects in our century. They like the flowers in this area."

Amy moved closer to the women. She began to imitate their movements then picked a few herbs. Her dress had a little apron and she rolled this over to place the herbs within the folds of the apron, similar to the women. Most of them had little pouches they filled up. They appeared to be made of hide.

Brittany moved to her mother's side then began to copy what Amy did.

Kara ignored them and stared off into the distance.

Amy stole furtive glances at the women nearby. She wondered how to start a conversation. As she got closer, she realized they spoke in their native language. She had no idea what they said. How could she communicate when she didn't know how to speak their language?

Amy sighed, now that was irritating.

Abruptly, the women stopped what they were doing. As one, they turned to gaze past Amy. Although they smiled and wore a welcoming expression, Amy thought they seemed shy and at awe.

She turned to see what had caught their attention.

27

It was a woman.

Not an ordinary woman though.

This one had a presence that rivaled that of a queen or diva. Amy thought Kara could take pointers from her. As she watched the woman approach, Amy made a conscious effort to stand straighter since she had terrible posture. This woman held herself very erect.

The women seemed mesmerized as they watched the newcomer move towards them. Their chatter ceased while they gazed expectantly towards her.

Amy was wildly curious to know who the woman was. With an eagerness she could barely conceal she watched the scene unfold before her.

In her wildest dreams, Amy never would have imagined she would meet the woman who walked sedately toward them.

History books mentioned her name. Her poetry and articles would be recorded for future generations. As an Aboriginal rights advocate she would blaze across Canada nineteen times, celebrating the First Nations point of view. She promoted the dignity and historical importance of First Nations people. As an actress and poet, she delivered ballads and readings on stages across Canada.

She wore a buckskin dress, leggings and a bear claw necklace. Her brown hair was down. It curled gently past her shoulders. On her feet she wore simple moccasins. The outfit seemed out of place here in the wilderness, it was more suited to that of a dance hall or theatre stage. The other women, in contrast, wore unadorned leggings and tunics.

"Who is she?" Amy whispered.

"Do you want to guess or should I tell you?"

Bird of Paradise Drums Beating

"Tell me, tell me quick before she gets closer." Amy grabbed Brittany's hand as if to steady herself.

Kara paused, for dramatic effect it seemed.

"Her name is Pauline Johnson or Tekahionwake. That's her Mohawk name."

Amy gawked. "What?" she squealed. Amy turned to Brittany, wide-eyed. "Have you heard of her?" she whispered.

"Yes, I have," Brittany whispered back. "Wow, totally awesome."

It was all they had time to say before Pauline Johnson arrived beside them.

The women moved closer, creating a little circle around Pauline. Amy, Brittany and Kara stood on the outer perimeter.

Amy and Brittany were spellbound. With mouths slightly open they stared at Pauline.

Amy nervously tucked her hair behind her ears. What luck to arrive here, in this place, at this time, when Pauline Johnson was in attendance.

Was it luck though?

Amy turned to ask Kara, but stopped short at her friends' appearance.

Again, Kara had changed into someone else. This time she was an old First Nations woman with reddish bronze skin, black hair and plenty of wrinkles. If Kara hadn't been standing beside them moments before, Amy never would have believed it was Kara.

Amy gaped, speechless at her friends' metamorphosis.

Kara smiled. Then she nodded at Amy as one would to an underling. She turned abruptly back toward Pauline Johnson then began to address her in a native tongue.

Pauline listened intently for a moment, nodded then spoke in English.

"Honoured Elder, I feel much gratitude for your kind words. Unfortunately, I can understand your language but not speak it. Do you know English?"

Kara shook her head, no.

"I do," Amy blurted out.

All eyes turned to Amy.

"I mean, if I can be of any assistance, I would like to help out," Amy stammered. She felt her face redden from the attention her comment generated. When Brittany squeezed her hand for reassurance Amy gratefully squeezed back.

"You know the language?" Pauline asked.

"Uh, no, I mean, yes, sort of," Amy mumbled.

Kara nodded toward her.

"We'll manage," Amy added.

"Wonderful. I wonder, could you tell the women here I will give a performance tonight at the church? Tickets are fifteen and thirty cents. It's inexpensive since I know people won't have much money. Oh, and what is your name?" Pauline asked kindly.

"Amy Ross," she stammered.

"A pleasure to meet you Amy, I'm Pauline Johnson."

Pauline graciously held her hand out. Amy dropped Brittany's hand then eagerly reached forward to shake Pauline's. She was surprised at how tiny Pauline was. Barely over five feet in height, her stature gave her the appearance of being taller, until one was face to face with her.

Brittany nudged her mother with her shoulder.

"Oh, this is my daughter Brittany."

"That's an interesting name," Pauline commented as she nodded at Brittany.

Brittany turned bright red then curtsied.

"What a charming girl."

Brittany gave a wide, pleased smile then murmured, "Thank you."

Amy turned then whispered to Kara. "Did you understand what Pauline said?"

"Yes, of course," Kara whispered back. "Pretend you're interpreting for another moment. Then I'll tell the other women what you said."

Bird of Paradise Drums Beating

They conversed quietly. Then Kara turned and spoke to the women in their native tongue. They nodded then smiled politely at Pauline.

Pauline turned back to Amy. "Are you related to George Ross?"

"Uh, no, I don't think so."

She raked her brain for the possible date they'd arrived at. Why hadn't Kara been more specific than the late 1800s? Then again, it had to be either late 1880s or early 1890s for Pauline to be touring the country. At least Amy thought those were the dates. Since she'd recently read the book *'Flint & Feather'* about Pauline Johnson the dates were relatively fresh in her mind.

If that was the period, it meant Amy's grandparents hadn't even been born yet. She rapidly calculated where everyone was in her family tree. It seemed safe to mention her great grandfather and great, great grandfather's names.

"My relations are Elzear Ross and Roderick Ross."

"Oh and where are they from?" Pauline inquired in a pleasant tone.

"They live in Manitoba, near Winnipeg, in the Red River Colony."

Amy held her breath. She hoped she'd phrased it correctly.

Pauline nodded. "I loved Winnipeg. I've recently returned from a cross-country trip where I went by train from Ontario to British Columbia. I performed on the way back. The people in Winnipeg gave me standing ovations every evening."

She laughed. "Of course most of the audience was male. They probably hadn't seen a woman on stage before or at least not for a very long time."

"I've read about your performances," Amy raved. "I'm excited to meet you and be able to see one for myself. I never imagined in my wildest dreams I'd have this honour. It's incredible to stand here and talk to you. Your poetry is outstanding. I love it."

"Thank you. Where did you read about me?"

"Uh, I don't know, it was in some newspapers." Amy gave a vague wave of her hand, quick to change the subject before Pauline could ask further questions.

"Is that your costume?"

"Yes, do you like it?"

"It's lovely. Did you make it yourself?"

"No although I added many things to it. I originally bought it from the Hudson's Bay Company in Winnipeg. Then I added these." Pauline touched the rabbit pelts. "It needed more style and decorations so I put these silver brooches I got from my grandmother here."

Pauline laughed. "I also added my father's hunting knife. You know for authenticity." She winked. "I often wear a scarlet blanket over one shoulder. It's too hot out today though. I'll put it on tonight for my performance, that and my other sash."

Pauline made a face. "I don't normally parade around in these clothes to drum up business. I insisted we do some of these shows for the people in the area here though. I knew they wouldn't come if I were dressed in European finery." She shrugged. "So I'm dressed already."

"Was there anything else you wanted me to tell the women here?"

The women had dispersed and gone back to gathering herbs.

"No, I should walk around the rest of the reserve and tell people about the performance tonight. I need to have a good turnout. I usually perform for large crowds and bring in quite a bit of money. My manager doesn't think we'll do very well on the reserves. I don't usually do my own promotion but I want this to work."

Pauline bit her lip.

"How many performances will you give at reserves?"

"Just a few, we do them this week then I'm off to Toronto again."

"Do you mind if I walk with you a bit?"

"That would be wonderful. Perhaps you'd interpret for me and tell the people about my show tonight."

Amy knew a moment of panic. How could she do that?

Bird of Paradise Drums Beating

Out of the blue, Kara appeared at her elbow and nodded with a sage look.

"Yes, my cousin will accompany us and help out. Oh, and my daughter as well," Amy added with a quick glance toward Brittany.

"Oh, this is your cousin. What's her name?"

"Uh, Mabel."

"Hello Mabel, I'm Pauline."

"Does your cousin have a last name?" Pauline inquired with a polite nod.

Darn, thought Amy. Thinking of a first name had been hard enough. Now she needed a last name. Then she had an idea. She'd use her grandma's maiden name. That should work.

"Yes, it's Bellegarde, Mabel Bellegarde."

Kara smiled brightly at Amy when she said the name. Amy noted she was missing two of her front teeth.

"A Bellegarde and a Ross," Pauline mused as they began to walk toward the community. "Those aren't names from around here. What are your people? Where are you from?" Her tone was curious.

"I'm Métis, actually Métis, Cree, Scottish and German. Mabel is from the Cree Nation. She's a Plains Indian. My people are originally from Manitoba and Saskatchewan…."

Amy began to cough uncontrollably. She pretended something was caught in her throat. Pauline thumped her on the back. Amy whispered a thank you then turned away.

Amy hoped the fake coughing fit would hide her mistake. Just as she said the word Saskatchewan she had a flash of her grandparents' birthplace. Saskatchewan was called Northwest Territories until it became the province of Saskatchewan.

Amy knew it wasn't until early in the 1900s when it became Saskatchewan. Her grandparents had been born in 1899 and 1900 and their birthplace had been Northwest Territories. Amy had always thought that was a fascinating fact, that's why it popped into her head.

"You were about to tell me where your people are from?" Pauline reminded her.

"Oh, right, sorry about that back there. As I was about to say, my people are from Manitoba and the Northwest Territories while Mabel's are from the Northwest Territories."

Amy nodded then smiled at Pauline. She sincerely hoped Pauline wouldn't ask for a specific band. If she did, Amy would name her grandma's band. It was Little Black Bear Reserve. She also knew it was part of the File Hills Qu'Appelle Tribal Council located in Saskatchewan, well, Northwest Territories, originally.

Amy began to sweat. She felt the pressure of keeping everything straight. It could be a problem to mention her grandma's birthplace since she hadn't been born yet. She didn't want to get too bogged down in detail or she might fold under the pressure. As if sensing her mother's distress, Brittany moved to her other side then bumped her shoulder.

Amy smiled at her daughter, then mouthed *'Thank you.'* She grasped Brittany's hand in hers for comfort.

Thankfully, Pauline didn't press further.

"How exciting," Pauline gushed. "To meet Métis and Cree women who are from the prairies. I can't believe it."

Amy could hardly hide her surprise. "Huh," was all she managed.

"I've traveled around the country hoping to chance upon Aboriginal people who aren't from Ontario." Pauline leaned closer. "Everyone here is from the Six Nations reserve. I've never encountered authentic Aboriginal people from other areas of Canada, especially from the Plains."

Amy raised her brows. Pauline had just referred to her, Brittany and Mabel, uh, Kara, as authentic Aboriginal people.

Kara gave a toothy grin.

"What are you doing here though? If you're from the Winnipeg area and Northwest Territories you're far away. Where exactly is Mabel from in the Territories? You must not be first cousins," Pauline noted. "Otherwise one of you wouldn't be Métis and one Cree. That's right,

Bird of Paradise Drums Beating

isn't it? Forgive me," she gushed. "I've asked questions while not waiting for answers. I'm excited to talk to you."

Pauline paused, her expression expectant.

Amy gulped. She looked at Kara who smirked. Amy shook her head. Obviously it was up to Amy to come up with a plausible account. Kara had bowed out when she'd pretended she couldn't speak English.

Thanks a lot, Amy thought. She wiped sweat off her brow with her free hand then smeared it on her apron. Brittany gave her a reassuring squeeze but remained quiet.

"Well, Mabel, Brittany and I have come to visit our Ontario relatives."

Kara and Brittany nodded.

It gave Amy encouragement to continue.

"Mabel is my cousin on my grandmother's side of the family. My grandmother is Cree. Mabel's father is my grandmother's brother. So you're right, we're not first cousins, but we're very close."

Amy took a deep breath. There, that should handle the cousin issue, she thought.

"Mabel lives near Regina, in the Qu'Appelle Valley," Amy continued. She purposely left out specifics. "I live north of Winnipeg. Our families visit one another a great deal. Mabel lives on a reserve but I don't."

Pauline nodded. "Was your family involved in the North West Rebellion? Since you're Métis, I mean?"

Amy honestly didn't know. She'd never heard stories of relatives who'd been in the Resistance. Amy knew it was referred to, in present time, as the North West Resistance but couldn't mention that. She glanced at Kara, with wide eyes, beseeching her silently to give Amy a clue.

Kara took pity on Amy then shook her head no.

"No, all Métis people weren't involved in the..." Amy cleared her throat. "North West Rebellion."

"Of course not, how silly of me. If Mabel is Cree, how did I understand her before?"

"Oh, she speaks many languages," Amy was quick to reply. "She's a medicine woman," she confided, "And an Elder."

Pauline gasped. "What good fortune to come upon you. This is too good to be true. I've been trying to figure out more about Aboriginal people in Canada. Then I stumble upon Métis and Cree women right out of the blue."

Pauline held her hand to her breast, overcome by her good fortune.

"What happened?" Amy murmured. "Where did Pauline go?"

Amy blinked, puzzled. She was seated between Kara and Brittany on a blanket on the floor of Kara's conservatory.

Kara was calmly drinking tea.

Brittany was rubbing her eyes as if she'd just woken from a deep sleep.

"Ah, you're back I see. Would you like tea, I just had Carl bring it."

"What do you mean I'm back? When did Carl come? I never noticed him walk by."

"You were," Kara paused, "Not yourself there for a while. Neither of you were." She shrugged. "You should be back to normal now."

Amy glared at Kara. She felt like throttling her. Why was Kara so annoying? Was it time to play guessing games again?

Fortunately, Kara was in a talkative mood.

"Do you want to know what happened?"

"Yes, yes I do."

"You had what would be known as an out-of-body experience."

"What?" Amy shrieked. "How, when, I mean, wait a minute, you never mentioned this before. You said we'd go on a journey together."

Kara shrugged. "It was a journey, of sorts."

Amy frowned.

"Now don't be upset. It wouldn't have been as effective if you'd known it wasn't real. Tell me where you went and we can discuss what you experienced."

"What do you mean, where I went? You were there, right beside me."

Amy turned to Brittany. "You were there too Brit. Tell me you remember."

"Well, you know mom, everything seems a bit fuzzy. I feel like I was asleep, or drugged maybe." Brittany glared at Kara as she mentioned being drugged.

Kara laughed. "I did not drug anyone Brittany." She turned to Amy. "To answer your question, no, I wasn't right beside you. Neither was Brittany. You might have projected someone who looked like me and Brittany, into your experience. Trust me, I wasn't there. I would have known."

"I wasn't there either mom," Brittany admitted as she held her hands out in apology.

"So I was there by myself."

Kara and Brittany nodded.

Brittany leaned over, grabbed her notebook and pen then started a new page.

"Yes, I helped you progress through various states of consciousness. When I sensed you'd transported to another place I knew you'd reached a higher level. It would allow you to experience that which was important to you."

"So I wasn't in the late 1800s?"

Kara shook her head. "Afraid not, but your experience was worthwhile. The content is what we want to explore. An out-of-body experience is similar to a lucid dream in many ways. It's more spiritual and occurs when you're awake. Tell us about it and we can interpret what it meant. We'll look at what you came across and your perceptions. Then we can determine how important it was to you."

Amy nodded.

"Was your experience vivid?"

"Yes, very, I thought I was there. Everything was so clear. The First Nations women were relaxed while they gathered herbs. They greeted Pauline in a quiet way when she arrived. Pauline seemed eager to talk to me. I guess in retrospect that was odd. After all, she was a stranger and famous, yet she befriended me immediately. Plus, she used the phrase Aboriginal people a lot and that wouldn't have been a common word back then."

"What Pauline was this?" Kara inquired, her tone polite.

"Why, Pauline Johnson of course. Don't you remember? Oh, right, you claim you weren't there." Amy waved her hand as if she doubted Kara's word.

"That's because I wasn't."

"Mm hmm," Amy murmured, skeptical.

"Neither was I," Brittany confirmed. "I would have remembered Pauline Johnson. Wow mom, you're so lucky. What was she like?"

"Pauline was a gracious, charming woman. She's not as tall as I thought she'd be. We had this long conversation as I interpreted for her. Well, I imitated an interpreter. Kara was a Cree woman so she's the one who told the other First Nations women what Pauline said. Pauline spoke English and I pretended to tell Kara what she said."

Kara made a face. "Your stories certainly leave something to be desired Amy. I find you ramble so." She shook her head. "Let's get back to the matter at hand shall we? The experience you had included First Nations women and a famous Aboriginal woman who was a poet, activist and actress."

"Yes, and Pauline wanted to know about my relations. She was excited when I mentioned we were Métis and you were Cree. She hadn't met any Aboriginal people from the prairies. Everyone she knew was from Ontario."

Kara arched her brows.

"Well, I had to say you were something. You were dressed like an older First Nations woman. You turned into one. I mean, you had some sort of physical metamorphosis and then you spoke Cree. No, it wasn't Cree. It was some native language Pauline understood."

Bird of Paradise Drums Beating

Amy frowned. "Wait, now I remember. You were a medicine woman and an Elder, so you knew many languages."

Kara smiled then bowed her head as if acknowledging a tribute.

"She called us authentic Aboriginal people." Amy smiled at the memory. "Pauline was particularly enthusiastic since we were from the prairies."

Kara nodded, "Ah, yes, she would have liked that. Nice touch Amy."

"You know, it was odd how enthralled she seemed to meet us." Amy noted. "In a book I read about her, it said she traveled across Canada many times. She highlighted Aboriginal issues in her performances. So why was it a big deal to meet three native women? Shouldn't she have met many Aboriginal women in her travels?"

Kara shrugged. "I have no idea."

"I wonder if Pauline was so enthusiastic with everyone she met. She made me feel special. I could have talked to her for ages." Amy grinned. "I wanted to exchange ideas and hear more about her background. It would have been great to hear what it was like for a woman to travel extensively back in the late 1800s. I can't believe I came back here so abruptly. We were right in the middle of a conversation." Amy frowned as she shook her head.

"Perhaps you can go back there one day."

"Next time, take me with you mom."

"That would be great." Amy patted Brittany's arm. In a musing tone she added, "You know Pauline made me realize a few things."

Kara sat up straighter. "She did. Like what?"

"Well, for one, she seemed uncertain about her Aboriginal identity. That makes me feel better since I've been mystified about mine. She was eager to hear about what it was like to be Métis and Cree women. If we'd stayed there longer we might have been hard-pressed to elaborate since, well, you're not Cree."

Amy laughed.

"Of course I could have talked about being Métis. I do know a few things. If I'd told stories about my grandmother I could have given some perspective from a Cree woman's point of view. It would have been secondhand but I guess that's better than nothing." Amy chuckled. "I got confused with dates and places since my grandparents weren't born until after the time period we were in. That made it trickier," she admitted.

"Did Pauline notice?" Brittany glanced up from her notebook.

"I had a coughing fit at one point so she thumped me on the back," Amy confessed. "That threw her off."

"Always an effective ploy." Kara flashed Amy a mischievous grin.

"I'll say. I had the sense Pauline seemed unclear about her place in the Aboriginal community. Since she was a performer and wore what was clearly a costume she mentioned she felt out of place with the other First Nations women. They treated her with reverence though.

Even though she was uncertain about her native identity, the other First Nations women accepted her for who she was. They weren't judgmental. That's because true Aboriginal people aren't. Judgmental, I mean."

"You noticed a great deal."

"Yes, I did. Pauline appeared proud of who she was. She was eager to hear about what it was like to be Métis and Cree. To me, that showed Pauline was on her own journey."

Amy nodded. "Even though Pauline might have been uncertain about her Aboriginal ancestry, she embraced it. That must have been hard to do. She lived in a society that equated First Nations people with tomahawks, ponies and scalps.

Awareness in that century was limited. North Americans were influenced by the European viewpoint. The Aboriginal perspective was non-existent. Pauline was a woman blazing a trail across Canada with her poems and articles, who was of Mohawk and European bloodlines. She had to be incredibly strong, don't you think?"

"Most definitely," Kara agreed. "It would have been difficult to be a famous woman of mixed blood back in the 1800s. It's a wonder she managed to maintain any sense of identity. It was impressive how Pauline was able to embrace her native roots then write about them."

"You're right Kara. It's easier to acknowledge being Aboriginal now since society, as a whole, is moving towards acceptance. Twenty, thirty years ago, maybe not even that long, one did not admit to any native ties. It's almost trendy now to be Aboriginal."

Amy laughed. "Imagine that, we're suddenly on the forefront of a trend Brittany."

Brittany mumbled as she continued to take notes.

"I've noticed some people have magically created a long forgotten Aboriginal ancestor," Amy continued. "Yet they only have a dribble of native blood in them or none at all. When people hear I'm Métis they talk about First Nations benefits, or what they perceive as benefits. In actuality, there are no free rides and no free money."

"Yes, that's true for most things in life. Did you have anything else to add about your people?"

"Well, I've read First Nations and Métis history quite a bit in the last while. It's fascinating. As with any culture, there are many points of pride for Aboriginal people. Of course, being the First Peoples in Canada is a fact society has acknowledged. The history of the First Nations and Métis nations is being taught in schools now so that's a positive development." Amy rubbed her chin.

"Even though there's still a great deal of racial intolerance, society seems open to the fact Aboriginal people have a long and noble ancestry. We are an integral part of Canada's history. There are books and resources to tap into these days with the correct facts about Aboriginal people. They've been written from an Aboriginal perspective. I see that as a positive step in the right direction."

Amy turned to Kara. "We each have a journey. As you said before, it's our personal path. You can't help with mine any more than I with yours. As we seek to find our own truth and meaning, our promise to ourselves will be realized."

Kara nodded. "Your journey has begun in earnest Amy. The positive effect of your experience will determine your path. We are part of all things, of the natural order. To become who you will be, you must be prepared to make sacrifices along the way. At the same time, be aware of the endless possibilities that surround you."

Kara tossed her hair back.

"The power of self comes from within. You have the courage to face whatever comes your way. Your inner strength will guide you. As your heart lightens and your soul is nurtured, you'll reach a point in your passage where you recognize the power of self."

"Will I still have questions?"

"Yes, but you'll know who you are. You'll be comfortable with your level of consciousness. You'll find your own answers. Happiness and satisfaction can be reached."

They were quiet, each lost in their own thoughts.

"When I hear the drumbeat that ties in with my journey," Amy mused.

"You hear the drumbeat and that's personal for you. The meaning is of significance to you, and you alone."

"So no one else hears the drum?"

"It symbolizes something relevant to you. You'll decide the degree of importance it will have."

"That must be another part of self-discovery and my journey. I'd say it relates to my Aboriginal ancestry. That's something I'm exploring right now. Perhaps as I learn more about my culture, I'll figure out the significance of the drumbeat."

"Yes, that sounds right."

"Did you know the drumbeat reminds us of our mother's heartbeat?"

"No, I didn't."

"When we hear the drumbeat, it makes us feel safe and loved. It's a similar feeling to being in our mother's womb. The drum is our link with Mother Earth and Creator."

Kara smiled. "Thank you for sharing that with me."

"I think I'm getting it." Amy wiped away a tear.

"Yes, you are."

Bird of Paradise Drums Beating

Kara reached out then squeezed Amy's hand. The gesture was more than one of comfort. It represented their new friendship and forged a turning point in their relationship.

Content to sit and be quiet, they sipped tea, each lost in their own thoughts. The only sound was the scratch of Brittany's pen in her notebook.

Amy glanced at her watch.

"Oh no, look at the time. I have to run. The boys will be back already. I should have been there when they arrived."

Frazzled, Amy jumped up.

"Can you drop by tonight with your family?"

Amy stared at Kara for a heartbeat then grinned. "You bet, we wouldn't miss it for the world."

Impulsively, Amy reached over to give Kara a quick hug.

"Thanks Kara, see you later, around seven."

Brittany joined her mother then added, "I've got a date tonight so I won't be here."

"Have fun Brittany. Make sure you drop by tomorrow. I have a surprise for you."

"Sweet," Brittany replied as they headed out the door.

"So, hot date with Brad tonight huh," Amy remarked as they turned toward home.

"Yeah. It should be fun. Wait till you meet him mom, he's nice, you'll like him."

"I'm sure I will. You have great taste in friends."

Brittany made a face.

"And guys," Amy was quick to add. "Going anywhere special?"

"He wants me to meet some of his friends. I think we're going out to grab a bite to eat then I'm not sure what we'll do with his friends."

"Do you want the car or are you bussing it?"

"I'll take the bus. That way if I want a drink I won't drink and drive."

Amy reached over to give her daughter a quick squeeze. "That's one of the things I love about your generation," she praised. "You're responsible when it comes to drinking. When I went to school a lot of people got behind the wheel after a few drinks. Sometimes they were even drunk. It wasn't a great trait of our age group."

"Yeah, that's just weird."

"You could invite Brad for supper tomorrow night. Of course then he has to meet the whole clan."

"Hmm, I don't know. It might be kind of early for that. Then again Brad mentioned how he'd like to meet you. He does like his siblings but they're older than him. Maybe he'd like to drop by and meet everyone. I'm not sure. Can we play it by ear?"

"Of course darling, I won't plan for it and if it happens, bonus."

"Thanks mom. Hey, the boys are here," Brittany yelled as they neared the house. "There's grandma and grandpa. Cool, I can visit a bit before I have to take off. Eric, Sam," she called as the boys stepped out of the car. "Over here."

The boys turned, grinned then ran towards them.

Amy quickened her pace and waved. She loved having the whole family together.

28

"So what do you think?" Brad whispered in her ear.

"Umm, I'm not sure. This wasn't exactly what I had in mind when you suggested a fun filled evening with your friends," Brittany admitted.

She chewed her bottom lip then glanced down. The high heels had definitely been over the top. Now she had on oversized runners one of Brad's friends had given to her when they'd seen her shoes. At least she'd worn dark clothes. Of course it was impossible to see her outfit since they'd gotten suited up upon arrival. The clothes she'd painstakingly agonized over were presently covered by an ugly vest.

Too bad Brad hadn't mentioned the word runners or grunge, yeah, grunge that would have described the place. Then she would have known how to dress. Sometimes surprise locations for a date weren't all they were cracked up to be.

"Get ready, I hear them coming," Brad whispered somewhere off to her right.

Brittany peered into the gloom. She saw the flash of Brad's teeth as he grinned. She smiled gamely back at him then raised her weapon, ready for action.

Moments later they were surrounded. It was an ambush.

Brad was calm as he rapid fired his phaser.

"Argh, no," Brittany groaned as someone got her in the arm. "Man, that sucks," she griped. After that she couldn't count the hits. She hadn't even fired off one shot. What a loser. She spied Brad crouched down by a wall. Their enemies had moved off, probably to re-group since Brad had managed to hit a few.

She carefully edged toward him as he'd instructed earlier. "Whatever you do, don't run or you'll call attention to yourself," Brad had coached. "You'll get hit a lot."

"What a loser," she repeated aloud as she hunkered down beside Brad.

"Na, you're doing great," Brad praised. "Don't be so hard on yourself. It's your first time. These guys meet regularly. They're good. I'm lucky they let me join them since they're way better than me."

The *'guys'* were a motley crew. Brittany was sure two of them were girls. They had a feminine air yet wore dark, oversized clothes so it was hard to tell their sex. Plus they'd put paint on their cheeks for camouflage. They seemed tough. They hadn't said a word to Brittany when her and Brad arrived, just smirked at Brittany's outfit.

Brittany sighed.

"Here, let me see this." Brad checked her phaser. He flashed the laser beam against the wall to test it. "Yup, it's fine," he said as he passed it back to her.

"Yeah, that's not the problem," Brittany griped. "It's me."

"Shh, listen, I don't think they've moved too far away."

Brad started to move toward another wall still crouched over. He appeared to do a slow motion crab walk.

Brittany mimicked his actions.

They made it safely across the space.

"OK, remember what I said about corners. That's when they get you if they're on the other side. We've gotta move in that direction though. I'll go first. You stay a few steps behind me. Oh, and protect your body sensors."

Brad stood up then turned to Brittany. "You're doing great," he praised as he bent to kiss her quick.

Brittany smiled up at him then shook her head to clear it of distractions. She had to get in the game. Competitive by nature Brittany did not like to lose. If she could get a few shots in at least she'd manage to save face. It was better than the alternative.

Bird of Paradise Drums Beating

They rounded the corner and didn't spy anyone nearby. Brad motioned for her to follow. As they found another wall to crouch by Brittany caught a motion out of the corner of her eye. She turned quick, aimed then fired a few rounds off.

"Hah," she crowed as she finally hit an opponent. She'd actually caught someone by surprise.

"Hurry, over here," she heard Brad urge as she stood for a moment, caught in her moment of victory.

Right, she just had a few seconds to get away before the enemy fired back at her. Brittany turned then ran quick into the shadows. She heard a muttered oath behind her. The enemy was not pleased. She grinned as Brad grabbed her then pulled her deeper into the gloom.

"My hero," he murmured into her ear as he embraced her. Brittany raised her face for his welcoming kiss.

"Mm, maybe this game is sort of fun," she whispered after a few minutes.

Brad chuckled.

Everyone talked at once as they handed their stuff back to the guy at the desk. Brittany grinned at Brad as she listened to him and his friends do a play by play of their moves.

"You gonna join us for drinks?" one of the guys asked.

"Sounds good, that OK with you Brittany?" Brad grabbed her hand.

"Sure."

As they made their way outside they clustered in a group to discuss where to go next.

"Oh, I forgot my shoes and purse inside. Where's that locker key?" Brittany checked her one pocket.

"I've got the key. You gave it to me since your outfit didn't have deep pockets." Brad pulled the key out for Brittany. "I love it by the way," he whispered in her ear. "The shoes don't match but once you get those heels back on you're like, wow."

Brittany chuckled. Her eyes met one of the two '*guys*' she'd identified earlier as a girl. She blushed. The girl was way beyond angry as if she could hear everything Brad said. Brittany turned away, quick.

Brittany got her high heels out of the locker then sat down on a nearby bench to remove the clunky runners she wore. She grabbed her purse, rummaged around then pulled out her brush. As she gave her hair a vigorous yank she idly watched Brad and his friends through the window. Yup, the two girls definitely were of the fairer sex. One had a make-up remover cloth and was currently cleaning her friends' face. That was definitely a girl thing.

Brittany quickly applied a bit of rose tinted lip balm to her lips, threw everything back into her purse, grabbed the offending pair of runners then slammed the locker door. She poked the guy who'd leant the shoes to her to get his attention, thanked him then edged back towards Brad.

Brad grinned as she rejoined the group. He grabbed her hand. "We'll just walk from here since there are lots of great places on Osborne and Corydon. You OK walking in those?" He pointed at her heels.

"Yeah, I'll be fine as long as it's not too far away. The shoes are actually comfortable believe it or not. They're just not the best for laser tag or running."

"Guess I should have mentioned the location. Then you would have known what to wear. I do like your outfit though. You look hot." Brad whispered the last part in her ear so no one else could hear.

Brittany grinned as he leaned in for a quick kiss.

They stayed near the back of the group as they crossed the street then headed up Osborne. Brittany was content to stay near Brad. His male friends seemed nice but she still wasn't sure about the two girls.

It was a short walk to *The Toad*. The guys grabbed a table then a few of them jumped up to get some beer. Brad sat beside one of his buddies and pulled Brittany's chair closer to his.

Brittany leaned over to hear their conversation as Brad and his friend, she thought his name might be Paul, continued to talk about

Bird of Paradise Drums Beating

laser tag. Brittany leaned back in her chair a few minutes later then glanced around the bar. She spied the washroom, grabbed her purse then headed in that direction.

As Brittany touched up her make-up she heard the door slam. One of the girls who'd been at laser tag poked her face beside Brittany's in the mirror. The girl was prettier than Brittany had thought. Up close Brittany could appreciate her features.

"Can I borrow your mascara?" the girl asked.

"Uh, sure."

"It's not my fault we have to be mad at you."

"OK." Brittany was at a loss as to what to add.

"My sister Kara, I'm Kiera by the way, has been crushing on Brad since we first met him. So she's really bummed that he has a girlfriend. Really bummed," she added for emphasis.

"Oh, wow, thanks for clearing that up." Now this Brittany could understand. That's why the girls had given her the cold shoulder. That made sense. It wasn't anything she'd done personally. It was because she was with Brad.

"Yeah, my brother Mark said we could come for these laser tag games as long as we behave. That means no monopolizing the conversations, no flirting with his friends, no getting drunk, no meeting up with strange guys at the bar, no, no, no, he's got a million rules. We love laser tag though so we put up with all his crap." Kiera shrugged. "I guess he's not bad for an older brother."

"Which one is Mark?"

Kiera raised her brows in the mirror. "You don't know who's who."

Brittany shook her head.

"Kay, Mark looks like us except his hair is redder. We're lucky we got the chestnut colour."

Brittany nodded. It was a good description.

"Paul is the one Brad was talking to at the table."

"I knew that one."

"Then the guy with the dreamy chocolate brown eyes, thick lashes and tousled hair is Jonathan. Don't you just love that name?" Kiera cooed.

"Got a thing for him, huh," Brittany noted as she brushed her hair.

"Yeah, he doesn't know I'm alive though. I don't even know if Mark's friends have figured out Kara and I are girls yet."

"You should wear hotter clothes. To be honest when I first saw the two of you in your oversized dark clothes and face make-up I wasn't positive you were girls either. Just saying."

"Really, hmm, maybe you're right."

"You're very pretty. If the guys saw you in nicer outfits they'd notice you for sure. Want to borrow more of my make-up?"

Kiera grinned in the mirror. "Thanks, yeah, I'd like that." She glanced down at Brittany's shoes. "I'm not sure about wearing those though. Make sure next time you come for laser tag you bring along your own pair of runners. You could have applied for clown school in Mike's shoes."

Brittany giggled. "OK, so that was Mike who gave me the shoes. Who's the blonde guy with the glasses?"

When they parted a few minutes later Brittany felt better about the group. Even though Kiera had to pretend she didn't like Brittany for Kara's sake, Brittany knew better.

∽

"Thanks for inviting us over last night."

"The boys seemed to get along, didn't they?" Kara offered.

"Yes they hit it off. Eric mentioned going to the park today to play soccer. They'll call your boys to see if they want to join them."

"Splendid." Kara clasped her hands together, pleased by the comment. "Your husband is a funny guy. We had an amusing conversation."

"He does have a great sense of humour," Amy agreed.

"Yeah, dad's a riot."

Bird of Paradise Drums Beating

Amy turned to Kara. "I have more questions I'd like to ask today."

Kara grinned. "Of course you do. I've come to expect that."

"Mom, remember," Brittany hissed.

"Right, of course dear, you go first," Amy urged as she met Brittany's scowl.

Brittany huffed. "Kara, when we left yesterday you mentioned a surprise. Is it the vampire story?"

Kara laughed. "I thought you'd forgotten Brittany," she teased. "Yes, that's the tidbit I've saved for today. Why don't I answer your mother's questions first? I'm sure we'll have time for the vampire story after that."

"Really," Brittany crowed as she flashed an eager grin. "Cool, I thought you'd blow me off again." She pulled out her notebook and pen. "Go for it mom. I'll take notes while you talk."

"Great." Amy cleared her throat. "Kara, why did you choose to tell your story to us? How much more will you share? When you talk about despair, have you reached the depths of your misery or are you only part way there? Will you continue as pain indefinitely? Will you move along to experience another emotion or state of being until your days are eventually used up?"

"Whoa, those are a lot of questions." Kara gave a quick laugh. "I see we've reached a critical point. I wondered when you'd ask these questions."

Kara spread her arms out as if addressing an audience. "One wonders, why did I conjure you here or produce you from thin air? Will I continue in my present situation? What is in store for Kara or whatever my name is?"

Kara's smile took the sting from her words. "I had an ulterior motive I must confess. As I mentioned before I want you to record what we've discussed. You and Brittany will write the words I speak for all eternity.

The notebook Brittany has started over the past week will provide a skeleton we can build upon. I need your help to compile my thoughts, to maintain them as part of history. I desire a moment, fleeting though it may be, when I am in the spotlight."

Kara grinned. "I asked *Her* to allow me this indulgence. This is a special favour, to record the accomplishments of great women. It will be more though, since I'll speak of despair, grief, pain and depression. The rose coloured glasses will be off as we convey their depth of emotion. History as we know it will be rewritten."

Amy gave a quick nod.

"I also want to talk about truth and identity. Culture is of the utmost importance to people. I think we need to emphasize how acceptance and pride in what you are, help make one stronger. Denial is self-defeating, don't you think?"

"Oh yes, definitely."

"Think of the women you've met through me already. We'll emphasize their goodness as well as their faults. Dedication to a cause indicates strength, tenacity and boundless resolve. If we capture the essence of these women while we highlight their determination, energy and zest for life, it will be a honourable message.

We'll include actual characterizations, incorporating good and bad elements. We can cover emotional tidbits and events that led to their ascent or downfall. Imagine the extent. There's so much to say. The potential is limitless. I'm not sure how much we can include. There could be volumes," Kara teased.

"When would you like to begin?" Amy urged. Kara's excitement was contagious.

Kara's voice held a hint of relief. "We already have begun Amy. The foundation has been set." She nodded toward Brittany. "We'll read what Brittany has written, then expand from there. I have so many stories to share. The hard part will be to decide which are worthy."

Brittany glanced up from her notes. "I have a sentence we could begin with."

"Let's hear it," Kara urged.

Brittany flipped through some pages. "Well, I guess I actually have two ways to start," she admitted. "Kara has secrets. I wrote that sentence the other day. Then the next sentence would be. One of her secrets began in 69 B.C.."

"That has merit," Kara praised. "I like it. What's the other choice?"

Brittany gazed at her mother, flashed a quick grin then returned to her notes. "History, fiction and fantasy unite as a Métis woman embraces the reality of her culture. I wrote that one to describe mom's personal journey of awareness. You've spoken about it a lot the last few days mom."

"Brittany, wow what a captivating first sentence. I love the hook, it really grabbed me." Amy giggled. "Of course, I enjoyed how it's about me."

"Hmm, seems there are two paths we could take. Perhaps we can incorporate both themes. Or, we might need to write two novels. I'm interested to read your notes Brittany. You could have the makings of an author."

"Thank you." Brittany gave a little bow. "So, Kara, what about that vampire story?" she urged with an eager nod.

Kara laughed. "Yes, I think you deserve to be rewarded for your efforts Brittany."

Kara got up, went to the intercom, spoke to Carl then returned to her seat.

"I've ordered coffee cake and iced tea since I know those are two of your favourites."

"Yum, special treats, thanks Kara."

When Carl had left and they'd helped themselves to his culinary delights Kara sat back to begin her story.

"The slight breeze stirred my hair as I rode atop my favourite unicorn. My legs gripped the sides of his back as I held on steadily. I reached toward the horn that protruded from his head."

"Don't even think about it," Hank admonished.

"I shrugged then brought my hand back to grip Hank's mane again. It was freaky how he always knew when I was about to grab his horn. I guess unicorns really are magic, or at the very least psychic."

"Come on Kara, do you really want us to believe you rode on the back of a unicorn?" Brittany taunted. She raised one brow, shook her head then wagged a finger playfully. Brittany leaned across her mother to grab another piece of cake.

"I rode many unicorns and this is what happened." Kara tossed her hair back. "If you insist on interruptions Brittany it shall grow tedious," she warned.

Amy shook her head at Brittany. "Please continue Kara, of course we believe you rode unicorns if you say you did."

Brittany snorted but held her tongue.

"Princess, we should head back," Hank reminded me. "We have wandered far from the castle. We are on the outer edge of the realm."

"Just a bit further Hank, please," I pleaded. "It's rare I get time with you alone. Father is usually tiresome and insists on sending a companion with me. I feel free on my own with you."

"All right Princess, we must be on our guard though. We could be taken upon by one of them if we are not vigilant."

I laughed. "You sound just like father when you speak like that Hank. What a wonderful impersonation."

"I'm serious. Those are my thoughts, not his."

"Since when are unicorns serious? You're supposed to be light, airy, mystical, and care only for fantasy. That's what all the stories about you claim."

Hank snorted. "I'm too old to be frivolous and flighty. That's for the young crowd of upstarts. Travel with one of them if that's what you prefer."

"Oh Hank, you know I love you best."

"Hmm, perhaps," Hank conceded.

"Wait a minute. So Hank is not actually a guy you're riding with. He's the unicorn," Brittany interrupted. She made a face at Kara.

"Of course, Hank was my favourite. I rode him often."

Bird of Paradise Drums Beating

Brittany laughed. "Yeah, right, well I guess if you claim you rode unicorns you can also pretend they talked to you."

"Brittany," Amy scolded. "I'm surprised at you. You loved unicorns when you were young. Imagine if you'd gotten a ride on one or better yet been able to talk to one. Wouldn't that have been a dream come true?"

Brittany rolled her eyes. "Mom, unicorns don't exist. That's the point. They're part of fantasy and magic. I could never ride one or talk to them. They were something I daydreamed and dreamt about. They aren't real."

Kara glowered at Brittany.

Brittany stopped her tirade as she noted Kara's expression. "Oops, I mean, yeah, well, OK, if you say they exist of course we believe you." With wide eyes she raved, "Your stories have been fantastic Kara. It's just that, well, this one is a bit more out there than the rest."

Brittany frowned. "No, I guess that's not true. Cleopatra was pretty farfetched. Hmm, OK, I'm sorry Kara. I apologize. Of course you rode unicorns and talked to them. Hank said you were a princess right. Where did you live?"

Kara sniffed, still peeved at Brittany's words.

"Please, tell us who you were Kara. I believe you, honest," Brittany coaxed.

"Hmph, well, if you insist. Yes, I was a Royal Princess. I lived in, you know, I think I'll wait and tell you who I was at the end of the story. If I tell you now, I'm sure you'll doubt my word again." Kara glared at Brittany. "Now, may I continue?"

"Of course, thank you Kara."

Kara sniffed. "Suddenly, Hank pulled up short. I almost fell over the top of his head. Hank raised his front hoofs slightly to keep me from toppling forward."

"Hank, whatever is the matter with you?" I cried.

"Careful, do not look forward," Hank instructed. "Avert your eyes Princess. Quick."

"What, why?" I shouted as I did the opposite of what Hank directed. "As I stared straight ahead, my mouth opened in a little '*o*'. Dumbfounded by what appeared in front of us, my gaze held the being. I could not tear my eyes away, even had I desired."

"Oh no," Hank uttered. He bent his head forward as if to avert his own eyes further from the disaster he'd forecast.

"Who is he?" I murmured. "I must meet him. He's perfect."

"No, please, I beg you Princess. Look away before it is too late."

"I cannot," I admitted. "His beauty blinds me yet I cannot avert my eyes."

Hank groaned then began to paw at the ground.

"What upsets you so?" I wondered. "Who is he?" I repeated. "I must know." The man before me gazed straight into my eyes. I found myself unable to blink let alone glance away. It was as if I was bewitched."

"It's true," Hank said as if I'd uttered the words aloud. "You have been bewitched. You are under his spell now. Should he decide to take you, we will be powerless to disobey him. I cannot accompany you. You will be alone Princess."

"What?" I murmured. "I don't understand Hank. What say you? He is too beautiful to be feared. Why do you quiver beneath me? Who is he?"

With an eagerness I could not hide, I was keen to take everything in about this man. His hair was black while his eyes were dark and smoky. They smouldered with intensity. Sunlight bounced off his skin as if shimmering crystals brushed over him. I saw a faint layer of facial hair as if he'd not had time to shave this morn.

I heard Hank moan as if he were a great distance away.

I shivered. "Witness the strength of his arms," I uttered aloud. "I wager he could lift me effortlessly should the urge arise within him."

"No, don't encourage him. Your words will give him leave to approach you."

Bird of Paradise Drums Beating

"I cannot help it. I want to meet him. No, I need to meet him." I dismounted from Hank. I never broke my gaze from the stranger before me. Although we'd never met I was sure I knew him, and he me. This was my destiny.

"Please, don't go," Hank pleaded.

I brushed his mane with my hand then stepped forward toward my future. Little did I know it was the last time I would see Hank for a long while.

29

Kara shuddered. "I didn't return to Hank, the other unicorns, my family and friends for what seemed an endless time. My life changed at that moment." As she gazed down a tear grazed her cheek. "I was powerless to stop it."

Amy reached out to touch Kara's hand. She gave a quick, reassuring squeeze.

"Who was he?" Brittany whispered.

"You asked if I ever hung out with vampires."

Brittany gasped. "You mean he was a vampire."

"Yes, his name was Silvano."

"Wow, so did he make you into a vampire?"

Kara laughed. "No, silly, that would have complicated my life even further. I was part of his realm for years though." She sighed. "I left my realm where unicorns, butterflies, faeries, dancing flowers and beautiful birds were an everyday occurrence. I was surrounded by light, goodness and purity."

Kara closed her eyes then shivered. "When I joined the realm of Shibot I was forced to unite with those who reveled in darkness, evil, hatred and debauchery. I associated with vampires, werewolves, giants and dwarfs. Flowers and plant life were pretty but either poisonous or large enough to eat you. It was quite the eye opener for a virginal princess."

"I'll wager you didn't keep your virginity long?" Brittany guessed.

"Brittany," Amy gasped. "Really, how inappropriate. No need to put Kara on the spot about such a delicate subject."

Brittany rolled her eyes, "Mother," was all she said but the word held endless levels of reproach.

"How rich Brittany," Kara praised with a chuckle. "Yes, as you so aptly pointed out I did not remain in my unspoiled state for long."

Brittany gave a wise nod. "Thought so, that's what all the books, TV shows and Internet say about vampires. They have a large appetite for those sort of things." She said the last part with a quick, fleeting glance at her mother.

Amy shook her head. It was her turn to roll her eyes.

"I walked over to Silvano, eyes locked with his. He picked me up, turned then carried me into the forest. He didn't say a word to me. Just broke into this fast run.

It was wild and carefree, reckless even. I felt as if we flew through the woods. He ran a great distance in a few minutes. My heart beat fast as I wondered what I'd done. That's when I began to realize my actions might have been foolhardy."

"Might have been? Ya think? That's an understatement if I ever heard one."

"Yes, you're right Brittany." Kara flicked her hair back. "As Silvano held me in his arms, I noticed he was stronger than I'd imagined. His chest felt like granite. That unnerved me, as I'd never been held so close by a man. I put one hand to where his heart should beat to see if it thundered in his chest. I could not feel a thing. With wide eyes I whimpered. I wondered what type of man was so powerful, ran like a great wind and had no heartbeat to speak of."

Kara bent her head as if embarrassed by her next words. "I heard tales of the dark realm. Shibot was a place parents warned their children of from a young age. We knew not to go too close to the perimeter. To this day, I don't know what brought me there at that fateful moment."

"He did," Brittany whispered.

"Do you think so?"

"Definitely, they can compel you, everyone knows that."

"Well, I did not know that."

"I guess technology helps nowadays. We know everything about vampires. The sunlight and shimmering crystals bouncing off his skin were a dead give away. Your buddy, Hank, the unicorn, was right. You should have glanced away. Once they lock eyes with you, you're sunk."

Brittany nodded.

"Yes, that's true. I should have known," Kara admitted. "When we came out of the forest and into the clearing, Silvano placed me down. His gentleness surprised me. He raised my face to his, stared deep into my eyes and I was a goner again. My fears evaporated. I was under his spell for years. If Selene and Eva hadn't come onto the scene I might never have escaped."

"Who were they? Those are beautiful names."

"They were female vampires. All the vampires I met had ancient names. Silvano means '*from the forest*' while Selene is '*moon*' and Eva '*life.*' I learned many things from them. I danced countless nights by the light of the moon. I began to appreciate everything that surrounded me even though it was dark and foreboding."

Kara gazed at some memory only she could see. "When I first entered the clearing with Silvano I was unaware of all the creatures and beings that surrounded us. They were invisible to me. Silvano raised my chin then placed his icy, hard lips upon mine. I gave an involuntary shiver. It was as if something cold, heartless and dead stroked the back of my spine with a long, sharp fingernail. I would have protested had I not been under his spell."

Amy shuddered as she heard Kara's words. She imagined how eerie it had felt. Amy always empathized with the helpless victim in creepy stories. She glanced toward Brittany. Did this freak her out?

It didn't seem like it to Amy. Brittany held Kara's gaze. With wide eyes she appeared spellbound by the tale, not in the least unnerved by it.

"He ravished me with kisses for endless moments. When Silvano showered me with a show of affection it was as if time stood still. I think it did. In the here and now anyhow, since the realms of good and evil are between what we recognize as real time. He turned me around and I got my first glimpse of Shibot."

"How are the realms of good and evil between what we know as real time?" Amy interrupted.

"Mom, everyone knows that. It's explained in comic books, graphic novels, video games, Dungeons and Dragons, magic cards, tons of areas."

"Well, maybe people your age understand it. I need more info though Brittany."

"Well, it has to do with dimensions and stuff. Like the fourth and fifth dimension have a lot happening in them. So, Kara, you must have fallen through a crack or a fold or something, right?"

"Hmm perhaps, I think it was just something that happened though. The catalyst as you've mentioned, was Silvano. I fell under his spell. It took a while to correct but eventually I landed back where I was meant to be."

"I'm still confused," Amy confessed.

"I'll continue my story. It might clear matters up a bit."

Amy shrugged but remained quiet.

"It was like a magic kingdom landed right in front of me. It was gloomy though, as if a veil were wrapped around the sun. There were all manners of beings there, some tiny, others the size of an average man while several were horrid and large. Those were the giants."

"Did you see any werewolves?"

Amy thought Brittany sounded a little too eager to hear about werewolves. Perhaps she should add something else to her reading list besides *'Twilight'* and the host of other books that dealt with the dark side.

"Not at first. The werewolves came later, when there was major trouble. It turned out Silvano was king of the realm. There were constant wars. Beings fought all the time. They were a bloodthirsty bunch. It became rather tedious after awhile, I must confess." Kara rolled her eyes.

"Of course when I arrived, Silvano's queen was pissed. She tried to kill me on many an occasion. Silvano made sure to surround me with loyal guards day and night."

"He had another chick and he brought you there? Wow, that guy had balls."

"Brittany, really, you sound coarse when you talk like that," Amy scolded.

"Yes Brittany, I do have delicate princess ears, you must remember." Kara smirked.

"Yeah, sure, that's a word I equate with you Kara, delicate," Brittany joked.

"Well, I was slightly fragile the other day when I took on the hag image. I'm infinitely stronger now though." Kara tossed her long mane behind her.

"To continue, his queen's name was Semele, it means *'of the underworld.'*" Kara shuddered. "Semele bestowed a name upon me. It was Princess Despoina. Even though I wasn't a vampire it stuck the entire time I was in the realm of Shibot."

"What does Despoina mean?"

"Mistress." Kara gave another eye roll.

"Sounds appropriate from what you've said so far," Brittany noted.

"Yes, unfortunately it was an apt title. She pretty much spat the name at me whenever we were near one another. Semele made princess sound dirty and sleazy as well. We weren't together much though since Silvano made sure to keep us apart."

"That sounded like a good idea."

"Yes, I was fortunate as I got to spend numerous hours with the younger vampires and beings. I loved to dance, read and listen to music. There were a great number of talented vampires among the group."

"That's because they have centuries to devote to idle pursuit," Brittany pointed out.

"Everyone knows that," Amy quipped.

"Now you're with the program mom."

They chuckled as Kara continued her tale. "The status quo went on for years, a half dozen at least. Then one day, things changed. There was a rival king about to visit Shibot. It was rumoured he had great powers. Beings whispered he was one of the originals."

"Not an original," Amy gasped.

Kara and Brittany ignored her.

"Silvano was in a state. He held countless meetings with the beings in his realm. Then he invited compatible neighbouring heads of state to Shibot.

They came up with this immense, complicated strategy to out-maneuver the rival king." Kara turned to Brittany. "I knew things were serious when they invited the werewolves to join them."

"Did you get to meet any of them?"

"Yes, as a matter of fact I did. Since they didn't like to be in the same room they brought along a few emissaries, people like me."

"People like you?" Amy wondered.

"Yes, humans as compared to vampires or werewolves. There were a lot of individuals in the realm that were not magic or supernatural beings."

"Of course. Vampires need people to feed upon." Brittany added the last part for her mom's benefit.

"Yes, that was one use for humans. Another was entertainment and diversion. They got bored of one another easily. Another bonus was humans could converse with vampires and werewolves without trying to tear one another apart, hence the emissary role."

"So, were you Silvano's representative?"

"Yes, I didn't leave Silvano's side for months. He took me everywhere. When we had visitors I was summoned immediately.

In addition to being his mistress I became an official envoy of his court. It solidified my place and helped keep me out of the dangerous clutches of Queen Semele. She hated werewolves and many of the other beings. Silvano determined it was best to keep Semele in the background since he needed them as allies."

"Sounds like this Silvano knew his stuff," Brittany noted.

"Yes, he was knowledgeable. I incurred his wrath though when I began to chum with one of the werewolves. His name was Justin. He was a handsome young lad. He had dark, curly hair and tawny eyes that danced with glee when he was amused. I melted when he fixed his gaze on me."

Kara sighed as she clasped her hands. "Justin's physique easily rivaled that of Silvano. I imagined those strong arms around me and felt the first stirrings of puppy love." Kara's laughter pealed out. "Get it, puppy love, since Justin was a werewolf and wolves are from the canine family."

"Yeah, we get it," Brittany replied in a bored, dry tone. "Hardy, har, you're hilarious Kara."

"Well I do try. Storytelling can have its trials you know. I thought you'd be interested in Justin since you mentioned werewolves earlier."

"Did you get together with Justin?"

"Not really." Kara shrugged. "It wasn't meant to be. I left the realm shortly after I met Justin. I missed the ultimate battle between Silvano and the rival king so I'm not sure what happened to everyone."

"What? Why? How did you leave? I thought you were a prisoner there." Brittany gave a quick shake of her head.

"Yes, I was. Then an odd thing happened. Remember the two female vampires I mentioned earlier, Selene and Eva?"

Brittany and Amy nodded.

"Well, I was sure there would be a confrontation between Silvano and his rival. It was unavoidable. One afternoon, Selene and Eva pulled me aside. They convinced me I must meet them outside when the moon rose. I thought we would embark on one of our evening gambits. The ladies loved to dance by the light of the moon. We'd make this gigantic bonfire then dance and sing for hours. I loved it." Kara smiled at the memory.

"That's not what happened though. I ditched Silvano and made my way outside, accompanied by a few guards. They were my constant companions. Selene and Eva waited nearby.

They convinced the guards to drink some concoction they'd made. Selene and Eva were shameless flirts so the men were easy

Bird of Paradise Drums Beating

targets. The lady vamps pretended to drink as well but didn't swallow any of the liquid. Just as I was about to drink my share Eva grabbed my arm and the liquid sloshed out." Kara frowned. "Eva did it on purpose since the grog was poisoned. Moments after they drank, the guards fell to the ground, dead."

"Dead, what was the point of that?" Amy wondered.

Kara ignored the interruption.

"Selene picked me up then ran into the forest. As I mentioned, vampires are very strong. They find it easy to carry a human. Eva ran beside her. I was speechless, as everything happened so fast. When we were far within the forest with no pursuit, Selene put me down.

Eva explained they would free me. We were near my realm. Since I'd arrived in Shibot many things had changed. Selene and Eva thought I was responsible since Silvano should not have bewitched me in the first place. They wanted me to return to my own realm. Then things would go back to the way they were meant to be. I needed to get to my own time for history to play out."

"Did they tell you who you were?"

"Why would they do that? I knew who I was," Kara retorted.

"Oh, right, you just kept that secret from mom and I," Brittany griped. "So, are you going to spill and tell us your name?"

Kara chuckled.

"I'll give you a clue. I was a princess who became a well-known queen. She was part of the Monarchy and is still alive today."

Brittany turned to Amy. "Isn't the Monarchy part of the British Empire?"

"Yes, I think so darling."

"Right. So, Kara, you want us to believe this queen is Queen Elizabeth II and she was involved with vamps and werewolves." Brittany's voice dripped with sarcasm. "Come on Kara. You can do better than that."

"Why do you find that so hard to believe? Why is this different than anything else I've told you?"

"It's preposterous, that's why," Brittany cried. "Too unbelievable, it's way off the map, even for you Kara."

Brittany crossed her arms then glared at Kara.

Amy glanced from Brittany to Kara. "Before the two of you come to blows there's a point that's been bothering me throughout this story. I have to ask. How did you further the cause of women by hanging out with vampires?"

"I didn't. When I fell off the grid, so to speak, I was missing for a brief moment in time. The vampires were irrelevant to our history."

"How long were you gone?" Brittany demanded. "You claimed it was years."

"Yes. I was in the realm of Shibot for seven years. When I returned to my kingdom I'd only been gone for seven hours. Hank came home without me. A search party was formed and some of my father's men found me knocked unconscious near the perimeter. That's where Selene and Eva left me. I'm not sure why they thought it was necessary to knock me out.

No one was the wiser about what happened. I never shared my outlandish story with anyone. I knew it might land me in an asylum."

"Wise move," Amy agreed. "Wait a minute? Queen Elizabeth II never had unicorns. Those don't exist."

Kara grinned. "Well, as a child I do admit I liked to exaggerate somewhat. I played pretend a great deal. Unicorns, faeries and elves were my best friends."

Brittany laughed. "So let me guess? Hank was actually a horse wasn't he?"

"Yes, I must admit in reality Hank was a horse not a unicorn. He was white though and had a bump on the top of his head that reminded me of a unicorn horn. I loved horses, dogs, all manner of animals."

"This story is a total fabrication isn't it Kara?" Brittany accused. "Unicorns, vampires, werewolves, other beings, you were never in another realm. This is not like the other tales you've told us. Those were based on history and usually had something to do with the women's movement." Brittany glared at Kara. "Like my mom pointed out, this has nothing to do with that. It's pure fantasy."

Kara laughed. She wiggled her eyebrows in a playful manner then tossed Brittany a mischievous smile. "Gotcha," she announced, not in the least put out by Brittany's accusations. "Good job Brittany, you've found me out." She clapped her hands as if applauding Brittany's efforts.

"What?" Brittany narrowed her eyes.

"I admit it, you're right Brittany. It is preposterous. Queen Elizabeth II had a vivid imagination in her youth. These are her daydreams and thoughts she conjured up to amuse herself. It helped to pass the loneliness you see." Kara shrugged. "After all, we know unicorns don't exist so why would vampires and werewolves?"

Brittany closed her eyes. She took a deep breath then puffed her cheeks out as if releasing pent up emotions. "Seriously, mother, how will we ever figure out Kara's truth and reality from these admitted fantasies she likes to weave for her own enjoyment?" Brittany griped as her eyes flew open. "This is unbelievable."

Amy regarded her daughter. With arms crossed and a disgusted expression on her face Brittany was extremely miffed. As she tapped her foot and waited for her mother's reply Brittany narrowed her eyes at Kara.

Kara laughed at Brittany's anger.

"Don't worry darling," Amy soothed. "Between the two of us we'll sort through the debris and clutter to identify the gems beneath."

Brittany took another deep breath. She appeared about to burst.

"Brittany, it will be a best seller." Kara gushed. "I guarantee it. Readers love to be double crossed as they're led among various paths of confusion. As long as you tie this up in a nice bow then draw a reasonable conclusion by novel's end, the public will love it."

Kara clapped her hands as if the subject had been settled to their satisfaction. "Think of the reviews. We should have a contest to see which scene the readers love best. I bet you'd vote for the unicorn, vampire scene wouldn't you?"

Penny Ross

Brittany shook her head. She sneered at Kara, grabbed her notebook, reached into her purse, snatched her pen from within its depths then announced through gritted teeth, "I'm ready Kara. Do your best to amaze me."

Kara chuckled. "Of course Brittany, nothing would please me more."

30

One Year Later
"Hi Morey, is Kara there?"

"Oh, Amy, I'm so glad you called. Can you come see Kara today?"

"Sure, I want to show her the galleys for our new book. They just arrived. I thought we'd proof them together. I'll pick Brittany up then swing by. Imagine Morey, our book about Kara's journey of history, feminism and culture will be published within a few months. It's a dream come true."

"Yes, well, we'll see if Kara is up to proofing galleys today. I'm not sure. When she woke she didn't seem herself."

"Oh, what do you mean?"

Alarm bells rang in Amy's head. Could this be what Kara had prepared her and Brittany for? Was it time?

"You'll see when you get here. I need to warn you though. She might not remember who you are. So far, Kara hasn't recognized the boys, Carl, me, or the house. Kara claims she's never met any of us before. I hope you and Brittany trigger something so she snaps out of this. Otherwise, I might have to call in a doctor. What if she has amnesia?"

"Oh no, Morey, I don't know what to say. Let's see what happens when we get there. Maybe it's not as bad as it seems. I'll leave Gimli within the hour so we'll be there just after noon."

"Great, see you soon. Bye."

༺༻

On the drive to Winnipeg, Amy thought about what this meant. Kara had said something like this would happen. They'd discussed how she left one woman's body to go to the next person. Kara had emphasized the importance of carrying on as usual when the fateful day arrived. Was this it? Had the mysterious Kara left? If she had, then that meant the real Kara had returned to live with Morey and the boys.

It had never been clear to Amy or Brittany what happened to women when Kara came to replace them. They'd discussed a holding place. Kara never confirmed the existence of such a location though. It was unclear if Kara even knew what happened to the women.

Amy thought the women lived what they thought were real lives somewhere. How did they reorient themselves to their place in this world upon their return?

Kara, Amy and Brittany had come up with the possibility these women's lives were suspended for multiples of seven. That had been pure conjecture on Amy's part though. They'd discussed a variety of scenarios but come up with no concrete answers.

When Amy arrived in Winnipeg she pulled over to call Brittany since her last class should have ended.

"Hi hon, is your class done?"

"Yup, I just walked out. What's up?"

"I'm on my way to pick you up. We have to get over to Kara's right away. Morey just called and Kara's not herself."

"What? No, you mean, oh mom, has it happened?" Brittany wailed.

"I'm afraid so darling. Kara warned us of this."

"The book hasn't been published yet."

"I know. The galleys arrived so I was headed into Winnipeg today to show them to you and Kara."

"Aw, that sucks. Kara would have loved to see them," Brittany griped.

"Yes, well, we'll show them to her anyhow. It might jog her memory."

"It won't be the same mom. This Kara isn't going to know anything."

"We'll see. I'm going to hang up now dear and head your way. I'll pick you up in the loop in ten minutes."

Bird of Paradise Drums Beating

"Kay, bye," Brittany grumped.

By the time Amy and Brittany pulled into Kara's driveway they were eager to rush into the house and search for signs of Kara's disappearance. Brittany wanted to quiz this new Kara. Deep down they knew Kara was gone even though they were loathe to admit it. Their friend had left without saying good-bye. Amy couldn't believe she might never see Kara again. Brittany was pissed by the turn of events.

Amy forced herself to face the situation in a calm manner. She squelched the urge to run around like a lunatic. It would scare everyone. Kara would want them to behave as ladies.

Amy rang the doorbell then waited patiently for Carl to answer. She grabbed Brittany's hand for support.

"Oh, thank goodness you're here," the unflappable Carl gushed when he opened the door. "We've been awaiting your arrival. Everyone is most anxious. They're in the living room."

He helped Amy and Brittany remove their coats.

"Thank you Carl." Amy gave a cool nod.

"Amy, Brittany, we're so glad you've arrived." Morey jumped up from his chair to greet them.

"Kara, your friends are here!"

All eyes turned toward Kara. She rose from her chair then walked toward Amy and Brittany.

Amy held her breath. Was this her friend Kara, or someone else?

Kara stood in front of them. She stared fixedly into Amy's eyes, searching for something it seemed.

Amy thought it was similar to what Kara would do. Perhaps it was the same person. Kara had a habit of staring at people for long moments before she spoke.

Kara's words drew them up short.

"I've never seen this woman before," she sneered. She tossed her head toward Brittany in a dismissive manner. "Nor you, why do you claim I know you? How tedious you are."

Morey stepped back alarmed by his wife's statement.

"But Kara," he stammered. "This is your best friend Amy and her daughter Brittany."

"Hmm, so you say."

Kara waved her arm in their direction like a regal queen dismissing her servants.

Morey motioned for Amy and Brittany to take a seat. There was an uncomfortable silence while they waited to see if Kara had anything more to add.

This Kara seemed more reserved than Amy's former friend. Should she broach the subject of their book? No, Amy decided, now was not the time.

While they remained in the same positions, similar to children playing a game of statues, Amy glanced out the window. Birds had gathered in the trees. They sang as one, while something in the distance held their attention.

Amy reached over, poked Brittany in the arm then silently motioned outside.

Amy and Brittany rose then walked to the window. Amy's hand flew to her mouth as she stifled the cry that came unbidden to her lips.

Flying towards the sky, in all her brilliance, was the paradise tanager. Startling colours heralded her departure as she rose straight up, towards heaven. As a special accompaniment to the bird, drums beat quietly in the distance.

Amy heard a voice whisper softly near her ear. It was Kara's voice.

"It's time for me to move on. I'm needed elsewhere. Help them get to know one another. Remember who you are and be true to yourself. I promise we'll meet again one day. Until then, good-bye my good friend."

Brittany felt a tickle near her ear an instant before she heard Kara's voice. "Take care of your mother Brittany. Her and I will meet in the far future. I leave her in your loving hands. Good-bye my young friend."

Bird of Paradise Drums Beating

Brittany smiled while Amy was quick to brush tears from her cheeks. They waved to Kara as the bird turned slightly toward them then waved her wing in farewell.

Kara had remembered to say good-bye after all.

As Amy watched Kara fly away she recalled one of their conversations a year earlier.

"Why the bird?" Amy had asked.

"It's my muse, my familiar, the way I journey from one mission to the next. I used to sing. I always wanted to be a nightingale or a bird of paradise. Now I am. I'm a paradise tanager from the tropical rainforest.

Even if I'm never the same woman I can always count on my bird of paradise. It's the part of me that's mine, and mine alone. As long as I have this, I can make it. It's part of my personal identity. You have your drums while I have my bird."

Amy gulped. She'd never forget her friend. Now was not the time to mourn Kara's departure though. They needed to be strong, for Kara.

Amy reached over to grasp Brittany's hand. They squeezed one another's fingers in silent understanding.

When she felt sufficiently composed, Amy turned to face the room.

"Kara, I have exciting news. I brought the galleys for our book. It sounds even better than we hoped."

The drumming increased in tempo and volume.

Amy smiled, nodded toward Brittany then let go of her hand to move to Kara's side. Brittany joined her. Amy held her hand out to their new friend.

Kara frowned.

"Don't worry, we'll figure it out together," Amy promised. "We have all the time in the world."

Drums faded away in the distance.

ACKNOWLEDGEMENTS

Thanks to my awesome group of readers who read various drafts of the novel to provide valuable comments and encouragement Katelyn Favell, Ryan Sigmundson, Randy Semenek, Amber Semenek, Danny-Jo Sigmundson, Roman Munroe, Hillary Furgala, Amy Monkman, Jared Irvine and Markee Ross.

Thanks to my illustrator Cathy Wickett for her cover art and ability to create yet another outstanding work of art from the depths of imagination. Special thanks to my editing team Ryan Sigmundson, Tanya Johannson and Cheryl Bailey. To Tanya Johannson, thank you for swooping down to rescue me on a regular basis.

Special thanks to my family. To my husband Danny-Jo, and sons Ryan and Dylan for your love and encouragement. I could not write without the patience and understanding of those who surround me. Thanks to my readers for their support, warmth and generosity.

ABOUT THE AUTHOR

Penny Ross lives in Gimli, Manitoba with her husband and has two adult sons, Ryan and Dylan. Proud of her Métis heritage, she loves to create stories that appeal to all ages. In addition to *Bird of Paradise Drums Beating* Penny has also published *Cave of Journeys* and *Mrs. Muggles Learns to Read*. She is currently working on a sequel to *Cave of Journeys* and a legend for young children.

Visit her website at www.butterflydreamspublishing.com

www.ingramcontent.com/pod-product-compliance
Lightning Source LLC
Chambersburg PA
CBHW051748040426
42446CB00007B/266